BOND

ALAN BOND

WITH ROB MUNDLE

HarperCollins*Publishers*

HarperCollins*Publishers*

First published in Australia in 2003
by HarperCollins*Publishers* Pty Limited
ABN 36 009 913 517
A member of the HarperCollins*Publishers* (Australia) Pty Limited Group
www.harpercollins.com.au

Copyright © Alan Bond and Rob Mundle 2003

The right of Rob Mundle to be identified as the moral rights
author of this work has been asserted by him in accordance with
the *Copyright Amendment (Moral Rights) Act 2000* (Cth).

This book is copyright.
Apart from any fair dealing for the purposes of private study, research,
criticism or review, as permitted under the Copyright Act, no part may
be reproduced by any process without prior written permission.
Inquiries should be addressed to the publishers.

HarperCollins*Publishers*
25 Ryde Road, Pymble, Sydney NSW 2073, Australia
31 View Road, Glenfield, Auckland 10, New Zealand
77–85 Fulham Palace Road, London W6 8JB, United Kingdom
2 Bloor Street East, 20th floor, Toronto, Ontario M4W 1A8, Canada
10 East 53rd Street, New York NY 10022, USA

National Library of Australia Cataloguing-in-Publication data:

Bond, Alan, 1938– .
  Bond.
  Includes index.
  ISBN 978-0-7322-7495-5.
  1. Bond, Alan, 1938– . 2. Businessmen – Australia –
  Biography. I. Mundle, Rob. II. Title.
338.092

Cover and text design by Gayna Murphy, HarperCollins Design Studio
Front cover photograph by Newspix
Rob Mundle author photo by Ian Mainsbridge
Typeset in 11.5 on 15 Berkeley Book by HarperCollins Design Studio

*I dedicate this book to My Princess . . .
my beloved Susanne.*

*Never a day goes by without me thinking of you,
remembering the good times and wishing you were here
with the family and most especially your darling, Charlie.*

CONTENTS

	Acknowledgments	ix
	Prologue	xi
1	Beginnings	1
2	The First Million	19
3	A Pioneering Spirit	44
4	Rising to the Challenge	63
5	Taking Care of Business	85
6	The Day We Stopped the Nation	104
7	Riding the Wave	130
8	Dark Clouds	158
9	The Tide Turns	182
10	Shattered Dreams	214
11	Trial by Media	244
12	Bad Times	268
13	Indifferent Justice	285
14	Reflecting Forward	306
	Index	319

ACKNOWLEDGMENTS

Alan Bond and I crossed tacks in Cowes, England, during the America's Cup Jubilee Regatta in 2001. We'd known each other for more than 30 years and this was the first time that we had caught up since his release from prison. More than three years of incarceration had obviously impacted his body and his emotions, yet it was apparent to me that not far beneath the surface much of the dynamic and energetic Alan Bond I had known for so long was still there. We chatted over a couple of cups of coffee about our respective plans for the future and that was when we realised there was potentially a common thread — this biography.

My thanks go to Alan for giving me the opportunity to put into print the story of his incredible life. When we began the project I thought I had a good outline of his achievements, but as we progressed I realised I was dealing with a far more remarkable man than the world had known.

While writing this book I also became well aware of the high regard so many Australians still hold for him. The number of people who would come up to him while we were walking in the street, shake his hand and tell him how much his contributions to Australia were appreciated amazed me. He is also well respected for having remained in Australia after his corporate world collapsed to face the music.

Creating this book was not the easiest of tasks, especially with Alan spending most of his time living in Europe. But the hurdles were cleared and to that end I must thank my ever-efficient assistant, Nicky Ronalds, for her on-going support. She made an exceptional contribution to this project while also keeping my other business activities on a steady course. Another associate, Linda Hamilton-Evans, was invaluable when it came to the final proofreading while Christine Hopton did a great job with the research.

And yet again I had the extremely pleasant experience of dealing with a super team at HarperCollins — Shona Martyn, Alison Urquhart, Vanessa Radnidge et al. Their support was outstanding.

I also extend a special thanks to my many friends who were so supportive during my 18 months of commitment to the book. In particular I must thank Peter and Kay for the many times they let me escape to their wonderful little riverfront cabana in Yamba so I could concentrate on my writing without interruption.

PROLOGUE

I'd describe myself as the ultimate entrepreneur who pushed the envelope of development and pioneered projects others were afraid to pursue. I could also be described as a corporate explorer — pushing out into the unknown, just like the great explorers of yesteryear and the corporate pioneers, such as Bunker Hunt, the Vanderbilts, Joseph Kennedy, and more recently Ted Turner, along with our own Lang Hancock. At no stage did I ever think that the shores of Australia were the boundary for my dreams. My world was beyond the horizon — a world that I knew was out there because I had travelled halfway around it as a youngster to start a new life in Australia.

Just like the dangers any pioneer faces, there was always a risk associated with my corporate exploration, but the risks I took were calculated. I was the one who gambled on four challenges for the America's Cup, who sailed the oceans of the world, who dared from a very early age to build the tallest buildings and who developed a global business that would ultimately benefit Australia and Australians. I was always of the view that just because someone said that something hadn't been done before didn't mean that it couldn't be done — it might only need to be looked at a bit differently.

What I do in my life requires an enormous amount of energy, and energy is something I've always possessed. I've also had the ability to do more than one thing at a time because I have been able to 'compartmentalise' my brain to the point where, when I'm dealing with a particular project somewhere in the world, that subject has my full focus. It didn't matter if I was working on developing a property in Rome, racing for the America's Cup, building a mine in Canada's Arctic Circle or developing the Super Pit, Australia's largest goldmine. I can lock my attention onto that one subject and not be distracted.

So what went wrong? Why did my world collapse, and why did I go to prison? I will obviously expand later, but in hindsight I can say there was too much gearing, too much borrowing, and as a result mistakes were made. But that doesn't mean that we weren't pushed over the precipice when we were still able to recover. The biggest mistakes came when I tangled with Tiny Rowland, and at around the same time bought into the Bell Group. Through my managing director in Australia, Peter Beckwith, the Bell deal saw me get mixed up with the government of Western Australia. His relationship with the government would prove to be a very unhealthy alliance for Bond Corporation. We became too close.

The real growth for Bond Corporation came after I won the America's Cup in 1983. The euphoria that followed had many people believing I was infallible and that the Company could achieve whatever goals we set. As a result we carried a support team of bankers and lawyers along with us on the way to Bond Corporation becoming one of the world's great conglomerates. It was a time when money and opportunities were literally forced upon us, and they were very difficult to refuse. Now, older and wiser, I look back and see opportunities missed — times when we should have raised capital rather than debt, although raising capital was the long-term plan that would have seen us become world dominant in our chosen arenas. Among the things we should have anticipated was the massive blow-out in interest rates in the 1980s — we had the opportunity to restructure debt to equity ratios then, but we didn't.

PROLOGUE

Even when I was 21 I was a global player, always thinking of the bigger markets and the power you achieve if you can control the market. From the very start my business philosophy was to develop businesses with cash flow and to buy assets that we could substantially increase in value, for example buying a raw piece of land and developing it or having its zoning changed. In Bond Corporation this same philosophy had us thinking bigger and thinking global because that was where we believed true success was to be found, such as when we bought the Channel Nine television stations in Western Australia and Queensland. I quickly realised that we were unlikely to succeed in this branch of media if we didn't make it part of a bigger project, so from there we developed Bond Media as an international media company. A similar attitude was in place when we established Sky Channel, the first satellite television service in Australia. We had no licence for it because there was no legislation governing such an enterprise, so there was nothing to say I couldn't do it. From the outset there was a massive risk just in developing the satellites to deliver the signal because we were dealing with new technology, and there was the added risk of getting them into orbit — if the satellite failed the money invested was lost because, even if it was insured, the time and expense associated with replacing it couldn't be recovered. But I went ahead and took the risk, had the satellites developed and put the Sky Channel television sporting service into pubs across Australia. We then thought 'Why have Sky Channel only here when the bigger markets of the world are unfolding?' So we went to the UK and established British Satellite Broadcasting.

I was never totally ego-driven when building Bond Corporation, but of course my ego was part of it as it is something that drives you to do greater things. I never ever thought of saying 'enough is enough'. The money didn't really matter to me — I had enough money to retire when I was 21 — £1 million — a huge sum of money in 1959. And even when I went on to become one of the wealthiest men in Australia money still didn't matter. My life was not about money, it was about developing projects and achieving world market share, particularly as a pioneer in specific areas. That's what I thrived on. I saw Australia becoming recognised and respected on the back of my international achievements, and that really mattered to me. I also derived great satisfaction from giving, in the form of donations to charities and community projects, such as support for people who had lost their homes in bushfires, building a replica of Captain Cook's *Endeavour*, opera scholarships and many other things.

To start in life with nothing and grow to where you are the head of a worldwide business empire employing 25 000 people in more than 20 countries was immensely satisfying. We had good assets and in the process of building the empire we created wonderful opportunities for thousands of people. I always wanted to give people the chance to succeed beyond their expectations by showing them the way — how to rise way beyond what they believed were their limits. I gave them the opportunity to leapfrog through life instead of standing in a queue. I can say with great satisfaction that this attitude is part of the reason that all of the major entities we developed remain hugely successful today.

We were on our way to far greater things when we made our mistakes and exposed our companies to the enemy to the degree where we were eventually sunk under a barrage of hostile fire. I have my suspicions as to who took aim and fired first, but I will never be able to prove it. I do know that the first shot came from high up in the Australian corporate world and that this assailant was backed by government troops. That shot hit hard via the Sulan Inquiry, which was established to look into Bond Corporation, and once we were hit that first time we were unable to save ourselves, primarily because we became extremely vulnerable as interest rates climbed from 10 per cent to 20 per cent and beyond. The media feeding frenzy that came with this government inquiry crippled any ability we had to restructure our company through new international funding, despite the fact that we had not been found guilty of any misdemeanour and still held exceptionally strong assets. This was a case where an accusation was as good as a conviction. No company could have survived what we had to contend with.

PROLOGUE

Personally, I knew that my entire world crumbled to dust when I heard the keys rattle and the prison cell door lock behind me for the very first time. That's when I slumped to rock bottom — totally alone, exhausted and depressed, but I knew that from that point there is only one way you can go, and that's up! In prison your life revolves around a miserably tiny cell measuring less than 2 metres by 5 metres. You have fallen from grace and you have hurt your family, and you begin to realise just who your true friends are in life. You also wonder what went wrong and why you are in prison when other people are still walking the streets freely after having failed in their business and gone bankrupt, or when company directors have lost billions of shareholders' dollars. For example, look what happened to AMP in Australia when in two years to mid-2003 more than $15 billion of shareholders' funds were written off the value of the company. I ask, could they survive a Sulan-type inquiry after that? Probably not.

I have no doubt that I would have died in prison if it wasn't for the great support of my family — my ex-wife Eileen, my new wife Diana, my children John, Craig, Susanne and Jody, and my true friends who stood behind me and maintained their belief in me. That's what made the difference between life and death. At the same time I have been extremely disappointed by the number of supposed friends who haven't gone the distance and who today seem to think that because I have been to prison that I must still walk around wearing a suit emblazoned with arrows. There are also a lot of people in the business community and media who don't believe that I have a right to a second chance. Sadly, it's an attitude that is endemic in Australia today.

Yes, I let my shareholders down, there's no question. If I could change something then I'd change that. It is extremely unfortunate that while the shareholders lost out, the bankers did not lose much at all because most of the companies within the organisation continued operating and continued to pay their debts. As I see it now, there was no need for this calamity to occur.

I remain adamant that the charges that sent me to prison were wrong — there were no offences committed under the laws that were the foundation for the charges. But if society saw it as fit and proper for me to serve a sentence because I lost money for shareholders and bondholders, then I accept the penalty. I don't accept the penalty for the charges that were laid, although I took a plea bargain on two charges.

I have paid a high price for what happened and having paid that price, the best thing I can now do is relate the lessons that were learnt, the experiences I have had in my life, and explain, from my point of view, what went wrong. And because the flame of ambition has been ignited once more, as has my belief that Australia and its people are unique, I can detail a plan for the future. That's why I have written this book. Rarely have I given even a remote insight into my life, and accordingly there has been considerable speculation and assumption made and published. The majority of it is wrong.

Now here's my story.

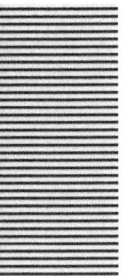

CHAPTER ONE
BEGINNINGS

It was an incredible adventure for me as a six-year-old to go down a coalmine in Cwmtillery, South Wales, with my grandfather and some of my uncles, an adventure that left impressions that I've never been able to erase. I was amazed how hard the men worked, how hard it was for a man to shovel a load of coal. There was no machinery down there, more than 300 metres below in a horrid, dank environment — the men were working only with shovels and picks to hack out the coal before loading it by hand into the trolleys. They were working 12-hour shifts and when they came to the surface they were as black as the coal they'd been digging. I also felt for the poor pit ponies — little Welsh ponies bred specially to work in the mines — that were trudging along underground, heads down, dragging the heavily laden trolleys. They suffered from what was called 'pink eye' because they worked and lived underground. They never saw the light of day, something a six-year-old struggled to comprehend.

Another time when I was there on summer holidays there was a cave-in. I didn't know what the whistle shrieking from the top of the mine meant, but the looks on the faces of everyone in my grandparents' home told me it was something very serious. I soon learnt that men were trapped below, and I can vividly remember being part of the crowd rushing towards the top of the mineshaft. Everyone was looking for family and loved ones emerging from the mine. No one was sure who was dead or alive or what exactly had happened. It was a terrible scene. I can still see the fear etched on everyone's faces, the people not knowing if their lives were about to change forever because a family member was not coming home that night.

It was a wretched life that trapped many courageous men. Safety conditions in the mines were never very good, yet the miners showed true guts by going back underground as soon as it was clear for them to do so, always knowing that next time they might be the ones who were trapped. Poor ventilation and dust were other dangers they faced, so serious lung infections were commonplace.

I have carried those images with me, so much so that decades later, when I became involved in major mining projects, I always had particular regard for a better quality of life for the workers. I wanted to improve their situation because I knew how hard they worked. They deserved respect and dignity.

My father, Frank, was born in Pontypool before moving with the family, to Cwmtillery a small village where if you looked out to one side of the town you saw lush green hills and ferns in abundance while out on the other side it was just slag heaps from the mines that stretched across the valley. There were 10 children in the family, nine boys and one girl, and all the boys followed the family tradition by going to work in the mines alongside my grandfather.

Every time I visited my father's family in South Wales as a child I was impressed by the pride everyone in the village had for their homes. The men worked underground all day in dirty conditions, but their houses were spotless. Every piece of copper in the house was polished and the gardens were always neat and full of flowers. There was an amazing contrast between the life underground and life on the surface. The men's attitude to cleanliness started the moment they arrived home from work. They would immediately go to the outhouse and fill a tub mounted into a wooden bench with water. They were out there scrubbing themselves seemingly forever, trying to get the ground-in black grime out of their skin. It always seemed to me to be a losing battle.

Dad started working underground when he was 12. His first job was as a lamp man, carrying the special lamps and birds in cages to check on the gas levels while the men worked. He was a very strong young man who, as he matured, began working in his spare time as a gym instructor, teaching gymnastics and sometimes boxing. He lasted underground until he was 16, realising at that young age that there was little future in being a miner for the rest of his life. Miners were paid a pittance for an incredibly hard day's work, and after that the highlight of town life was to go to the local pub. A really big night out was to go to the fish and chip shop to buy dinner. He wanted to better himself, and the best alternative he could see was to join the army. The problem was that he was too young, but being well-built meant he looked older than his years, so it was simply a matter of putting his age up on the enlistment papers and off he went into the army.

He was transferred to a garrison in Leeds, and about a year after he had been stationed there he was one of a group of soldiers invited to a garden party organised so they could meet local people and feel welcome. I recall my father telling me how he and a bunch of the lads arrived at the venue and walked into the garden where he immediately became infatuated by the beauty of a young woman who was standing there. His fascination was such that he was later compelled to ask her for a date. But her father did not approve, saying something along the lines of 'of course if he was a member of the Royal Air Force (RAF), that would be more understandable'. Being in the army was simply beneath the status of the young woman's family.

The young woman, Kathleen Smith, obviously passed on to Frank the news that her father did not consider it appropriate for her to go out with an army man. Undeterred, Frank simply resigned from the army, joined the RAF as a physical trainer, and got his date. Kathleen was to become my mother.

After a time both Frank and Kathleen went to London where they met up again, established a relationship and eventually married in a registry office there in October 1934. My only sister, Geraldine, was born in 1936 and on 22 April 1938, I arrived on the scene.

Fortunately for the family, my mother had received a small inheritance and that allowed her to buy a typical two-storey, semi-detached London house as the family home: 22 Federal Road, Perivale, Middlesex. My memories of my father are of a very kind, genuine and charismatic man. He was also a man's man. I'm sure those were the characteristics that appealed to my mother when she agreed to his marriage proposal. Another thing about him that impressed everyone was his wonderful Welsh voice. He could really sing. When I was very young I remember him regularly singing 'I'll take you home again, Kathleen' for my mother while we all sat around the piano at home.

I was almost four when he went off to war as a member of the RAF's 13 Squadron. I can remember it very clearly. At Waterloo Station my mother bought me a bag of cherries and I was eating them while watching all the RAF men board the train for the first leg of their journey to the front line. There were hundreds of people farewelling them, some standing on the platform chairs waving flags and balloons. The men were leaning out of the windows of the train, waving as it pulled away from the station. Amazingly, I can still see my father there waving as if it was only yesterday.

As a youngster in London during the war, I found it as exciting as it was dangerous. My father had built a bomb shelter in the garden which was made out of corrugated iron and concrete. We had all the basic provisions in there that would be needed in the event of a serious attack. We also had a huge 10-centimetre thick steel table built in the house, the thought being that we could shelter under the table if ever there was not enough time to get out to the bomb shelter during a blitz. My sister and I actually slept under the table on the nights when it was thought that heavy raids were coming.

The blitzes were frightening. You could hear the bombs whistling towards the ground, and then there was an empty silence before the sound of the explosion reached you. We always thought the Hoover appliance factory, which was on the opposite side of the lane at the rear of our house, would be a target because they were making munitions there. Lucky for us it was spared, but there were still some terrible nights when a number of streets around us were completely bombed out. For a period of about ten weeks, when things were at their very worst, Geraldine and I were evacuated to Somerset with a lot of other kids, all of us with identification labels attached to our clothing. We were put on a train then met by people at the other end who organised for us to be billeted out to families on farms. Mother, who was working as a secretary for the Air Ministry, stayed in London.

I can't say I enjoyed my school years. This was partly because the war was such an interruption during that period. I also missed having my father around, not having the influence of a man. Initially I went to Perivale School, which was only a few hundred metres from home, and while I did very well there I never felt challenged. As far as the teachers were concerned, I was very bright but also fairly rebellious. They wouldn't call me bad, it was just that I wanted to do everything my way. Even the headmaster recognised that I had leadership qualities, saying to me one day: 'Look, you have the ability to be the Prime Minister of England if you want.'

I did well with maths and algebra but I could never spell properly, so I'd write things down phonetically. Even to this day people comment on my poor spelling, but it was something that I just could not grasp at school.

My parents could see I was unsettled at Perivale so it was decided that I'd do better at a private school. I was sent off to Wembley College, a small school with fewer students in each class. I enjoyed that because we were doing more advanced work than what I'd been doing and we also studied French and Latin.

With my mother working at the Air Ministry from early morning until late at night there was plenty of time for me and my friends to get up to plenty of mischief playing in the streets after school — not bad mischief, just the plain, healthy mischief that most kids get up to. When I was seven years old I had my own gang comprising five other little kids. We used to jump the fence and pinch apples from people's trees, let off a few firecrackers in letterboxes — those sorts of things. We discovered that there were a lot of the old metal army helmets and other equipment lying around the Hoover yard that were going to be processed for munitions. We'd clamber over the fence and grab some of that stuff, like the helmets and shell casings, polish them up and sell them. The shell casings were considered to make nice vases. Mind you, we weren't always successful getting the stuff. Once I impaled my hand on a spike on top of the factory fence as we went over it while being chased away by an army security patrol and a couple of their dogs. I still have the scar.

I guess selling that stuff was my very first business enterprise. I also sold jam jars which I got by going around the streets pulling a little cart, knocking on doors and asking people if they had any empty ones to spare. I'd take them home, wash them out and then sell them to people who wanted them for pickling.

Religion was also part of my upbringing. Frank was a non-practising believer while Mother was High Church of England. Whether I liked it or not, Mother made sure I went to Sunday school every week. A photograph of me standing outside our house in my church choir outfit was one of her favourites.

Father was badly injured during the war and subsequently repatriated a very sick man. He suffered a collapsed lung and other internal injuries when the boat he was on was torpedoed off the coast of Italy. It was obvious from the moment he arrived home unannounced that he was in great pain and it wasn't long before he had to be carried off on a stretcher to hospital where he was to spend much of the next three years. The doctors had to remove one of his lungs and also put a steel plate in his chest to keep the rib cage apart. I remember part of his therapy in hospital was to make a huge carpet, stitch by stitch. My sister and I would sit there totally mesmerised when we visited him, watching him working on the carpet while chatting with Mother.

When he came out of hospital and was well enough, he established a small milk delivery business in London that he operated out of United Dairies. He used a horse and cart and I often joined him for the early morning delivery rounds in our area, including our street, selling milk, eggs and butter. It was a good little business.

Eventually, however, his respiratory problems returned and became so severe that the doctors were convinced that they wouldn't be able to keep him alive for much longer than a year. They said that's all they expected, but that he might do better in a warmer climate. As a result my parents sat with my sister and me and discussed moving to South Africa or Australia for the sake of Father's health. The plan was made for Frank to go on ahead of us to decide which country was most suitable. Mother already had a soft spot for Australia because she'd been distributing food parcels that had come from families there. Food rationing in the post-war years was a fact of life, regardless of how much money you had. I remember us getting a package from Forest Downs Station in the north of Western Australia and wondering where on earth that was. It sounded like the end of the earth to me. The parcel contained Christmas cakes, tinned ham and other non-perishable items.

It was 1949 when Frank set off to first check out South Africa. He had been there during the war, and because he had met a lot of South Africans and Australians and become very intrigued by their stories of their respective countries he felt comfortable about visiting both in search of our new home. His impression of South Africa was very interesting. I remember a letter he wrote to Mother saying:

> I've been here six months now, and I've had a look at Johannesburg and Cape Town. One of the things that concerns me is that they don't treat the black people very well here. I think there will be problems in the years ahead and I don't think we should risk our whole future if there's going to be problems.

I'm sure it was an attitude influenced by his upbringing, a coal-mining background where he worked hard. In South Africa he saw that it was only black people, not whites, in the mines doing what he had been doing as a miner. He didn't believe in discrimination at all — he felt people should be treated equally. I think he showed great foresight in his analysis of a future life in South Africa.

He then travelled to Perth, or more specifically Fremantle, and quickly decided that it was where we should settle. Mother agreed, so we were told that we were going to move to Australia. I hated the idea, especially the thought of the outback. As an 11-year-old I just couldn't come to terms with the change because I didn't want to leave London and all my mates. There was only one thing to do — run away. I jumped on a train and headed for Brighton where I got a job with a circus. I just walked in and asked if there were any jobs on offer. They probably thought I was a local lad looking for some pocket money, so they gave me a job cleaning up after the animals, including picking up huge lumps of elephant dung. There were lots of small hotels on the beachfront at Brighton so, being the confident young working man that I was, I booked into one of them. But my escape was short-lived. A couple of days later a policeman came around and asked me where I belonged. He took me off to the police station and arranged for my mother to come and collect me. I ran away once more, that time staying in London where I met up with a lot of street kids and slept in the ruins of bombed-out buildings. But the thought of home eventually got the better of me that time and I went back less than a week before we were scheduled to leave for Australia.

Because of his disability, my father couldn't migrate to Australia as a 'Ten Pound Pom' so he had to pay full fare, but the rest of the family took advantage of the cheap passage. Being a great organiser, Mother planned the move exceptionally well. She checked on everything that we could and could not take, discovering most importantly that no means test — family wealth status — applied. That meant we could take a car, so off we went to the Ford Motor Company where she bought a new, fawn coloured Ford Prefect four-door sedan. It was a beautiful looking motor vehicle, and I was really impressed because we had never previously owned a car. Mother also learnt that you could take a lot of household effects, so we shipped crates and crates containing all the silverware, antiques and other items that we owned.

Reluctant as I was to leave England, the three-week voyage to Fremantle turned out to be a very happy time that I enjoyed immensely. We were aboard the *Himalaya*, a brand new ship on only its second voyage. Because there were so many children on board the crew went to great lengths to keep us entertained. To celebrate the crossing of the equator, we had a big party where we all dressed up before being dumped in the swimming pool. The pool was such a focus for fun that we swam almost every day.

We arrived in Australia on 5 February 1950, and my first impression of Fremantle when it came into sight from the ship was that we had gone to the moon: 'My Godfather, where am I?' Desolate was the only way I could describe it. And it was so hot, hellishly hot — more than 100° Fahrenheit (38°C) — a temperature that I'd never experienced and never imagined. As the ship moved towards its dock we could see big Norfolk pine trees, but the tallest building was only three-storeys high. But my shock turned to excitement as soon as I saw Father standing on the dock to welcome us with so many of his new friends. There were families there on that day who would remain lifelong friends.

Father had set up a small painting business in the nine months he waited for us to arrive and also found the new family home, a small weatherboard and tin-roofed cottage at 276 High Street, Fremantle. He paid £1750 for it, money that Mother had sent out from England after she sold our house there.

Having come from London, a high-density city with suburbs that had the houses all wedged together, our new home was another shock for me. It was relatively small and set well back on a big, wide block of land with a long driveway up the side. I was happy to see that there was plenty of room to kick a soccer ball around, but I would soon learn that Australian kids didn't play soccer. And I was amazed to see we had chickens in the backyard.

Father had done some renovating in preparation for our arrival. My room was a small, covered-in part of the front verandah that had louvres for windows, while Geraldine had a room inside the house. One thing for sure was that having a car was seen as a big deal in the street. There were only two or three other families with vehicles, so every time we went out people stared at us.

My Father's health had improved considerably and his painting business was doing well. Mother, a great believer in working hard and intelligently, soon found employment as a bookkeeper/accountant at Sylvester's Dry Cleaners in Subiaco. From the outset she very wisely invested any spare money we had in stocks and shares, and later she invested £1500 in a block of land at Melville, on the highway leading into Perth.

I was sent off to the local primary school within days of arriving and quickly became frustrated because, yet again, there was no challenge. They were doing maths and algebra studies that I'd already done in England. It was like stepping back in time for me, and I didn't like that. I was also experiencing that awful change-over period where you are between one country and another country and you don't quite fit in. I got on okay with the local kids, but I didn't play Aussie Rules football, and if you didn't play Aussie Rules you didn't play anything.

Soon it all became too hard so I took the only option and ran away from home, getting on a train and travelling 600 kilometres east of Perth to Kalgoorlie, a place that I had decided looked interesting on the map. After a week of wandering around the town I became bored so I got a lift home with some people I'd met there and went back to school. When I eventually finished primary school I went off to Fremantle Boys' High School which, ironically, was located in the building where today you'll find the Film and Television Institute, an organisation I established years later to teach people how to make movies and short films.

We stayed only a couple of years in the house in Fremantle. Mother had bought another block of land in Melville and we built a large but modest brick home there. When I was 14 my father said:

'Look, you've got to do something with your life. If you're not going to get your head down and do well at school then you should learn a trade. I've arranged for you to be apprenticed at Parnell Signs and you're due to start there on Monday morning.'

I had no say in it — I was on my way to becoming an apprentice signwriter. Father had met Fred Parnell through the Freemasons' Lodge, and because I could draw he asked Fred if he needed an apprentice. I was paid 15 shillings a week — not very much, but it was a start. I really did enjoy the work, even though Fred gave me some God-awful jobs where I felt like I was being used as child labour. We had the contract to paint and signwrite all the big trucks for Arnott's Biscuits. They were beautiful looking trucks on the outside, but the trimmings and the chassis were covered in grease. I would be under them all bloody week, scraping all the grease and paint off, then painting the chassis. Still, it was a good bit of discipline and I eventually progressed to learning how to paint the trucks, and then the signs they carried. The one thing about my work was that I was very quick. Some people are slow and methodical signwriters but I would splash it on and get it done.

My weekends usually involved work or sport. Soccer was out of the question so in winter I started playing rugby for Fremantle, making my way through to A-grade playing as a five-eighth. And when I was 14 I joined Leighton Beach Surf Club to become a lifesaver.

My signwriting apprenticeship required me to go to Leederville Tech School one day a fortnight to learn about the trade. Mother also suggested that I continue my education so I signed up for courses in carpentry, tinsmithing, accountancy and art at the Fremantle Technical School, something I did on and off for three years. When I was 16 I decided I wanted to learn about operating a business so I teamed up with three other apprentices from Leederville Tech to work over the weekends and make some extra money. We had it all covered — painting, signwriting, carpentry. If you wanted any job done on your house we could do it. I was the team leader, the one who went out and got the business, usually by door-knocking. It was a challenge that I loved. I'd price the job, negotiate a deal and work with the team all weekend, starting at 7am and finishing when it got dark. There was no mucking around. We were there to work, and work hard. The team grew to six and soon we were earning more than we did in our regular jobs. And to make even more cash I used to write signs in any spare time I had at night.

It was during that period that an Irish priest, Father O'Sullivan, from the Order of Oblates, approached me while I was doing some signwriting on a street in Fremantle. He was a fantastic man who had once been a policeman on the waterfront in Ireland and who'd obviously seen some hard times before he joined the church. He came up to me and said: 'We'd like a few things done around the church. Would you like to earn a little pocket money? We can't pay you much ... just a little.' I agreed and soon found myself re-painting all the Stations of the Cross in St Patrick's Church in Fremantle. Father O'Sullivan must have liked my work because next he said: 'The church hall out the back needs some attention. We have some social functions, some dances, coming up and we'd like to cover the back wall. Do you think you could paint something to cover it?' I suggested that the best thing to do was to hang a big canvas up there and that if he found the canvas then I'd paint it. He didn't say he wanted a religious scene, the subject was up to me; I decided that what was appropriate was a painting of the Resurrection of Christ. I created the image in my head as I painted, the biggest challenge coming when I had to paint feet and hands, which I was never able to do very well. The solution was simple — I had Christ coming out of clouds.

What I liked about Father O'Sullivan was that while he took time to talk to me he didn't preach. He spoke about the things that mattered in life. It was quite inspirational and left a big impression on me, so much so that I thought 'if this is what the Catholic Church is all about then I should join it', and I did.

I'd had a very strong, very strict High Church of England upbringing by my Mother, and I didn't enjoy it. It was a case of 'you will join the choir now', or 'if you don't do that now you will not get dinner tonight'. She never did understand the Catholics and was quite unforgiving in that respect. I remember her saying to me after I joined the church: 'You'll rue the day you joined those Catholics.' She was very Victorian in her attitudes and held those views until she departed this life in 1987 aged 76. In fact, she was so Victorian in her approach to life that when I had established myself in business and wasn't living at home any longer I would have to make an appointment to see her. I would arrive at the designated time — usually after she'd been to the hairdresser — and enjoy silver tea service from the maid she had employed. She always had a list of the things she wanted to talk about, and then when we'd talked about all those things I could bring up what it was that I wanted to talk about. I found her opinions on business and the economy to be full of insight and of value to me.

The thought of dances at St Patrick's appealed to me, but there was one small problem. I couldn't dance. Mother had the solution — book myself into Wrightson's Dance Studios for some lessons, a suggestion that I was quick to adopt. As it happened, the very first day at Wrightson's would prove to be a turning point in my life. I was standing there in the hall wondering what to do when a dancing teacher came across and asked why I wasn't getting involved. I explained that I was new and couldn't dance a step, but I was there to learn. She then introduced herself as Eileen, and explained she was there so her elder sister, Maureen, could teach her how to become a dancing instructress. Before I knew it I was the trainee teacher's training partner, and it wasn't long before I sensed something else was happening. While I was trying to concentrate on my dancing another part of my mind was telling me that Eileen was very attractive, this was a special young woman. Until that time I'd never even thought about girls and girlfriends; I didn't have time for them. But all of a sudden the thought of a relationship was entering my head. Needless to say I became a very enthusiastic pupil — I couldn't get back to Wrightson's soon enough for more lessons, and because of the special attention I was getting I was learning to dance pretty quickly. Eileen always thought I was a bit outgoing, she even described me laughingly at the time as being 'a little shit', but we just hit it off and before long I became her partner for ballroom dancing competitions. More importantly I found myself with my first true love — a redhead with a vibrant personality who was very much an individual. I met her family, including her brother Don who was an Oblate priest in the Catholic Church, and got on very well with them, partly because Eileen's previous boyfriend had a motorbike, and that was taboo. I was considered to be okay because I had a bicycle. As time passed, my relationship with Eileen became increasingly intense and more enjoyable and it wasn't long before I'd go around to her home every morning to meet her and walk her down to where she would catch the bus to work in Perth. I'd see her again in the evening, every day. We became pretty much inseparable.

I can't speak highly enough of Eileen's father, Bill 'Doozer' Hughes. He was a very good man who couldn't do enough to help anyone in need. In the 40 years I knew him I did not hear him say a bad word about anybody. Fortunately for me he became my friend and mentor. He was a Fremantle City Councillor, had played football for South Fremantle Football Club in his early years, and was the commissioner of the Fremantle Harbour Trust, the body that ran harbour operations. He was also the managing director of a large wool firm in Fremantle.

It was Doozer who came to our rescue at the Leighton Beach Surf Club when we needed to transport surfboats to carnivals in country towns. He would lend me a truck, which I got one of the older blokes from the club to drive. We used to put the surfboats on the back and off we'd go for the weekend to surf carnivals at places like Albany, Bunbury and Geraldton. And apart from being the source of trucks for the club, I also got the job of painting the surfboats and surf reels. It was considered a community project so Fred Parnell didn't mind me doing the jobs at the workshop either at lunchtime or at night. I remember one particular night when I was working late on one of these jobs that I got the shock of my life. Parnell's was opposite a funeral parlour that was being renovated, and it was arranged between the undertaker and Fred Parnell for all the coffins, with the bodies inside, to be stored in the back of our workshop while the renovations were being done. This particular night I was working away quietly under dim lights, when suddenly there was a horrible, haunting sound coming out of the darkness at the back of the building: 'grrrrrrrrrrrrrrrr'. Then a body in one of the coffins sat half upright, knocking the unlocked lid off in the process. The noise was gas exiting the body.

The work I was doing on the surfboats and reels was made easier by the experience I was getting in the design office at Parnell's. This was where I got involved with the painting of the famous red dingo, the big logo for a flour company that still dominates the side of a huge, multi-level white shed facing the ocean in North Fremantle. Over the years there have been plenty of stories going around about my involvement in the project. The fact is that I worked on both the design and the painting of it. We first made up a small drawing of the dingo then divided it into squares and scaled the drawing onto the side of the shed with big templates, and then a team of us went out and painted it. It was a huge team effort, being the largest sign painted in Western Australia at that time. My involvement with its creation led to this sign appearing on the cover of *Time* magazine when we won the America's Cup in 1983.

I was thriving on work, so much so that at one stage, when I was just 15, I was doing three jobs. The apprenticeship at Parnell's was important to me, but it was the two hours I spent each afternoon working at Gibney's Dry Cleaners in Fremantle that gave me the real foundation for the business career that lay ahead of me. The dry-cleaning business was owned by Kurt Lessheim, Mr Lessheim to me, a short and rotund German Jew. He was one of the richest men in Western Australia, but because of his low profile — apart from owning the only new, imported Chevrolet sedan in the state — no one knew it. I met him because Parnell Signs had the contract to paint his shops. I got chatting with him while working at one of his stores and we immediately hit it off. One day he said in this very, very thick German accent: 'Why don't you come and work for me each day after you finish at Parnell's. I'll pay you and you can learn a bit about business.' I did just that, staying in the job for a couple of years.

Kurt had originally made his money through owning brickworks in Germany before the war. While he was a quietly spoken, tough guy to work for, he was very, very good to me. I always appreciated that he was prepared to take the time to explain everything about business in detail. This would prove to be a great grounding in later years. A successful businessman took some of his valuable time to teach another generation what he had learnt from his mistakes and I was the one who benefited. One of the first things he taught me related to branding, and that if you can't have a monopoly then go no worse than a duopoly. Few people knew that he also owned the only other dry-cleaning business in Fremantle, Sylvester's, which was where my mother worked. Both were major operations that he insisted kept their own trading names. That way, if anyone ever took a dislike to one business they would go to the other, and he got their business anyway.

He had 40 or 50 European women working on the presses in the dry-cleaning plant, which was an ugly corrugated-iron sweatbox built behind a glass shopfront in the main street of Fremantle. My job was to do the tally sheets, to keep a tab on the productivity of the pressers. It sounded relatively easy, but it wasn't, because I had to fire the women if they weren't working well enough. Kurt had a little annex above the workshop floor where he could stand and watch the workers sweating away at the presses. He'd be dressed in an immaculate suit, peering over the edge, watching every move. If he decided a woman had to go she could look up and see him talking to me, telling me, a 15-year-old, to go down and sack her. I got very emotional about this role, but one thing I learnt from the experience was to be gentle, to talk the women through it. I used to say: 'You have to go, but look, you can find a better job. It's silly sticking around here. He's too hard.' One of the women put her arm around me one day and said: 'I know it's not your fault. Don't get upset.' It was a tough school run by a tough master, but there were some real lessons there for me.

In taking me under his wing Kurt talked a lot about making money. He said one day: 'Alan, I want to tell you something; you earn 7 per cent on your money and you sleep well. But if you earn 12 per cent on your money, you eat well. It is up to you, how much you want to eat.'

In Perth he saw a shortage of accommodation so built blocks of flats everywhere. Every time he had the money he'd build another block of flats. I was really interested in what he was doing, so he'd take me along to meetings with his architect, Harold Krantz, to let me get a better appreciation of how projects were developed. I really got to understand the Jewish business mentality and their approach to business. He said to me: 'If you build a straight line with no indents then you need fewer bricks, so you build it cheaper. If you don't have overhangs and only fit gutters then you save on that much timber on the eaves. And if you have bricks on the outside and bricks on the inside, there's no maintenance. Bricks are very good.'

So, all the bloody flats he built were just brick walls — no maintenance, no painting and no plastering. He'd put down parquetry flooring. He also explained that as windows were very expensive, to make sure to only use the standard size, and to make sure the sill comes with the window because then you don't pay for the sill. He built many blocks of flats around Perth, keeping all of them as rental properties. It was Mr Lessheim who really taught me about building projects — how to borrow the money, collect the rents and ensure your capital assets grew.

My weekend work with the team from the Tech School continued unabated. It was all going very smoothly until the day I took on a job that would lead to the parting of the ways with Parnell's. I knew a guy wanted a caravan he used as a hot-dog stand painted, so I asked him if he would like me to quote on the work. He agreed, saying he wanted to have cartoon characters, like Dagwood, painted all over it. We got the job and promised we would start work the following Friday night so it was finished by Monday morning. We got stuck into it, the two other guys who I had working with me painting the background, while I was busy designing and painting the cartoon characters. We used the headlights of my old car to illuminate the job while we worked at night. I was so proud of my cartoon work when we finished that I signed my name in one corner of the job. Little did I know that the caravan owner had also asked Parnell's to provide a quote, and Fred came around on the Monday morning to price it. It was all too much for Fred when he saw my signature on the job. He came straight back to the office and said to me: 'We're not going to put up with that. Off you go.' That was it. I was out of a job and still had more than a year of my apprenticeship to go.

I could have gone to another job and completed my time but I decided that I'd had enough experience as an apprentice signwriter at that stage to sit for my final exam. So I went to the Tech School in Leederville and applied to sit there and then for my Journeyman's Ticket, the final apprenticeship exam. They let me do it, and I passed.

CHAPTER TWO
THE FIRST MILLION

When I was 18 I set myself a target to have £1 million in the bank by the time I was 21.

The driving force behind this was the lasting image of the coal miners I saw in Cwmtillery when I was young, working so hard underground and essentially trapped in a lifestyle that was a never-ending financial battle. And when I remembered how tough it was not having my father around during the war, I also knew I wanted to be happily married with a financially secure family life around me.

When I left Parnell Signs I was determined to have my own business, so I set about establishing Nu-Signs at the rear of the Waterside Workers' Federation building, just half a mile away from Parnell's. I rented the space from the Federation for £1 a week. Fortunately Eileen's father had taken a real shine to me and offered to guarantee a £300 overdraft with the bank, and this, together with the £500 that I had saved from my extra work activities, allowed me to start the business. That was the total capital that started Nu-Signs and, in essence, the total amount that got me started in my business career.

While it was most unusual for anyone to have a business within the Waterside Workers' Federation building in what was a very strongly unionised port, my relationship with the union would be one that worked well for both parties. I would get first choice of the qualified migrant workers coming off the ships, and the Federation got its money because anyone who started with us automatically got a union ticket — no ticket no work. There was an added benefit in being there — the secretary of the Federation would come out and sit down with us during the morning-tea break and talk about what the union stood for. His explanation of labour relations was something that in later years helped me to better appreciate positions from the side of both the employees and management in a dispute.

I needed cash flow quickly if I was to get Nu-Signs off the ground, so I went around town quoting on every possible job, almost always undercutting the opposition just to make sure I got it. The formula worked because the cash came in and I had the business making a profit within a few weeks of opening. This situation didn't, however, come without incident, like when my exuberance for finding more work for the fledgling company saw me finish up on the wrong side of the law. One day I went around to measure up a property for a job and was arrested for trespassing. It turned out that in my haste I was clambering all over the wrong bloody building. The whole thing was a total inconvenience, but I went along to the court, pleaded guilty and was put on a bond for six months. It was all over in 20 minutes. I was £25 poorer but a lot wiser.

My first big break came not long after I started Nu-Signs when I developed an idea for using a silkscreen process to mass-produce signs. I knew that L. J. Hooker had been paying £3 for each real estate sign that they had erected to sell property across the city, so I went to them and said: 'Look, instead of buying a sign each time you need to sell a block of land I'll just rent you the sign for one-third of what you're paying now. But to do the deal I need all your business.' Hooker's liked the idea so I got the job. That meant I could use the same signs six to eight times, and on top of that Hooker's paid me to deliver and erect the signs then pick them up when the properties were sold. It was a big deal, the first one that made me a lot of money. Within 90 days of starting Nu-Signs I took on my first apprentice, a young chap named George Cotton, and within a year I had 28 employees. Four years later I was employing 250 people.

My Mother did the books for the business because she was the closest thing to a qualified accountant there was without actually being one. I learnt a lot from her and also did a three-year stint at night school, studying basic accounting, which was essentially very simple bookkeeping, but it was enough for me to understand a balance sheet.

My Father's health had improved considerably once he was living in Western Australia and he was going from strength to strength. He was still working as a painter and decorator so when Nu-Signs began to grow he came aboard to run the painting division, managing hundreds of workers until the long-anticipated deterioration in his health finally arrived and forced him into semi-retirement.

Frank remained a very convivial man who spent almost all his spare time down at Claremont Yacht Club where he had a small boat that he used for fishing on his much-loved Swan River. He and Mother had distinctly different influences on my life; Mother was a very determined and strong individual who knew exactly where she was going and what she wanted to achieve. She was also a good businesswoman in her own right — whatever she wanted to do she did well — while Frank was a hard-working, nice man with a lot of friends. He was the sort of chap who was quite happy just growing a few potatoes in the garden and going fishing. Looking back at their marriage it's safe to say that it was the perfect example of 'opposites attract'. They were quite different people. Certainly there was a big difference in intellect, with Mother always striving to do something new while my father was content with enjoying his life exactly the way it was. The fact that he was still alive was enough for him. He died in January 1971 aged 59 from war injuries.

Both my parents showed great affection towards Geraldine and me, but I never saw them show any affection towards each other. It seemed to be a very Victorian relationship and I've no idea what their personal life was like. They kept that side of their life, if there was such a side, very much to themselves.

My relationship with Eileen had grown stronger with time and soon we decided we should marry. It was a huge step for a 18-year-old and I was a little nervous, but outweighing that was the fact that we were very much in love and excited about our future together. However, while Eileen's parents supported the plan my mother told me I was making a big mistake, probably because the Hughes family was Catholic.

Our wedding was interesting, to say the least. We got married in St Patrick's Church and the guests were very definitely divided — Catholics on one side, and the Anglicans and Freemasons on the other. The reception was in the hall at the rear of the church where my canvas painting of the Resurrection of Christ dominated the scene.

Marrying Eileen made me feel for the first time that I was an Australian. I had married into a fourth generation Western Australian family and, as a consequence, I became part of Fremantle. At last I belonged there.

Our marriage was built from very humble beginnings because as a 18-year-old with a new business we could only afford to rent half of an awful little house with a tin roof at Hamilton Hill, outside Fremantle. We had no refrigerator, only an icebox, and when the iceman didn't turn up all our food went rotten. We wanted to build a house of our own so I worked towards getting enough money to buy a block of land I'd seen in Melville for £365. With that purchase complete we built a double garage before anything else so we could live there, and then I took out my first loan to pay for the construction of the house, a loan that I managed to repay in three years. John, our first son, arrived soon after we moved into the garage and from that moment Eileen essentially became a full-time mother.

Life was getting to be more exciting by the day and I was thriving on the challenge of expanding the business, doing the deals, making them work and making money. I was looking for every opportunity that was out there, even deciding to go for contracts with car sales yards because I thought their signs needed brightening up. This was how I became friendly with Eileen's cousin, John Hughes, who managed one of the largest car sales operations in Fremantle. We got to know each other very well and did a considerable number of successful business deals together, and we still do deals today. It is a friendship that strengthened with years and one of the few that has stood the test of time.

The momentum continued in Nu-Signs, partly because Bill Hughes's influence in town led to us getting a lot of work around Fremantle Harbour, including painting cranes and ships. I also started to look for more business via government contracts, knowing that while we were only registered painters we could employ builders and whomever else we needed to complete jobs. I won contracts to paint railway stations right through the state, even up to the Kimberleys in the north, the most famous job of all being at Geraldton where the station is a huge structure with massive frames supporting a very high roof that covers the platforms. Just about anyone who could quote on the job did so, all confirming that scaffolding costing around £25 000 would be needed to paint the underside of the station roof. I worked out that instead of using scaffolding we could suspend some timber planks between the roof struts then get up there and swing like monkeys over the top of the trains. That's exactly what we did, so we eliminated the cost of the scaffolding. The frustrating thing was that there were a few areas very high up that we couldn't quite reach to clean off the dust before painting, until I came up with the idea that if I mixed kerosene with the aluminium paint then the kerosene would penetrate the soot and bind it to the corrugated-iron roof. At the same time everything would be painted silver. It worked — the paint never came off. But there was one problem in that the kerosene made the paint we were spraying very thin and this fine silver mist, the over-spray, drifted down onto the trains underneath. Suddenly we had silver-topped trains departing the station. I thought we were in for a lot of bother with the state's railway department, but much to my amazement nothing was ever said about it. Maybe the Western Australian government liked their new-look trains.

The other memorable train station painting experience was at Mukinbudin, which is a little place 450 kilometres northeast of Perth. We were moving from station to station each day and this particular time we had only managed to spray-paint the main building before it got dark. There was a little shed at each end of the platform where people could shelter from the sun, and from the rain on the rare occasion that it occurred. We were faced with two options: come back the next day, or paint everything there and then in the rapidly fading light. I said to the guys: 'Bugger it. Crank up the compressor and we'll spray the sheds now. This place is too far away to come back to tomorrow.' With that decided one of the guys grabbed the spray-gun and went inside the then very dark shed, spraying silver paint everywhere. Suddenly there was an incredible bloody scream from inside the shed . . . and an Aboriginal man came staggering out, coughing and spluttering and painted silver on one side. He'd been lying in the corner of the shed sound asleep.

Signwriting was quickly becoming just a part of a rapidly expanding business. We got the contract to sandblast and paint many of the big oil tanks at the BP oil refinery outside Fremantle, and with that came the job of lining the refinery's catalytic cracker with bricks. I got specialists in to do that for me, but I developed my own concept when it came to building the concrete dams that were required around the base of every tank to contain any spill that might occur. Instead of an expensive concrete structure, we simply laid chicken wire over an earth wall around the tank and sprayed concrete onto the mesh. That way there was no need to have thick concrete walls forming the dam. When you consider the hundreds of tanks BP had, you'll see that this idea saved them a lot of money. We also picked up a huge state-wide contract with the Public Works Department doing complete maintenance jobs — plumbing, concreting, plaster work and painting — on batches of 50 and 100 houses at a time. I used to drive a team of men to the town where the job was located, usually in the far north of Western Australia, where we would work for 7 to 10 days straight. The workers were all new immigrants: Germans, Italians and Slavs who'd come off migrant ships and immediately gone to the Waterside Workers' offices to see if they could get a job. Before they knew it they were around the back of the building at Nu-Signs and we were signing them up.

My next big break came in 1958 as a result of my very first contract, the one with L. J. Hooker. A major east coast land development company, T. M. Bourke, was doing developments around Perth and came to me for signs. As a result of this and the Hooker deal, which had us delivering signs all over the city, I started to see which estates were selling quickly. Fortunately it got to the stage where Marcus and Adrian Bourke would fly into Perth from the east and take me to look at their new properties so I could advise them on the signs that would be needed. Before long I was learning about how they subdivided the estates and the procedures they used for building the roads. I thought: 'That's not too difficult, and look at the money they're making. I can do this. I'll go and buy some land myself and give it a shot.'

The first land I bought was in Kalamunda in 1960. Everyone I told about it said I'd lose money. How wrong they were. We did three subdivisions in quick succession in the hills to the east of Perth — Kalamunda, Lesmurdie, then Gooseberry Hill, which I called the Beverly Hills Estate. Most of the developments were around 40 or 50 acres and I marketed the blocks on television and in newspapers. In the early days Eileen and I would go up to the estates every weekend to do the selling. Back then people would pay you £4000 in cash for a block, so Eileen had this great big bag and she'd just keep shoving the money into it. When we'd get back home — or more appropriately garage — in the evening, she'd tip £20 000 or £30 000 out of the bag onto the table. It was then that I realised that I was on my way to having the one million pounds in the bank that I wanted before I was 21.

Those estates pioneered the development of the hills area. We built the first bitumen road up there, right along the escarpment. No one wanted to build roads there because it was considered too difficult and costly, especially because of the drainage, but we developed a cost-effective way of doing it and as a consequence were able to open up the estates. That project led to me forming a wonderful business relationship with a road building company, Bell Brothers, a relationship that saw them do all my road-building work for the next 30 years. Little did I know that this company, which became Bell Group and was eventually purchased by Robert Holmes à Court, would be the centrepiece of my business downfall decades later.

Working out how to build those roads was just one example of my approach to many of the challenges that faced me in my business career. So often we took on projects that people thought couldn't be done, or were considered just plain too hard. My approach was to look laterally at each challenge and work out a way to get through it. What was a problem for someone was for me just a challenge in need of a simple solution.

We utilised the cash flow from Nu-Signs to finance these estates and buildings that we were buying. We had the backing of a finance company from Adelaide which had just set up business in Perth, but still we had to keep juggling the finances on our side to keep the developments moving and the company progressing. We would take as long as we could to pay our Nu-Signs' creditors so we could use the money in the real estate deals. It was no different from what happens in business today, but the great thing back then was that we made solid financial gains because the margins for each block were so great — about 100 per cent on each fully developed block that we sold.

There was another secret source of funding I had that enhanced the development finance available to me. People in the know in the building business were often mystified by the fact that I had so much building activity going on at the one time. They couldn't work out how I was getting such large amounts of money to build all the roads for the estates in the hills, and the blocks of flats around Perth. The secret was that the brickworks I dealt with gave me up to two years credit on bricks while the Bell family gave me six months credit to pay for the roads on the estates. Rick New owned the biggest brickworks in Perth so I went to him with a proposition: 'You have all these bricks stockpiled in the yard that are going to take a long time to be used, so why not give them to me on credit so I can put them into a building. I'll pay you for them as soon as I get the money out.' It was the same with the road maker. I said: 'You've always got machines standing idle so why don't you utilise them by building all my roads and I'll pay you when the land is sold.' Both parties agreed, so I gave them all my business. I'm sure they used to charge me a little bit more for the bricks, and a little more for the roads, but it worked well for both sides — they got all my business and I got the credit. I was required to keep the deals secret because they didn't want to be forced into giving extended credit to everyone. The added benefit for me was that getting the long-term confidence of suppliers like these was crucial to the expansion of my business. Also, it was a deal where both sides had improved profits.

The only time things got really tight for us in the early days was when we built a shopping centre in Fremantle, primarily because it was a big development and the market turned against us while we were building it. We had to work very hard to keep that project going and turn it into a success. I was then 22 and had already learnt a lot from building my first block of shops in a disused quarry not far from Fremantle, but still it was tough going. Fortunately Eileen's father organised and guaranteed a big loan for me to build the centre, which had about 20 shops and a supermarket in it. My big break came with the supermarket site when Tom Wardle, of Tom the Cheap grocery fame, committed to becoming the supermarket tenant, an agreement that gave me the commitment I needed to get the finance to go ahead with the development. Tom, who became a great friend, went on to become the Lord Mayor of Perth and was later knighted, Sir Thomas Wardle. As the years passed and I established a track record in property and land development it became increasingly easy to finance projects. I had no trouble back then, in my mid-20s, getting millions in finance out of a single finance organisation, IAC, with just a telephone call to the Chief Executive, Bill Edmonds.

Just prior to doing the Lesmurdie development, when I was 20, one of my mother's better investments, the block of land she had bought on the Canning Highway at Melville, gave me a good leg-up in life. She gave me the block as what might be described as an early inheritance. I remembered everything that Kurt Lessheim taught me about building, so I had plans developed for 11 European-style townhouses to go on the block. Kurt had also taught me enough about financing for me to go out and get my first serious loan to fund the project. That loan came from the AMP Insurance Company, which was offering 5 per cent as the fixed rate over 30 years, but not to me. They decided I was a 'bit risky' because of my age and inexperience in such a development, so I had to pay 6 per cent over the same period.

I built the townhouses by employing contractors and working with them from the foundations up. I was there for three or four hours a day and any available weekend while still running the painting business and keeping everything else on track. I rented out all the flats and kept them for five years before trading the block for 10 000 acres of farming land at Westonia, 300 kilometres east of Perth on the edge of the wheat belt. I did the transaction with Leonard George Casley, the self-proclaimed Prince Leonard of what he called Hutt River Province, an unofficial principality that he proclaimed in Western Australia to bring much-desired publicity to himself and the region. He had a glass eye, and I can't tell you how difficult it was dealing with him because you never knew which eye was looking at you. One minute you'd think it was his left eye, and then you'd say to yourself 'oops, no, it's the other one'. It was very disconcerting. Dealing with him taught me a great lesson very early in life — call it a misunderstanding or whatever — but he showed me on the map of the property that 7000 acres had been cleared and 3000 acres were still bush, when the reverse was the situation. So, while I thought I was getting a good deal, I actually got a bad one because I had to go out and clear the land at my cost so I could establish the crop acreage I needed to make the place financially viable. I checked the sale contract later and realised that it didn't specify how many acres were uncleared. But as distressing as the deal was at the time, I did end up having the last laugh when I sold the property for a huge profit because the touch of luck that has been with me most of my business life was there for this project.

From the outset I went into it without hesitation, my gut feeling telling me it was time to venture into farming. My first bonus came as a result of meeting a chap named Mike Lindsay through mutual friends when we were water-skiing in Perth some time earlier. He was a farmer and a stockman from Cranbrook, more than 300 kilometres southeast of Perth, and he was the first person who came to mind as a likely manager at Westonia.

We were both at a party one night when Mike and I had the following chat:

> *Me:* 'I've bought this farm out at Westonia and it needs a manager. It's a bit of a mess. There are pigs and sheep running loose. I think you should have a crack at it for me. How about we get up there at five o'clock in the morning so you can take at look at it?'
> *Mike:* 'Alan, it sounds interesting, but it's now 11pm and besides, all my work clothes are hours away at home.'
> *Me:* 'Oh well, that's not a problem. Can you be up there at seven?'

I guess my enthusiasm was outweighing reality, but Mike turned up that day and soon decided he wanted to work with me. From that moment, and for the next 35 years, he was manager of all my rural properties, right through until he took an early retirement.

When I realised that I needed to clear a lot more of the property so it could be farmed I took to the task, driving out there almost every weekend, often with Eileen, who was pregnant with our second child, and John, and staying in the small hut we had built.

We cleared the scrub using two tractors pulling a ball and chain between them, then once the scrub was down it was bulldozed into long lines called windrows and left for a year so the timber could dry out enough to be burned. Normally it was a two-year process before you could plant crops because as well as the burn-off you had to get all the stumps out of the ground. I decided two years was too long to wait so, after some lateral thinking, I did what nobody else had done — made the windrows bigger than normal and planted a wheat crop between them. I found a Dutchman with the right gear to plough the stumps out of the ground so gave him the job. It turned into a real comedy because the ground was so rough that he had trouble staying in the seat of the tractor. We nicknamed him 'The Flying Dutchman' and laughed all day as we watched him bounce his way around the paddocks towing the plough. There was no laughing when he'd finished though; that was when the hard part came for us — picking up all the roots. It was backbreaking and tiring work that I soon realised was almost impossible to do by myself, so I finished up paying local Italian and French farmers in the area to help me.

We planted the crop and then the rain came, a beautiful 18 or 19 inches of it, about five inches more than normal. The wheat grew superbly, partly due to the rain and partly because the bigger than normal windrows protected the crop from strong winds. The result was quite amazing. We got around twice the normal harvest and I made a huge profit on the crop, hundreds of thousands of pounds. We finished up with about 8000 acres under crop the next season.

Working as long and hard as I was meant there wasn't a lot of time for social activities in those days, so cars, or more specifically big and flash imported American cars, were the go. They fascinated me immensely and became my form of pleasure. I had two mates, John Hughes and Peter Young, who imported these amazing and expensive machines that I'd buy, like a huge Oldsmobile V8. I'd just drive them around town for the fun of it, wearing my painter's overalls and enjoying the ride. At one stage I owned the flashest car in town, a stunning Chevrolet Impala that was great fun to drive. For me these cars were something that I could afford and represented a way for me to relax and enjoy my money while working such long hours.

With so much happening in my life I became very aware of the fact that I needed to manage my time carefully. I would 'compartmentalise' projects so that each one had my total concentration for the required period. I would separate myself from everything else so I could concentrate on that single project. I learnt this form of organisation very early in life — how to manage projects, put people in charge, delegate the responsibility and have a critical path in place. If the client wanted a project finished by a set date then we would work all night, if need be, to finish it. That's why we picked up so much work. We used to do a lot of shop renovations where we would map out the project then go in on the weekend and work in shifts around the clock until it was complete — new counters, completely painted and decorated, tiled floor, the lot — and ready for re-opening on Monday morning. One such project was the Roma restaurant in High Street, Fremantle. It's still there today and has on display a sign written by me in 1959 reading 'Roast chicken — £1'.

We were operating the entire business — signs, renovations, building maintenance, construction and property development — out of the office in Fremantle and were running out of space in proportion with growth. I found a suitable building nearby in Fremantle and paid £4000 for it, a big deal at the time. It had a retail space at the front, so I decided that with television just coming into existence in Australia there had to be a business opportunity somewhere. I was right. I started retailing television sets through the shop and it turned into a bit of a goldmine. It was easy money because all that was required was for us to take orders and arrange for the sets to be delivered by the distributor. People were paying a lot of money, up to £1500 for a set.

By the time I turned 21, in 1959, I had my £1 million in the bank and was building on it. Eileen and I built the house at Melville, sold it to her sister Maureen, then moved around the corner into a more 'up-market' residence, a beautiful home with a big terrace and wonderful views across the Swan River.

We'd also seen our second son, Craig, come into the world in January 1958.

In December 1961 I paid £40 000 for Rosehill Estate, a 188-acre property located in Guildford, that boasted a large historic home with a stunning garden and which was about two kilometres beyond Perth airport. There I struck up a friendship with a local Italian family and together we farmed the land for several years. I saw Rosehill as the perfect environment for the children so we moved there and enjoyed a fantastic lifestyle with wide-open spaces and a herd of cattle grazing along the riverbank. We made our own cheese and established a very impressive vegetable garden for the house. My vision was to eventually subdivide the property, but as that plan progressed I discovered there were too many problems to make that vision eventuate. After only a few years I sold the property for £96 000 and it became a golf course and country club.

About that time, in the mid-60s, I also bought Whiteman Brickworks, a rundown plant also in Guildford that should have been a museum piece. It had very limited clay reserves, antiquated equipment including inefficient timber-fired ovens, and the workers hand-stacked the bricks. The owner, Lou Whiteman, was a very rich man who offered to sell the business to me confident in the knowledge that it was a very good deal. He simply wanted to retire and get out, a move that was influenced by his knowledge that the old style brickworks, with their high labour content, could not survive. He also recognised that there would be few, if any, buyers and that he was almost certainly destined to have to close the plant down just to get rid of the problem. I was a simple solution to his dilemma.

When I first looked over the plant before buying I asked myself what the hell I was going to do with it. It was a case of modernise or perish. But I also remembered Kurt Lessheim's stories of how he made a fortune from bricks, so buy it I did for £375 000. It turned out to be like buying a goldmine instead of a brick pit when I discovered a tin box in the office, containing various title deeds to pieces of land around the brickworks as well as details of cash deposits belonging to Whiteman Brickworks. I knew when the deal was done that there was some land attached to the site, but nothing like what there really was. Some of the property was not even part of the main asset. Apparently Lou Whiteman knew what was in the tin box, but as he wanted out he let it go. The money was enough for him. Fortunately it meant that we were able to liquidate the deposits and land holdings and get our £375 000 back within a few weeks of the purchase — and still own a brickworks.

I had already learnt a lot about the brick business through my dealings with Rick New, whose company, Midland Brick, was next door to Whiteman's. First up I had to ensure the long-term future for the business so I purchased more land at Red Hill where there was a good clay deposit. But I still had to modernise. Eventually we spent $15 million (decimal currency had been introduced in Australia) developing the company into a highly efficient, gas-fired brick-making facility. I went to Germany and acquired the most modern automatic brick-making equipment ever introduced into Australia, something that allowed me to challenge the big boys and take 15 per cent of the market. Even though I was in competition with Rick New we remained good friends and eventually I sold the business to him for $35 million, a deal that gave him a monopoly and me a $20 million profit.

I had joined the Junior Chamber of Commerce in Fremantle when I was 21 and the following year became the Australian Jaycees delegate to the World Congress in Paris. I was one of the youngest delegates and delivered a paper on Australia and the interesting times that I saw coming to the nation. I met people from all over the world and started to establish solid business contacts, many of whom would cross my path in later years and lead to many profitable transactions. I wanted to learn everything I could from people at the Congress, so my most interesting challenge was to ask what business they were in, and how they were tackling the problems that faced them, what efforts they were making in new directions and whether they were doing things that other people hadn't done. These conversations with such a wide cross-section of people again convinced me that nothing was impossible. It confirmed my belief that problems are like mountains — you have to decide how to get to the other side. While some people said: 'It's too difficult. You can't go around it or over it,' I'd be saying: 'Okay then, we'll go through it.' This was an immensely valuable trip for me in so many ways, and in particular it introduced me to international business and I learnt how to negotiate a deal on the world stage.

I went by ship to France and on the way stopped off in South Africa, visiting Cape Town and Johannesburg to look primarily at gold and diamond mining ventures run by the Anglo American Group. It was a visit that would prove to be very beneficial to the development of my mining businesses in the years ahead. For example, Durak Mines, which I formed and subsequently floated when I was in my early 20s, was influenced by that trip. Someone brought the Durak project to me for consideration because I was seen as a risk taker. Yes, I was a risk taker, but what many people didn't realise was that I only took on calculated risks. In other words, you can't get a good reward without taking risks, but you have to analyse the extent of the risk. As a result of accepting the Durak deal I secured some large exploration leases in the Pilbara region of Western Australia. That made me one of the very early mineral explorers up there. We were looking for copper and gold, and after a while it became evident that there was copper in the region that might rival deposits in Zambia. I went to Anglo American with a view to them coming to Australia and investing in the project, and after their own geologists came to the site and confirmed the drilling results, they agreed. They spent a considerable amount of money on the exploration and the early results showed that we had copper intersections that were very, very rich. I organised the entire float of Durak Mines and within days of the big event someone came along and wanted to buy the company at a price that would see me double my money. My instinct told me that I should take the profit, and I did. A couple of years later it became apparent that the copper that everyone had hoped for wasn't there. What had been found was what was called a cap. There was nothing below the surface material. Ironically, the leases I held then covered all of the ground where years later the Argyle diamond deposit was discovered. But even if we had been looking for diamonds back then we probably wouldn't have found them. The technology needed to locate them didn't exist.

Even so, the opportunity came along much later to acquire control of Northern Mining, a company that had a 5 per cent interest in the Argyle Diamond Mine before diamond production began. I already knew that there were two parts to the diamond business, the actual mining of diamonds and the marketing of the product, so unlike all the other participants in Argyle, I decided to set up my own sales and marketing organisation in Antwerp. It meant that I sold our share of the diamonds directly into the Antwerp market, an action that caused great consternation to the big diamond traders, De Beers. They made many, many offers to buy the Argyle marketing rights from me to keep me out of the business, because they knew that if I could succeed in selling there then other people would realise how easily it could be done. De Beers would have competition coming at them from every direction. I didn't sell.

There was another interesting sidebar that came as a result of that trip to Paris. While the ship was en route to South Africa I met Cam Deakan, who would later introduce me to the Kuala Lumpur Kepong Amalgamated Group, a London-based company that owned rubber plantations and sugar cane farms in Malaysia. This company's board had decided that they should also be farmers in Australia, even though none of them had been there, so I seized on the opportunity and went into their boardroom in London with the plans, photographs and details of my 10 000 acres in Westonia. I said: 'Here's a property for you in Australia to consider. I own it and I want to sell it.' They were a group of classically English, puffed-up old businessmen, gentlemen farmers heading a company that had been going for a couple of hundred years, and they didn't have a clue about Australia. One of the old chaps looked over the map and said in a most pompous manner, 'Mr Bond, out there, are there any tarred roads?' It wasn't easy explaining that the property was on the edge of the outback where tarred roads, bitumen roads, were only a dream. It was bull-dust and gravel roads, and that was it. They struggled to comprehend that. Anyway, luck struck again. They looked at the figures for the crops, considered that the property was 10 000 acres, and decided to pay me something like £1.25 million for it sight unseen, a figure that was unheard of at that time for a farm in the Westonia region. From this initial investment and my introduction of Kuala Lumpur Kepong to Australia, the company went on to spend tens of millions of pounds buying many farms throughout the state.

By the mid-1960s we had outgrown our headquarters in Fremantle so the decision was to move to Perth. In our first move I paid £160 000 for a block of 26 flats in a building called *Riviera*, off the main street, St Georges Terrace, combined two of them and moved my own office into there. The plan was to rent out the rest of the building but after only a few months it was obvious that I'd bought the right place at the right time and would be moving on. It turned out that Englishman Lord Alistair McAlpine had overlooked the fact that he hadn't purchased *Riviera* when announcing plans to develop the entire block. On the night the McAlpine plan was due to be finalised and announced I was playing darts and drinking with some mates in a nearby hotel. McAlpine's lawyer, John Adams, found me there and came back with three offers during the evening to buy the building before I accepted £360 000. I had sold what is now the site of Perth's Parmelia Hotel.

Next I bought the old Adelaide Steamship building in St Georges Terrace, renovated it and moved in, then not long after that I was the owner of the ANZ Bank building in St Georges Terrace, bidding a city record of £400 000 when it came up for auction. The price, and the fact that I proposed a 13-storey structure for the site, saw the local 'experts' declaring that I'd finally gone too far. The tallest building in Perth at the time was about seven storeys, so as far as they were concerned the project would not be sustainable — I was over the edge and heading towards going broke. But it was very viable because as well as putting my own office in there I convinced the Stock Exchange to move in, and as a result all the stockbrokers followed. You didn't need to be a rocket scientist to work out how to make that one work.

By the time I was 22 I had developed a particular friendship and commercial relationship that was to have a significant influence on my business activities for decades. I went to Singapore where I was introduced by an Australian stockbroker to Jacob Ballas, a Baghdad Jew who later became a director of Bond Corporation. He in turn introduced me to Tan Sri Dr Runme Shaw, a wonderful man of Chinese descent who was one of the wealthiest men in Asia. Throughout the relationship we developed, Runme Shaw, and later his brother Sir Run Run Shaw, invested in a number of my projects. Runme had direct shareholdings in West Australian Land Holdings and subsequently Bond Corporation. These holdings were structured through various trusts and foundations that he had set up which were not easily identified with him because, while he was a great friend and supporter of the company, he wanted to retain a low profile because he feared being kidnapped and held to ransom.

The brothers made their fortune owning movie theatres throughout China and hotels in Asia. My relationship with Runme

Shaw developed because he could relate to me and where I had come from in life — he and his brother also started with nothing, pulling rickshaws in Shanghai while pursuing an education. Runme became a real friend and I was privileged to share some memorable times with him when visiting his huge house in Singapore.

What was notable about Runme Shaw was that he was quietly spoken and had a very quiet nature, something that made for a surprisingly calm yet positive way of negotiating in business. The name Runme means 'kindness', and that was very fitting for the man. The brothers were very focused on any negotiations they were doing, and their attitude was quite unlike anything we are used to in the western world. I learnt a great deal from Runme over a long period about how to negotiate with people from an oriental culture. It was a slow but extremely valuable learning process.

Such was my relationship with Runme that a couple of times when we ran short of money on a deal and faced difficult times he would provide the cash to help us out. I'd just announce to the media and those who mattered that we had found the money we needed for a particular project and were proceeding with the deal, but no one knew where the money had actually come from. The media speculated about me being assisted by my 'Chinese mogul' even though they had no idea who it was. When he did come in to help he insisted that there was nothing in his own name; it was all left in my name, even though he was a partner. He trusted me implicitly and believed in what I was doing, his desire always was to be behind the scenes and help me achieve my goals. He had a very big impact on my life.

Runme remained in Singapore where he passed away in 1985 aged 88. Sir Run Run, whom I hadn't done business with at that stage, was based in Hong Kong, and Hong Kong is where I was, establishing my international business headquarters, when Runme died. As a consequence of Runme's passing Sir Run Run and I started doing business, our first venture being my acceptance of his invitation to be a major shareholder and deputy chairman of Hong Kong TVB. It was my first big entrée into business in Hong Kong and interestingly, when I accepted the offer of the TV deal, I was able to apply a cultural lesson that I had learnt from Runme. I made a very wise decision in the way I structured the TV business in that while I held a larger shareholding than Sir Run Run, I asked him if he would stay as the chairman of Hong Kong TVB while I took the lesser position of deputy chairman. It was a demonstration of respect that was very well received.

In my mid-20s, having already been into farming for some years, I decided that I'd go around the world and have a look at projects that might interest me. It ended up being the trip that led to me becoming the pioneer of live sheep exports out of Western Australia.

We became aware that an opportunity existed to export live sheep to Iran so I visited there on a number of occasions and agreed to a joint venture with a representative of the Shah of Iran, who was then head of state. It was a £40 million contract with the Iranian Meat Organisation, but having that order was one thing; getting the project together was another. For a start we didn't have any ships to transport the still to be found sheep.

When I got back to Perth I created a master plan and then set about implementing it. It started with a search for ships, and that led to the establishment of a joint venture with a Norwegian company that had two log-carrying vessels lying idle in the Netherlands which were suitable for conversion to sheep transporters. I signed up a group of Norwegian naval architects to design the sheep-pen structure that was needed to go on top of the ship, and while this was being done I had the ships sail to Taiwan where I knew I could get the conversion done for the right price.

Fortunately, just prior to doing this deal, I had employed a chap named Warren Jones as a troubleshooter within Bond Corporation, and this was the perfect job for him — he had to coordinate this entire project, find the sheep, get them on the ship and get them to Iran. He had originally come to me to ask if I wanted to buy his local machinery and building equipment hire business, Skipper Mayday.

We did buy it and tipped in some additional capital, but while it was a good business it was destined to never really go anywhere, so we sold out. But I kept Warren on and as it turned out he became a long-serving and very loyal lieutenant who had a great way with people. He would also become a pivotal part of my America's Cup campaigns in later years.

Logically, with sheep involved, Warren started talking to my farm manager, Mike Lindsay, and we soon realised that Mike should be part of the team. He came in to help when the first ship was approaching Fremantle for our first cargo of sheep.

Between them, Mike and Warren found the sheep we needed, got them to Fremantle and loaded them, with considerable difficulty I might add because the design had a lot of faults, something that wasn't really surprising when you consider it was our first shot at it. But the loading problems would prove to be minuscule compared with what we faced when the ship was underway and heading into the sweltering weather near the equator. Fortunately both Warren and Mike were on board to see first hand that there just wasn't enough airflow through the pens, and in the incredible heat the poor sheep were dropping dead at a rapid rate, so fast in fact that Mike and Warren started thinking that we would be lucky to have any left by the time the ship reached Iran. They had to find a solution and soon worked out that there was only one option — every so often the ship would do big figure-eight loops to get more breeze across the decks and through the pens. At one stage the ship even went backwards into the breeze just to keep the sheep cool. They also had to deal with disposing of the dead sheep, a problem compounded by the fact that the crew comprised mainly Indians whose religious beliefs wouldn't allow them to handle the carcasses. It turned into a very interesting confrontation with the crew but after some solid negotiations the dead sheep were dumped over the side.

The design faults were Lesson One. Lesson Two in how to survive in the live-sheep export business came when the ship arrived in Iran. The first interesting experience, as Mike would tell me later, was with the Iranian veterinary specialist who came on board to clear the cargo. Wearing pink pants and purple shoes, he looked more like someone from a circus. He came up onto the bridge and started hanging around, not wanting to do anything until someone slipped him some money and a bottle of scotch under the table. The moment he received his payola he declared that the ship was clear to be unloaded. He didn't even inspect it.

Next, when the sheep were being unloaded the local dockworkers would go in, pick one of them out and disappear off up the dock with it. We couldn't work out what was going on until it was explained to us that the sheep being taken were considered to be too sick to go to slaughter. They didn't look sick to our guys yet it was obvious that the Iranians were intent on knocking off hundreds of them. It turned out that the workers were Bedouins who were taking the sheep to the local butcher to be slaughtered for their family and friends. Every sheep that didn't get to the slaughterhouse was money out of our pocket, so Warren stepped in and paid the Bedouins what we called a living supplement, a payment to ensure they were more selective about how many sheep they knocked on the head.

As this first ship was so unsuitable for the job we sent it straight to Singapore for extensive modifications, and at the same time set about modifying the second ship before putting it into service. I sent Mike Lindsay to Singapore to oversee the job, along with a naval architect. To get the work done in the shortest possible time they had 900 Chinese labourers working in shifts around the clock while Mike and the architect worked 21 hours a day. Mike didn't know the first thing about ships when he started but he certainly knew plenty by the time the job was done. The good news was that we lost very few sheep on all the runs we did from then on.

After two years of operation and delivering nearly 500 000 sheep, good fortune was to follow us into this business as well. We got out of it less than a year before the Shah of Iran was ousted and the sheep import business collapsed. I had been approached by the National Australia Bank, which had a client who wanted to get into the live-sheep export business in a big way. I'd been going to Iran on a regular basis and could feel the tempo of the place changing, and you didn't have to be Einstein to realise political trouble was brewing. I told the bank that there was an element of uncertainty about the future of the business and that I didn't think it was a wise investment for their client, but they stayed firm and offered me a price that meant I would make millions of dollars in profit. I took it.

This project confirmed for me yet again that if you go into something first you make the initial capital gain by establishing the market. To be a pioneer shouldn't necessarily be a worry because you are showing the way. The followers may go on and do it better than you, but if you are the first into something innovative and do a good job then you can expect to make a significant profit because others will want to buy you out. We were first in many, many ventures over the years and made good profits as a result.

We formed West Australian Land Holdings in 1969 and that company, which soon after became Bond Corporation, was floated on the stock market as our first public company so we could buy 5000 acres of land just 14 kilometres north of Perth and develop it into an estate. I had many Asian shareholders in the company, including Runme Shaw and the heads of two Asian banks, and things were looking very positive on this deal because we were buying the land for $5 million and looking at a profit of around $150 million ... until the Western Australian government stepped in and said that we couldn't proceed with the development, stating the property was already subdivided into 50-acre blocks and that as it was to be part of the catchment area for Perth's water supply it could not be further subdivided. They froze me out and in the end all I could do was sell the land to the government for the price I had paid. That was to be my first unsatisfactory run-in with a state government, an experience that I didn't forget.

I looked on it as another lesson learnt and pushed on, soon going beyond the borders of Western Australia and developing projects across the country — land deals in Queensland and shopping centres in Melbourne for a start. Our reputation was such that while others were talking about doing developments we were seizing the opportunities and making them work.

Throughout this incredible time of establishment Eileen provided wonderful support emotionally, and as a mother. By then our family was complete. Susanne was born in 1959 and Jody in 1966, but while there was plenty of money around we still had our share of financial ups and downs and often experienced tight times. Most of the money we had was invested and we had to regularly borrow more to invest in new projects or to keep the existing ones going. Things became extremely difficult when land sales slowed but we always managed to pull through. My theory was that I always wanted our money to be working for us and not sitting around. And most importantly, that we didn't take it out of projects, an approach that a lot of people tend to forget. While shareholders in many other companies were taking their dividends out, we were turning our money back in to propel expansion.

As a result of this approach I had more than $25 million in net assets when I was 28.

CHAPTER THREE
A PIONEERING SPIRIT

The more I met successful people across the world the more I realised there were no real limitations when it came to where you could go in business, so long as you were prepared to take on the task and plan it properly. In hindsight though, I believe I did look too far ahead on some of my projects — I went into them too early and didn't account for the limitations associated with human frailties. Certainly in some projects I was ahead of the times in what I was doing and what the market could stand: while I had the vision and the energy to drive the project forward, others struggled to comprehend it fully and keep up the pace. I tended to force the market, but that's what pioneering is all about — you either have that pioneering spirit or you don't.

I also had what can be called a bulldog spirit, a fighting spirit in business, a trait that I'm sure was a direct result of being in England during the war years. The soul of Britain during the war, the spirit that defeated Hitler, came from Winston Churchill's words: 'Never give in, never give in, never, never . . . never give in.' I felt the same way in business. I was always willing to fight if I believed in something and wanted to achieve a result.

I did learn very early in life that if you could get hold of an asset and add value to it then its value increased and you could sell it at a higher price. That experience goes way back to the days of the jam jar business when I was a kid in London. The jars were filthy when I got them — washing and cleaning them made them worth more and the locals were happy to buy them from me for their pickling. The old shell cases we salvaged from the Hoover factory were scrap before we polished them and turned them into vases and ornaments that we sold for more pocket money. This approach to profit making was to hold me in good stead for the rest of my business life. Very simply, if you had an old caravan and painted it, it was worth more. There was no market for it in its dilapidated state, but there was when it was done-up. I used to buy old caravans and do just that — paint them and sell them for a considerable profit.

So 'value added' has been the basic premise for so much of my business activity over the years. For example, we would buy buildings, renovate them and therefore improve their rental value in the market. I bought an old quarry, quarried the rest of the limestone out of it and then used the site for a shopping centre — we changed the value of the quarry by adding something to it. And we took that same attitude to the big issues: Santos was just a gas company when we bought it, but then we spent $600 million building the pipeline and changing it into an oil producer. That was also a project that demanded persistence — I went to dozens of banks before I found three that would lend me $200 million each to develop the plan.

Improved value was the same approach we took to the Robe River iron ore mine when we bought it in 1973, then changed the value by increasing tonnage output and expanding the market. As a result we turned a loss-making venture into a profit maker. It was no different with the Chile Telephone Company. When we took it over they only had 450 000 lines in operation, and there were 400 000 people on the waiting list for telephone connections. What I did was look at the problem laterally and finished up putting in the first modern telephone system across the country using satellite communications. We were way ahead of our time in the communications industry on that one. In remote areas, where it was too expensive to put a line in, we were selling mobile phone handsets for $US3000 each. What we did was change the value of the company by putting in a modern communications system.

One of the most positive examples of thinking outside the square was my approach to Queensland Nickel, in Townsville. No one wanted it because it was losing $40 million a year. They couldn't see what to do with it because it was running out of ore. It was going to be run down within 18 months and liquidated. But I came up with the concept of importing unprocessed lateric nickel ore from Indonesia and New Caledonia. The plan made the purchase viable and added considerable value to the company. We made really big profits as a result of that approach. But even more importantly for me we saved thousands of jobs.

At all times I've had to have a vision of how a project could be developed, be it a mine in the middle of a desert or a property project. For me it was like looking into a crystal ball. I would look at a piece of land and visualise what could be done with it, and it's something I still do today. I can close my eyes and see the buildings rising, the houses being developed and the kids in the playgrounds at the schools we planned to build. I can see what is needed now and what will be needed in the future. These visions were a direct result of my travelling overseas regularly and extensively on exploration trips with two or three of my executives. We went just to look at projects and see what was going on in the world. We spent a lot of time in America and Europe, looking in particular at large real estate developments.

It has been no different in mining. I've been able to look positively at a remote location somewhere in the world where the problems have been extreme temperatures and impossible transportation. While others have not been able to visualise the opportunity and how to develop it, I've turned a vision into reality and made it profitable.

So often though, you would have your visions frustrated by people who just did not understand, or who had their own private agendas that were to the detriment of the community. For example, in the early days, we were doing a huge number of developments in Perth and, with almost every development where we had to deal with bureaucrats, I was left in no doubt that there weren't enough people with business experience elected to the Perth City Council. Poor decisions were being made by misguided, unqualified people. Costs were going up and rates were continuing to spiral. I wanted to do something about it, and the only way was to do it myself. My attitude was: 'It's all very well to criticise other people, but if you want to change things then you'd better get in there and do some of the work yourself.' So I stood for council and after some effort I was elected. Interestingly, I wasn't elected by big business people but by the ethnic minorities. They could relate to me because they were European people who had come to Perth and set up their own small businesses, and they held similar concerns about mismanagement in the council.

During my three-year term the face of the council changed dramatically. The rates never increased in that period and we saved considerable money by outsourcing things like rubbish removal. The council had been getting out of its depth by venturing into commercial enterprises, so we put a stop to that. It was the council's job to serve the community rather than compete with it. I got myself onto the finance and town-planning committees and encouraged them to free things up and get the city moving. I believed that the best way to add to Council coffers was to get more people into the city rather than penalise the people already there. Perth has always been a dead city at night because of council constraints. In Europe, and even in cities like Sydney, high-density residential is allowed near the city centre. This makes them living cities. There were some wonderful plans proposed for Perth but they've failed to materialise, beaten more often than not by blind bureaucracy. Perth as a city needs special attention when it comes to planning, particularly because it's a windy city where the inhabitants can literally get blown away. The entire city plan needs a major rethink and the north of Perth needs to be linked with the city proper. Today a railway line divides the two centres, and that divide creates a haven for vandalism and hooliganism. If they put that section of the railway line underground you'd bring the two halves of the city together and create an exciting new metropolis, and as a consequence it would become a much better city.

Another problem we faced on the council was that there were 27 councillors, which was far too many. While they all thought they had the right intentions there were too many chiefs. The same job could have been done with just five councillors and an effective administration. It's a problem we still face across Australia today — we are grossly over-governed and it all adds to the administration costs we face as a nation. All local councils should comprise no more than five people with a central planning authority in each state. Beyond local councils we need smaller state governments and fewer members of parliament.

The experience I gained from my trips abroad influenced many of my actions while I was on the council. The same trips also made a significant contribution to my first big vision in property development, Yanchep Sun City, the project that launched me into national prominence.

The property was a 19 000-acre farm 70 kilometres north of Perth that had some 17 kilometres of oceanfront. While we owned and operated the farm as a cattle property I always held the belief that there could be an opportunity one day for rezoning it for residential development, and that was what happened. When it was rezoned I initially did some small developments along the oceanfront and sold them off, but all the time I was contemplating the potential of the entire property, looking at the big picture, and one day I struck on an idea.

It was 1971 and my vision was to develop an entire city on the site, Yanchep Sun City, a city that would eventually accommodate a quarter of a million people, something that was unprecedented in property development in Australia. At that stage of my life I had become a very active sailor and had been campaigning my new ocean racing yacht, *Apollo*, in America and England, an experience that had made me aware of the America's Cup, the world's oldest sporting trophy and yachting's ultimate prize. So I expanded my vision to include a challenge for the America's Cup that would be based out of Yanchep, a move that would ensure the project hit the headlines both nationally and internationally. I went to the Western Australian government and presented my master plan for the project in the hope I would get the necessary approvals. The plan involved the construction of a harbour extending out into the ocean, a town centre, university, golf course, light industrial area and a high-technology park. Nothing was left out. I told the government that Yanchep was going to be the home of the America's Cup because I was going to build a yacht, race the Americans, win the cup and bring it back to Yanchep. I remember adding: 'if the Americans can hold the cup for 120 years then we can hold it for 120 years,' and I believed it because I was a brash young 33-year-old building a city for 250 000 people. For me this wasn't land development — it was a beautiful blueprint for a future that I was convinced was going to happen. What I was blind to at the time was how long it would take to both create the city and win the America's Cup.

When the government saw the master plan the then premier, Sir Charles Court, said, 'well why not? Why not let him have a go at it?' Going in our favour was the fact that the government had always envisaged developing the corridor along the oceanfront to the north and south of Perth. All I was doing by developing Yanchep was skipping 50 kilometres and moving 30 years ahead of their plan. Their approvals for the development came, but there were lots of provisos. They were concerned about the supply of services, mainly power and water, but I told them not to worry about that, as I'd put in my own water and power supplies.

My decision to base an America's Cup campaign out of Yanchep as the basis for the marketing hook came about because of what I'd learnt from looking at other big estate developments overseas. I'd realised that if I was going to sell 60 000 home sites then the project had to offer something special. I also knew that I would soon need a significant financial partner so I could get things moving the way I wanted, but in the meantime we would start by doing our own land sales and get the cash flow moving so we could pay for the America's Cup campaign. At the end of the first 12 months we had sold 1350 blocks of land at an average price of $6000, so there was no need to worry about cash flow.

The biggest problem I faced in getting property sales moving was that the land was primarily rolling sand dunes, and sand dunes wouldn't look too good in the brochures and advertisements we were proposing to use to promote and sell the concept of Yanchep. The other problem we faced was that whenever the wind blew — which is very often in Perth during summer — it took the sand dunes with it. So I needed to stabilise the sand as well as make the property look more appealing. The solution soon became obvious — just mix green paint and grass seeds with a light bitumen and spray all the sand hills with it, and voilà, you've solved both problems in one hit. Instantly we had green sand hills that weren't going anywhere. It made for great brochures as I then had presentable photographs — a beautiful blue sea and green land, land that eventually became naturally green because the grass seeds in the mixture took root and nature took its course.

While we were developing the land we were also starting work on the harbour. Yanchep was well known for its occasional ferocious seas, so we found a Russian designer, with experience in building seawalls that could withstand rough weather, to do the plan. The harbour walls were between 12 metres and 18 metres wide at the base and 6 metres across the top. Fortunately there was enough limestone on the property to build the wall, but it needed to be quarried. No problem — I opened a quarry.

My search for a financial partner for the project went on unabated during this initial development stage. Eventually I found the Tokyu Corporation in Japan, a company that had investments in property and retail stores and also operated railway lines. A part of my Yanchep plan was to have a rapid transport rail system linking Yanchep and

Perth, so Tokyu slotted perfectly into this project. I was convinced that rail was the logical solution for any big development because traffic only clogs up roads. Railways allow you to have effective high-density developments yet incredibly, here we are more that 30 years later and only now is the Western Australian government realising the importance of a rail system, and it's still only about two-thirds of the way out to Yanchep. Sadly, with such a rail system there is a political argument as to the wisdom of doing it, but it must be done, because no city functions well without good transportation.

Tokyu Corporation agreed to come into the project about the time of the America's Cup challenge in 1974 and paid $19 million for a 49 per cent share. I'd originally paid $1.9 million for 100 per cent of it and had spent about $10 million on the development at that stage. But I'd also received a lot of that money back from the land sales, so having Tokyu's involvement made it an even better deal. But my dream of a rail system for Yanchep turned blurry when the Tokyu people, who had originally led me to believe that they would proceed with it as soon as possible, changed their mind and decided against it in the foreseeable future. I think it was a question of economics on their part, but had we won the America's Cup in 1974 then Yanchep would have boomed and the rapid transit system may have been established very quickly.

Looking at how things have now developed, I can say that my vision for Yanchep was probably 30 years ahead of its time. Certainly the people who got in early and bought land can't complain today. Blocks they paid between $3000 and $4000 for now cost $50–100 000, while oceanfront blocks are now selling for $350 000.

Soon after I got Tokyu involved I realised that their philosophy for the development was diametrically opposed to ours. We wanted to push ahead while they wanted to wait for the natural progression of development to get there. And they had the money to wait, as Yanchep was only a small deal for them. Inevitably we were soon at loggerheads and within two years of combining forces we wanted out.

It seemed we were being confronted by problems on every side as we looked for a way to extricate ourselves. For a start we didn't win the America's Cup, and locally land sales had slowed. It was a time of tight liquidity for us and the company needed the money from the sale of Yanchep. However, the state government wouldn't let us sell our 51 per cent holding to the Japanese and give them 100 per cent ownership. We were between a rock and a hard place.

One of my biggest challenges while building Bond Corporation into a strong and diversified company, was to remain close to my children, something made possible by Eileen and the very stable home life that she had created for us. She did everything she could to make my life easier. She took the children to and from school, took her turn to work at the school canteen, and generally removed any pressure from me around the house. We went to church as a family on Sundays and found time for family holidays every year. We were a lot closer than most people think.

Eileen also excelled in her role as a hostess over many, many years for the business dinners and parties we had at our homes in Perth, Sydney and London, and while travelling around the world. These get-togethers were tremendously advantageous for the growth of the company, and Eileen played an invaluable role in creating the right atmosphere at all times.

John and Craig went to the local Aquinas Catholic College where they did very well academically and in sport. Both were in the school army cadet corps, something that I believe gave them a greater appreciation of discipline. I really encouraged them to play sport, because sport was something that I longed for but missed out on as a youngster because of the war. Their achievements throughout their school years made me very proud; Craig was in the top 10 in Australia in his age group as a breaststroke swimmer while John won many state medals for backstroke and freestyle. John could have gone on to be a great swimmer but chose to join Cottesloe Surf Club where he had considerable success in surf and belt races. At school he was a member of the cross-country running team. Scholastically he won a Commonwealth Scholarship and finished school with an aggregate high enough to get him into university to study medicine, which he started but then opted for two degrees in commerce and one in law. After working in a Perth law firm John went to London where he did very well working in merchant banking. Craig's other sporting prowess was in rugby where he was captain of the First XV and was recognised as the 'best and fairest' player as well as 'University Club Champion'. He was two years behind John at school and after leaving Aquinas went to the University of Western Australia to get a commerce degree in finance and marketing before going to London where he did the residential executive program at the London Business School.

I was grooming John to take over the empire I was busy building, so it was very satisfying to see him achieving such wonderful success in the business world. It seems anything that he has pursued in his life he has been good at — tennis, golf, football, triathlon. But it did come as a surprise for Eileen and me when he told us that one of the career paths he was considering was to enter a seminary and become a priest. On reflection, it was understandable because John is the sort of man you can look at and say that he had been touched by God to be a disciple in today's world. When he and his wife, Gemma, were first married they used to go out and help delinquent children. Today I wouldn't describe him as being overly religious, but I am proud to say he is a very good man. Everyone who knows him agrees.

Our eldest daughter, Susanne, got caught up in the hype of our first America's Cup challenge in 1974 and as a result decided she wanted to go to school in America, which she did. She was also an enthusiastic rider, something my father had encouraged both her and Jody to take up when they were very young. He loved riding and had an affinity with horses, but because of his illness was not fit enough to ride himself. Thanks in no small way to my father's support in those early years, Susanne went on to become a successful equestrian event rider and competed all over the world. She chose that as a career path instead of a university course and went on to be in the team that won the European Cup for Australia, and she narrowly missed selection to the Australian team for the

Olympics in Seoul in 1988. Sadly, Susanne died when she was only 41 in tragic circumstances that I will detail later.

Jody started her schooling at Loreto Convent in Perth but later became a boarder at Geelong Church of England Grammar School, an experience that included a year at Timbertop in the mountains outside Melbourne, the same school that Prince Charles attended when he was young. Jody was a boarder for three years, showing all along that she was an excellent student. During that time we'd established a home on a 1750-acre property, Wormbete, at Winchelsea to the west of Melbourne, because it was easier for me to work out of there when I had so many projects happening in the east of Australia. The farm provided a wonderful opportunity for Jody to get a break from boarding school. On many weekends, and during school holidays when she didn't come back to Perth, she would take a group of friends there to enjoy the country lifestyle and do lots of riding. Like John and Craig she later attended the University of Western Australia where she studied for a commerce degree with honours in marketing. She went on and completed an MBA at Harvard Business School in the United States.

Wormbete was a magnificent property that held special memories for the family. As much as I enjoyed the ocean and sailing I found great pleasure associated with life in the country, and fortunately farming and grazing became an important part of the business and our family life. Early on I learnt from Mike Lindsay that old phrase that was the theory of farmers on how to be successful: 'If you're going to buy land or cattle, you've got to be a real snob; you have to buy the best.' Certainly Wormbete was among the best, an absolute blue-ribbon property that we had from 1974 until 1987. It was on the Barwon River and had been owned by the Hopkins family for 137 years before we bought it. The house was a magnificent two-storey bluestone structure with a slate roof. Eileen and I had great fun completely refurbishing it, especially the interior. The bluestone shearing shed on the property was the original church in the district back in 1830 or thereabouts.

At the height of our rural operations we controlled seven properties and Mike Lindsay managed all of them. He was totally committed to making every one a success, and when things went wrong he really felt it personally. One day he bought a large number of sheep to spread across six of the properties, and almost as soon as he had done the deal the price of wool went down. He came along to me very distressed and said: 'Alan, I've made a prize blunder here, and you know it's going to cost us.' The only thing I could do was put my arm around his shoulder and say: 'Look, let's not talk about what we have done, let's talk about what we're going to do.' There's nothing else you can do in a situation like that when circumstances are beyond your control. You must always look to the future. I always enjoyed working with Mike.

Between 1972 and 1974 I discovered for the first time the pressures that come with a general shortage of cash in a business. Our problems came about primarily because of a savage credit squeeze and the fact that we were carrying about $35 million in debt. One thing that was going to help us out of the bind was the deal where Tokyu Corporation had agreed to buy 49 per cent of Yanchep, but we couldn't get federal government approval for the sale because it was seen as being outside the guidelines for foreign investment, even though the Western Australia government was in support. I finished up going to Canberra and had meetings with the Minister for Urban and Regional Development, Tom Uren, who remained adamant that the deal wasn't on, so I simply said: 'Well, if you won't let me sell it to the Japanese because you want to keep it in Australia then the government should match the offer.' I also told them that the Western Australia Premier, Charles Court, had pledged support for a state government buy-out, but because they didn't have the money they would need the federal government to back a loan. Still the federal government's answer was 'no', so we remained in a very tight financial situation until the approval for the sale finally came through from the Reserve Bank in the latter part of 1973.

Beyond Yanchep, our financial predicament wasn't being helped by the fact that land sales in Victoria had fallen in a heap, and two of our major financial backers for our projects were in trouble. We were involved in a huge development at Taylors Lakes, something like 4200 acres of home sites only 20 kilometres from central Melbourne. I had created a series of lakes as a centrepiece of the development and we were opening up subdivisions all around the site. There were a lot of front-end costs associated with building all the lakes and with land sales slow we were being stretched by our financiers.

Industrial Acceptance Corporation (IAC), who'd been long-time backers for us, agreed to finance the whole Taylors Lakes project, but they were in financial trouble as the result of the squeeze and eventually had to be bailed out by another American group, Citibank. This was a smart move by Citibank in many ways because in doing the bail-out they got their business into Australia without having to have a banking licence. So Citibank then inherited the commitment to keep funding Taylors Lakes because it was an open-ended, non-recourse deal. IAC's contract stated in essence 'we will fund all the development work and be paid out of the land sales'. But while the contract committed them to ongoing funding for the project they were unable to provide the necessary money and stopped supporting us. The big question however, was whether or not Citibank would keep IAC going through its losses. So here we were having the Taylors Lakes financier going down the gurgler and, to make things worse, CAGA, which was backing other projects we were doing, also looking dodgy because they too faced massive exposure from other developers across Australia.

I went along to Citibank and said: 'We currently owe you $16 million from Taylors Lakes, so now you can either lend us another $20 to $40 million, which you're obliged to do in this contract so we can complete the job, or alternatively I'll give you $4 million for the lot and you can walk away.' Citibank didn't like the idea that under the IAC contract there was still up to $40 million needed to finish the job, so they stopped funding, and that left us in a hell of a bind because we weren't able to finish the blocks and put them on the market for cash flow — and we already owed

$16 million to IAC there and then. Citibank puffed up their chests like big Americans and said: 'Well we're Citibank. We didn't sign that contract, that was IAC, and we're not going to honour IAC's commitments to you.'

My response? 'Okay, then we have no other choice but to sue you in Australia and America. However, if you want to get out of the commitment for the other $40 million you can sell me the debt.'

As I had no other choice, my threat of legal action was real, and it was done for a very good reason. It was at the time when I was challenging for the America's Cup, and my profile in the business world in America was quite high. A legal battle with me over a property development in Australia would have been a public relations disaster for Citibank. They soon realised this and decided to take the $4 million which, to get the development, I paid personally from one of my family companies because Bond Corporation at the time didn't have the money.

It was a smart way out for Citibank because they had the obligation to provide the rest of the money, and they knew that if the land sales didn't occur immediately, which was quite possible, then they wouldn't get anything back for a long, long time. Needless to say, Citibank were not happy chappies at all, but it was the only way to be sure that they'd cut their losses. They eventually agreed to take the deal but then it took a further two years to complete the development and turn the project around to where we pulled in a lot of money for us. In buying it personally I had protected the asset for Bond Corporation until the company was in a position to take over the deal once again. The important thing is that despite the most dire predictions by the media as to the demise of Bond Corporation at the time — based on assumptions and not fact because they didn't know what was happening behind the scenes and that we had the contract for IAC to cover us all the way — we survived. Unfortunately though, we couldn't fight the adverse publicity because it could have ended up in the courts. We couldn't come out and say what our position was commercially and that we felt we were on good ground because then IAC might have been forced into a very awkward position of compromise with other borrowers. They might have been forced into assisting others through the credit squeeze. It was a case of a good deal for us. Others weren't so lucky with the contracts they held with IAC, but that's what contract negotiations are all about. Fortunately for us, with me buying the debt from IAC personally, I was able to refinance the entire project because Bond Corporation then had no liability on the land. We eventually made a lot of money out of a project that took 20 years to complete. It involved around 5000 homes, and I guess the final profit was approximately $200 million.

At this time, the newshounds and doomsayers also had the house I was building on the riverfront in Perth under threat of repossession, but it was never under risk. The situation was that it was a big job — a four-level home that needed another $1 million-plus put into it to complete it, and because money was tight for Bond Corporation it was money that I didn't have. I needed to spend that $1 million elsewhere to help the company, so I stopped construction of the house. All I did was prioritise things — the house wasn't the priority, buying the Taylors Lakes debt back from Citibank was, so I had to find $4 million personally which meant pulling my horns in wherever possible. With the house it was a case of 'we can defer that for a while', and we did, but only for a few months. Yet again, because I had a high profile, the headlines had it sounding disastrous for us, but once we got the financial side of Bond Corporation reorganised and settled it took us only six months, not years, to recover our position.

Even though this was a time of tight finances we were continually looking for opportunities for the company because that's when you often pick up the best deals, and that is exactly what happened, for we soon found ourselves heading into our first large mining project, Robe River, one of the most significant iron ore projects in Australia. The company produced iron ore pellets and had a lot of international contracts in place, but it was in a bit of bother because it was an asset of Mineral Securities, a company that was facing bankruptcy and which had seen an administrator appointed in

1971. It was quite a messy situation with loans worth tens of millions of dollars outstanding and a lot of people wondering how on earth they were going to get their money out. The receivers were having trouble finding anyone interested in taking on Robe so I went along to see them in the hope we could strike a deal. We were interested in buying just less than 50 per cent of the company, or 16.2 million shares, to hold a controlling interest, and in pursuing the deal Bond Corporation found itself subjected to strong public scrutiny in the world of big business for the first time. The pressure was on from the moment we expressed an interest.

It was a massive deal for us, and we faced two very important questions during the negotiations — how were we going to pay for it and, considering that Robe River was still losing money, could it be turned around? The decision was 'yes, it could be turned around', just like we had done with so many other projects, so I negotiated to buy it, on terms. The purchase price was around $15 million and after agreeing to a payment schedule that I knew was reasonable we put down a 10 per cent deposit. Because we were seen by many to have again over-extended ourselves we came under heavy questioning every time a payment fell due. The headlines were along the lines of 'Bond Corporation mightn't make the payment', 'If Bond doesn't pay the $2 million that is due by 11 o'clock tonight then the whole Mineral Securities deal will collapse'. They were sensational headlines that made things unnecessarily difficult for us because they caused the financial institutions to look at us in a negative light, and as a result they were not prepared to come up with any of the finance we needed. The deal was very complex; it could not be financed directly through loans because it wasn't secured other than through shares in Robe River Limited. While the contract provided for a partial release of shares to us, the liquidator held the remaining shares until the final payment. Still, despite the headlines, we managed to raise some money from outside sources, and yes, I did once again turn to my 'Chinese mogul' for help. Runme Shaw put some money in on the quiet.

Not making our life any easier was the fact that the banks and lenders exposed to Minsec were suddenly breathing down our necks because they thought we might fall over on the deal and they could lose out. In particular Bill de Boos from the Bank of New South Wales was hounding us because the bank had the potential to lose about $15 million. No one was prepared to put their hand up to help us save their bacon, but they were quite happy to be negative and hinder us. Regardless of these obstructions and intrusions, we still managed to grind out the money needed when each payment was due, sometimes after getting an extension of a few hours, a few days or a week from the liquidator, Jim Jamison, just so we could keep the deal together. What no one realised was that this deal was a game of tactics between us, the liquidator and the banks. I always believed we had as much time as we wanted to come up with the money because it was too big a mess for them to unravel if the deal fell over — the banks were the big creditors and it wasn't in their interest to vote us out or see us fail, even though they made it as hard as they could for us to succeed. At the same time we decided to ignore the media as much as we could because we believed if we tried to explain our tactics to them they would either not understand or they would see it as a ruse, a stalling tactic to try to take the heat off us. So it was thought best not to deal with them and in doing so let them try to second-guess us for good or bad. Looking back now, it is obvious that building a better relationship with the media by taking them into our confidence would have been a wiser course of action. Our media advisers let us down on this one.

What drove me to secure the Robe deal was that we believed it was potentially a good mine. Our numbers people told us that while the company was going through a bad patch, increased sales and higher iron ore prices would quickly improve the situation. Also, importantly for us, it was a company based in the Pilbara region of Western Australia, so it was a Western Australian deal, and we believed we knew more about it than the guys sitting in Sydney making all the statements.

Another factor that influenced my enthusiasm for Robe River was that I'd been associated with Lang Hancock, the man who founded the iron ore industry in Western Australia, and I'd seen where he was headed. We had been virtual neighbours on the riverfront in Perth and I'd spent time with him over many, many years, professionally and socially. I'd been up to the north of the state with him when he was a relatively young man to look at the mining projects he had already established and to experience some prospecting. So I knew the Robe deal was a good one when it came up because Lang had already given me a strong insight into the mining industry.

My relationship with Lang reflected one thing that I've done all my life, and that is to take time to talk to people who know more about a particular subject than I do. I've also taken the time to go and walk around the assets and get a feel for them and talk to the people working there, something so many boards of directors don't do today. You must be acquainted with the assets you are managing and get a real feel for them. Lang was a great man who made the iron ore industry happen because he was able to bring together the big companies and the government to get things moving. He took them round and showed them what they could do; he sold them the big picture; what it would mean to their companies and the country if they were involved. In following Lang's lead I knew that what we were doing with Robe River was right. And I knew that even more so after we'd done the deal when he said he was interested in buying Robe River from us, his thought being to combine it with his existing business and make one big public company out of it. We got close to a deal but he finally decided it was best to stay with his specialty, lump ore, which was cheaper to mine, and not complicate things with the inclusion of a pellet business. For him it was a bit like being a specialist in the crude oil business then trying to include refined products.

There were two entities in the Robe River project — Robe River Iron Ore Associates, which was a joint venture with a number of partners principally from America and Japan, and Robe River Limited, a public company that we controlled which held the largest interest in that venture but which had the least say. Until we arrived, the Americans and Japanese had got together, worked out the prices and where all the money was going to be distributed, while the poor old Australian company that put $40 million in and was the biggest shareholder couldn't get a hearing.

Once we had control of the business I knew that if it was going to be turned around then I had to be on the board, and that's what happened. But I wasn't exactly welcomed to the party. From the outset I said to the others: 'This deal is not equitable and if it's not changed we will challenge the management contract in court and take the management away from the existing group. We, as an Australian company and the largest shareholder, will manage it and you boys will be out.'

The American group, Cleveland-Cliffs, weren't enthusiastic about this because they had a very cosy deal. They held only a small shareholding but were getting millions out of it through management fees. As a result the bottom line didn't really matter to them, so long as they were getting their fee. Their response was: 'You can't change it. That's what the contract says and we are not prepared to change'.

I responded: 'Well hang on there, the contract has to be changed and will be changed. And remember a contract can be read two ways. Think about this: you're going to the Japanese to renegotiate a pellet price with them that's different from the contract price — you want to change the terms with the Japanese because you think the circumstances have changed, so you want to change the terms of the pricing for Robe River. Correct? Well, I'm afraid, chaps, that circumstances have also changed now in the structure of the company and I want to change the terms of your appointment.'

We huffed and puffed to the extent where eventually Cleveland-Cliffs thought they'd have to buy us out.

The more we huffed and puffed the more a buy-out looked like happening. Then at the same time an American company, Phillips Brothers, bobbed up and wanted to buy our shareholding, so we sold it to them in mid-1976. We happily walked away because it was a good exercise for us. This entire situation spanned a couple of years and during that time I pushed and shoved for improvements in the existing contracts, and for new deals to be written at prices that were profitable for us and all shareholding partners.

CHAPTER FOUR
RISING TO THE CHALLENGE

Just as a property swap deal got me into farming, a similar situation got me into sailing. In the mid-60s a chap named Bill Lucas, who was one of Western Australia's best-known yachting identities, did a deal with me where he traded a yacht for some land I owned. I'd always been interested in water sports but I'd never thought about sailing. I hadn't even been aboard a yacht. However, I had done quite a bit of water-skiing over the years, and in fact the reason I have a slight limp today is because I lost a couple of toes when I crashed while I was going over a ski jump one day.

Suddenly there I was, the owner of a 51-foot racing yacht, the glamour boat on the Swan River, *Panamuna*, and never being one to miss an opportunity I decided I would give it a try. I organised for Bill to take me down to the Royal Perth Yacht Club and introduce me to the crew, who turned out to be a good bunch of blokes, and go for a sail. I liked it, so after just a few races on the river I stepped up for my initiation to offshore racing — a very memorable experience. The yacht was like a semi-submarine with water going everywhere. Bill wouldn't allow any excess weight on board so there was very little below deck when it came to crew comfort. The stove, for want of a better word, was just a Bunsen burner, and to cook on it you had to hold tins of food over the flame. Despite this I quickly discovered that I really enjoyed sailing and the camaraderie that came with it, especially in the offshore racing up and down the coast where you find an element of escape you just can't experience any other way on the planet. Not even the seemingly endless bouts of seasickness in those early days could turn me off, partly because it always felt so good when you finished the race. I also found that the more sailing I did the less prone I was to seasickness.

Local sailing legends Peter Nichol, Jack Summers and Dr Ted Griggs were the backbone of the *Panamuna* crew, and it wasn't long before we were talking about building a new boat. I'd already met Ben Lexcen, or Bob Miller as he was known back then before he changed his name, as I'd bought some sails from the Miller and Whitworth sail loft in Sydney. Ben had created some amazing 18-foot skiffs and other small sailing boats, but he had virtually no experience in designing an offshore racer. Still I just knew he was a natural talent with an amazing feel for sailboats, and I also knew he was the man that I wanted to design the new boat.

I liked Ben the moment I met him. He was a man I could relate to and in whom I held great faith as a loyal friend. Charisma and humour were in abundance with Ben. He was very much like me in some ways. He was a tradesman who had started his career at the very bottom of the ladder in the railway workshops. He was a charming, self-educated person who loathed school as a youngster, but as he matured he was forever trying hard to learn from his peers and get things right. He, too, approached problems with lateral thinking. He was not contained by existing boundaries and was prepared to experiment when others weren't. If he had a shortcoming it was that he had a short fuse and could not suffer fools. He was a doer, preferring to get in and do something himself rather than have someone else do it.

The new boat he designed for me, *Apollo*, was a reasonably radical boat for the time. It was a 57-footer built in Sydney and launched in late 1969. The shape was something like a cross between an overgrown Olympic Flying Dutchman class dinghy and an 18-foot skiff — two of Ben's favourite boats. We had a mad scramble to get the yacht ready for that year's Sydney to Hobart yacht race, so much so that we were screwing fittings onto the deck while we were heading out to the starting line. I can still see Benny pounding along the deck, totally annoyed because the boat was not ready. It all got to him in the end — in sheer frustration he ran forward, took off one of his shoes and hurled it overboard. It was typical Benny — he regularly did things like that to ease the tension. It never took much for frustration and impatience to take total control of him. I'd known him to tear telephones out of walls and to punch a hole in a wall, just to let off steam.

It was the 25th anniversary of the Sydney to Hobart race that year and there was a pretty impressive line-up of competitors. The man who was soon to become Britain's Prime Minister, Edward Heath, was competing, as was another Englishman, Sir Max Aitken, who owned our main rival and the favourite for being first to Hobart, *Crusade*. She was a very stylish, dark-blue yacht that was 5 feet longer than *Apollo*.

The Sydney to Hobart is a 1000-kilometre race and *Crusade* did as expected, leading the fleet away from Sydney and into the first night. My initiation to this classic race was as memorable as my first-ever ocean race out of Perth because a storm blew up and it was a pretty wild ride upwind through the dark hours. Inevitably I was pretty crook, and spent a lot of time with my head hanging over the side of the yacht barking like a seal, something that goes with the game for a lot of people. The storm brought hailstones as big as golf balls and when they hit the deck they sounded like rocks bouncing off a tin roof. I had a really experienced crew on board, including Olympian Dave Forbes, and they drove the yacht hard, opting not to reduce sail while other yachts around us did. I felt more comfortable when Trygve Halvorsen, one of Australia's greatest offshore sailors, came to me and said 'Alan, we're doing okay so we're going to drive this boat hard all night', and boy oh boy, was he true to his word. I thought that *Apollo* was going to break into wooden splinters every time she launched herself off a huge wave and pounded into the following one. She'd come down with a thundering bang and a massive shudder, just like a jumbo jet landing very heavily. Everything shook, and I struggled to understand how the mast stayed in the boat. It certainly said a lot for Benny's talents as this was the first offshore test for one of his designs. The next day the wind turned around and came from behind so we set a spinnaker and soon discovered what a great yacht we had under us. That boat could surf like no other — you could do over 20 knots down a wave, an amazing speed for that style of yacht. Our heaviest spinnaker was almost bullet-proof and whenever we had it set we knew we were in for a fantastic ride. I can't tell you how many times I thought we were going to blow the rig out of the boat when that sail was aloft, but somehow it all hung together and we charged on.

Crusade maintained her lead all the way down to Tasman Island and Storm Bay, some 70 kilometres from Hobart, so the crew was confident they would win line honours over us by a big margin ... until a rain cloud cleared and they spotted us just a few kilometres behind, closing fast. *Apollo* had made an amazing gain off the coast of Tasmania in the 40-knot southerly gale we experienced on the final night at sea. It was really rough and uncomfortable but we pulled 30 kilometres out of their lead in just a few hours. From there we had a fantastic race against *Crusade* all the way to the finish line. They beat us by less than 19 minutes after nearly four days of racing. Years later Sir Max, who became a friend as a result of that contest, would confess to me that in the darkness as we approached the finish on the Derwent River his crew could see our navigation lights not far behind. To have us think that they were sailing away and gain a psychological advantage, they progressively covered their white stern light with strips of tape, making it look dimmer and dimmer. Even though we finished second it was a great result for us, but more specifically for Benny, because this was his first crack at designing a fast offshore racer.

Sir Max Aitken was a flying ace from World War II, a very competitive and wonderful individual who took me under his wing and introduced me to many leading business people in London. He was the head of Beaverbrook Newspapers — his father was the first Lord Beaverbrook — and I spent some time with him at the company's offices where he published the *Daily Express* and *Sunday Express*. I also stayed at his home in Cowes. He was staunchly British but at the same time he loved Australia, so much so that he conceived the London to Sydney car marathon.

Meeting Sir Max confirmed for me why so many business people like to compete in ocean racing. All are very competitive by nature, and ocean yacht racing is an extension of that, but most importantly it's an arena where you can also escape the pressures of business. When you're out sailing you don't think business; we certainly had a rule on the boat that no one talked business. Sailing also stretches you mentally in a different direction. For me there's a distinct correlation between ocean yacht racing and running a business, yet it's not only a rich man's sport because for every wealthy yacht owner there are usually 5, 10, 15 or 20 crew members sailing with him who come from everyday life. In business and sailing so much of your ultimate success depends on how well you are prepared to face all the elements of a challenge. In both you must be prepared to face more than one challenge at a time, such as when the wind increases in strength and you have too much sail up and you break things because you are over-exposed to the elements. And chances are that while you are repairing that damage a giant wave will come along and create more havoc on board. You must then fight as a team and press on, making repairs so you can keep racing towards the finish and a possible victory. And what makes sailing even more appealing is that you must literally be able to weather the storm because no matter how wealthy you might be, you can't buy or beat the elements, you can only match them.

The sport is also a great leveller of human beings because you are only as strong as the weakest link in the chain. Nobody is any different when you are out at sea; every one is dependent on each other. There is also a great camaraderie among the crew as they face constant challenges — the race, the elements and the unknown. For me, there's nothing better than being out at sea on a clear night sailing along, seeing stars spread across a sky that looks as though it's been smeared with white paint. I think sailing reaches out and gives you a new perspective on life; it provides a great balance. It's a humbling experience when you realise that you are far from the security of land and home, as the unchallenged master of your own destiny.

There are plenty of bonuses to be had in sailing, but for me there was none greater than having Ben become a real friend. In fact, he became part of our family — when he was in Perth he had his own room at my home and a car space underneath the house. Over the years he became more or less an in-house yacht designer for me, working on all of my sailing projects. Sadly though, I can still hear him telling me time and time again over the years that he didn't expect to have a long life. Even when we mounted our first challenge for the America's Cup he said to me: 'I've got to win this Cup because I won't live long'. And it wasn't all that many years after we won in 1983 then raced for the right to defend in 1987 that Ben died aged 52.

Apollo continued to prove she was a fast boat, and as I had learnt enough by then to be a competent helmsman, I decided to take her to America for their classic offshore event, the race from Newport, Rhode Island, to Bermuda. After that we scheduled to sail her across the Atlantic to England for Cowes Week, Europe's premier offshore regatta.

This was 1970 and Newport, as I would soon discover when I got there, was the home of the America's Cup match, an event I'd never heard of. But with Benny in tow I was quick to realise how important it was in the world of yachting — the world's oldest regularly contested sporting event and a trophy held by the New York Yacht Club since it was first contested in 1851. Some amazing men, like Lord Dunraven, Sir Thomas Lipton and Sir Thomas Sopwith, had tried to win it over the years, but all had failed.

We had *Apollo* docked at Newport Shipyards and there was an American 12-metre class yacht, *Valiant*, lying nearby being prepared for the America's Cup defence trials. The challenger was Australia's *Gretel II*, owned by Sir Frank Packer and skippered by Jim Hardy. One day when Ben and I were on the dock we innocently walked over to have a look at *Valiant*. There was a crew member, Vic Romagna, on deck so we asked if we could step aboard. Romagna, who knew we were Australians, was very uppity and essentially told us to bugger off, saying: 'No way. This is a 12-metre. You can't come aboard. It's secret.' It was as if we'd started an international incident, so we had only one response for him: 'That's okay. Keep your boat and your Cup. We'll build a yacht and come back and beat you.' It was just a throwaway line at the time, but it started me thinking about the America's Cup, and that's where the idea associated with the Yanchep development was germinated.

The Newport to Bermuda Race really opened my eyes to the forces of nature. It was the toughest race I'd ever done, and conditions were so bad that I actually believed that there was a good chance we wouldn't survive. There were nearly 100 yachts taking part and as we headed out into the Atlantic we copped the tail end of a hurricane. It became so rough as we approached Bermuda that we were forced to lower all sail and run under bare poles, still doing a scary 12 knots. The waves were like mountains — big, big rollers that at times were higher than the mast, and they would just loom up behind and give us no option but to charge down the face like a giant snow plough, into the trough below. It was quite frightening when you were at the top of the wave knowing that you were about to be hurled down the face of a massive liquid cliff. Each time the yacht would partially submerge and send water one-metre deep cascading all the way back to the cockpit. It was really scary stuff. I kept saying to myself: 'She'll never come up. She's just going to keep submerging. We're gone.' But each time she did. Somehow. The adrenaline rush was so great I didn't have time to even think about being seasick, but we had a lot of injuries among the crew because we were being thrown around so badly. One of us had a cracked forearm, another had broken ribs, and a lot of others were down with seasickness. It was grey and overcast and the wind was howling through the rigging, and above all that you could hear the roar of the waves. None of us could stay at the helm for more than an hour at a time — it was just too exhausting, and it was bitterly cold. Surprisingly though, you were sweating like you were in a sauna under your wet-weather gear, and because it was so rough you couldn't take it off when you went below to rest. It was like sleeping in a cold, wet sponge.

As we closed on Bermuda the wind was gusting to 80 knots and the seas were still huge. It was too dangerous to make an approach to the island so when we were two hours away from finishing I decided that the only thing to do was to turn the yacht around and head back out to sea. That meant we were heading into the face of the storm, so instead of being in danger of submerging we were then under threat of being rolled over by one of the big waves. It was terrifying, especially when we got one gust that literally blew the tiny storm mainsail we had set into strands of fabric. It was shredded.

Incredibly, while all this was happening and I was telling myself that we weren't going to survive, I was only worried about what would happen to the rest of the guys. I had this ridiculous notion that being a good swimmer meant I would be able to swim my way to safety, even in those conditions. I have no idea why I thought that, but I did. I guess I was confident that I had an ability to survive, but it was false confidence because I knew that if the yacht was overwhelmed by a wave it would sink so fast it would take everyone with it.

Apollo was taking such a pounding each time she crashed over the top of a wave that we were wondering if she was going to break in half. We took that punishment for a couple of hours then conditions started to settle down, so we decided to turn back towards Bermuda. We finished fourth across the line and fourth on handicap, a great result, but what we found when we docked was a little disconcerting to say the least — every strengthening rib in the hull forward of the mast was either cracked or broken. There was no doubt that *Apollo* couldn't have taken much more pounding than she did. We had to build a steel frame into the bow while in Bermuda just so we could compete in the 3700-mile Race of Discovery from there to Bayonne before going on to England.

The Bermuda race had been a real learning curve for me. I realised how important it was to make the right decisions when sailing, and I learnt that you'll never beat the ocean. It can never be tamed. You can only utilise its strengths and you must accept that, even when it is having a weak moment, it might change its mind and rapidly come at you like a wounded bull. But the experience also confirmed just how intriguing, stimulating and challenging sailing could be. It certainly prepared me for the race to Bayonne, which was to be the longest offshore passage that I'd undertaken.

The Race of Discovery turned out to be an experience at the opposite end of the weather scale. It was supposed to take us 14 days to complete, but because we were becalmed in the mid-Atlantic we were out there for 21 days, and as a result we ran out of food two days before we reached the finish. We actually started running out of food seven days out, but luckily I showed the entire crew a bit of magic that replenished our supplies. While all of them had failed to catch a fish I managed to land two big ones within two minutes of putting my line into the water. Besides being hungry, the race was also memorable because at one stage we were surrounded by a pod of more than 100 whales, but fortunately none attacked us.

The thought of an America's Cup challenge kept gnawing away at me while I was overseas sailing, so much so that only weeks after I returned to Australia I was left in no doubt that a Cup campaign and the Yanchep development went hand in hand. On 29 September 1970 I forwarded a cable to the New York Yacht Club that read in part: 'I wish to inform you that I am heading a syndicate ... and wish to challenge for the America's Cup ... official notification will be forwarded from Royal Perth Yacht Club in due course.' When the challenge was accepted by the New York Yacht Club we became the most distant contender in the 123-year history of the cup, Perth being about as far away from Newport as you can get.

At Cowes Week that year *Apollo* had some great racing against American media man, Ted Turner, who was sailing the famous 12-metre, *American Eagle*. During the week we beat him twice and he beat us once racing on the Solent. But he got the better of us in the big one, the 605-mile Fastnet Race, leading us home by two-and-a-half hours and setting a course record at the same time. The entire overseas *Apollo* campaign was a superb experience for me because, apart from introducing me to the international sailing circuit, I met some wonderful people, including Emil 'Bus' Mosbacher, a commodore of the New York Yacht Club who would later introduce me to the Canadian Imperial Bank of Commerce, one of the banks that came into the Santos project.

With the thought of an America's Cup challenge brewing, I decided that Ben should design me a new offshore racer, one that could contest the Admiral's Cup as part of the Australian team at the 1973 Cowes Week. It would be a good stepping-stone towards the America's Cup challenge. The yacht was to be a sistership to another yacht that Ben had designed, *Ginkgo*, owned by Gary Bogard, which was proving to be a very competitive boat. We had discussed the possibility of building the world's first aluminium 12-metre for the America's Cup challenge so decided to build the new boat, *Apollo II*, from alloy using the same scantlings required under the America's Cup design rules. *Apollo II* was fast enough to be selected for the Australian Admiral's Cup team, along with *Ginkgo* and Syd Fischer's *Ragamuffin*.

The Admiral's Cup was considered the world ocean racing team championship, and when *Ginkgo* and *Apollo II* finished first and second in the lead-up race from Cowes across the English Channel to Dinard and the beautiful historic French port of St Malo, we were feeling pretty confident. We turned on a very memorable crew party in St Malo after the race — French wine, French women and song — before sailing back to England very happy but a bit worse for wear. For me this was the start of a love affair with racing on the English Channel and across to France over many years. In fact I did it 13 times.

Ted Turner was back in Cowes that year, this time as a member of the American Admiral's Cup team, sailing his yacht *Lightning*. In typical Turner fashion he kept us amused every time we were within earshot of his southern drawl. After three races, when the German team had taken the lead on points, a reporter approached Turner for a comment. It proved to be another of his legendary one-liners:

> *Reporter:* 'Mr Turner, your American team is still trailing the leaders, Germany. What do you think about that?'
> *Turner:* 'The Germans were leading in 1942 too!'

The final race to decide the Cup was the Fastnet Race. It carried bonus points and we were doing well as a team until we hit a calm about 80 kilometres from the finish. We were in the running to win the trophy at that stage because, apart from the leading German yacht, which was just near us, their two other team yachts were way back. Receiving information from outside sources was illegal in the race, but somehow the two trailing yachts sensed the calm, did a hard turn towards the French coast, and sailed around us. Australia had to be content with second place in the series behind the Germans.

My ocean-racing career would continue through to 1989 and cover a wide range of yachts through to maxis in size. In all I had five yachts named *Apollo* and competed in three Fastnet races, two Newport to Bermudas, five Sydney to Hobarts and a trans-Atlantic race from America to Bayonne.

While the 1973 Admiral's Cup regatta was happening we were also developing our America's Cup campaign. There's no doubt I was a little naïve about our chances in that first challenge, but in reality the Cup program in its initial stages had more to do with land development and real estate sales than winning the Cup. I was convinced that we would win the Cup because Ben had already designed me a great yacht in the original *Apollo;* the America's Cup was just another step up, it was a done deal as far as I was concerned. Of course I was in for a rude awakening.

While I chose Royal Perth Yacht Club as the challenging club for the campaign I decided to create my own club, Yanchep Sun City Yacht Club, so we had a real America's Cup focus around the property development. The actual clubhouse was a small building that had a much larger building attached to house the yacht during our sailing trials.

Soon after I had announced the challenge Sir Frank Packer rang me. He made Australia's first challenge for the Cup in 1962 and challenged again in 1970. He said in his usual gruff manner: 'Come and see me in Sydney. I want you to buy these *Gretel* boats I own, and I want you to go and do a proper challenge.' So I flew to Sydney and met him, did a deal across the table and bought the original *Gretel, Gretel II* and all their equipment. I also picked up Jim Hardy as part of the package, a big benefit as he had skippered *Gretel II* in the 1970 challenge.

We knew that previous America's Cup challengers had been launched too late and as a result were always confronted with a rush to be ready to race, so we decided to build early and have plenty of time to prepare the yacht. That, and the fact that we were the first syndicate to move from timber to aluminium for the hull, meant we had to build in secret — we didn't want the Americans knowing anything about the yacht for as long as possible. We rented a dilapidated old corrugated-iron cowshed in the backblocks of Terrey Hills, on Sydney's northern beaches for the job. But the New York Yacht Club still had us on toast in so many ways because they controlled the rules. Any time we came up with a new idea it had to be approved by them, especially when it came to so-called 'exotic' materials. Ben had this great idea to use mercury in the ballast so adjustments to the yacht's trim could be made quickly and simply. The New Yorkers banned that. Then he wanted to use tungsten in some parts of the boat. That, too, was not acceptable even though the Americans had used tungsten in one of their 1958 defence contenders. And while we were getting knocked back on our applications the Americans were working towards using a special new sailcloth for their defence that we would not be able to use.

The yacht was named *Southern Cross* after the cluster of stars on the Australian flag, and we broke from the tradition of having a plain white hull for a 12-metre by painting her yellow, in keeping with the sun theme for Yanchep Sun City. John Cuneo, an optometrist and Olympic sailing gold medallist from the 1972 Olympics in Kiel, was my choice for helmsman. I asked Jim Hardy to join us at our training base in Yanchep to act as helmsman aboard *Gretel II*, which was the trial horse. Much to the frustration of the New York Yacht Club I also departed from convention in employing an American match-racing expert, Andy Rose, as sailing coach — another first for America's Cup challengers. John Bertrand also became part of the sailing team after Ben had him work on the design of the rig for *Southern Cross*.

When our training in Australia was completed we headed for Newport feeling pretty confident. We took two yachts, *Southern Cross* and *Gretel II*, plus 23 crew, a shore team, 24 000 cans of beer that had been donated to us, and almost a container-load of beef, which would be consumed in the four months we were there. In the end the campaign would cost $6 million, but as far as I was concerned it was worth it. This was a commercial venture as much as a sporting challenge.

During the latter days of our time in Yanchep I became unhappy with the way John Cuneo was shaping up as skipper, so I decided that once we were in Newport the role of helmsman was up for grabs between him and Jim Hardy. In the end it was Jim who got the job, but not before I had stated my case: 'Jim, I want you to remember one thing. I once read where Napoleon was losing a lot of battles, so he took his most popular general out and shot him in front of his own troops. He wasn't very popular with his troops but he started winning a few more battles.' Jim just replied: 'I hear what you're saying, Alan.'

Baron Marcel Bich, the man behind the ballpoint pen empire, led the French campaign, and while we beat them easily to win the right to challenge the American defender *Courageous,* by this stage I knew that we would have our backs to the wall in the fight for the Cup. I had come to realise that the America's Cup was far more than just another yacht race. This was a race against the might of America, with rules that were made to be broken by them but not by us. We were at the bottom of a massive learning curve, both in design and how to outsmart the Americans in the psychological games that they played.

Ben's theory with the design of *Southern Cross* was that waterline length meant speed, so he came up with one of the longest yachts possible under the 12-metre class rule. But the rule is one where the Lord giveth, and the Lord taketh away. A long waterline meant the yacht had to carry less sail to fit into the class formula, and that meant that *Southern Cross* needed near-gale conditions to be fast. It was generally light weather in Newport that year, and we were trounced 4–0. So instead of getting to the top of Mount Everest in one stride as I expected we would, we got to the base camp, and there would be two more camps before we got to the top.

Baron Bich and I became good friends during the campaign and I accepted an invitation to join him on his estate just outside Paris after the Cup to go wild boar shooting. It was quite a remarkable experience. We went out very early in the morning with his 'beaters', men who would create a racket to drive the boars out into the open. The Baron said to me: 'There is a big boar in here. We've been trying to get this one for a long time. Now you stand over near this dam here, and because you're our guest, we'll let you have first shot at it.' With that he and the rest of the party stepped back 45 metres behind a thicket that was so dense it was as good as being behind a fence. Next thing the beaters started up and I could hear this rustle coming towards me at an incredible pace. Suddenly all I saw was a huge boar 5 or 6 metres away, coming straight at me, head down and flat out. I didn't take aim, I just fired the gun in the general direction in the hope that something would happen — and it did. I winged the boar and it veered away from me for a moment, only to then change course and head back at me. He just missed goring me with his tusks as he flashed by. Someone finished him off amid rounds of wild laughter coming from behind the thicket. We dined on wild boar that night, and while we were doing so one of the Baron's French friends joked: 'The Baron wanted to get you out of the America's Cup race, and he thought that if he couldn't get you on the water then he would get his boar to get you.'

During our discussions the Baron took time to explain his business philosophy and marketing strategies. He started with Bic ballpoint pens, but very cleverly bought the Biro name as well. His theory was that having a number of brands competing in the same market was very healthy for the company, a theory that reminded me of Kurt Lessheim back in Fremantle when I was young. The Baron was a self-made man who, I am told, bought his title, something you could do in Europe then. He thought that being a Baron sat very comfortably with the success he was experiencing in business.

I looked on our 4–0 loss to the Americans that year as a lesson learnt, and I came away from the event more determined to take the Cup away from them because I'd seen the true value of the event in every sense. I also realised that if we were to win it then we had to continue trying. I remembered Sir Frank Packer's famous comment that it was alcohol and delusions of grandeur that drove him towards challenging for the Cup, but for me it represented far more, and it was something I could not walk away from.

People forget that one of the most interesting things about this contest is that there is no big cash prize for winning. You don't even get to keep the Cup because it goes to the yacht club that issues the challenge. So as a sporting event there is no direct financial gain for the challenger, unless you approach it as I did through a commercial avenue. Mind you, it didn't always work that way either, as we were to find out in our next challenge in 1977. For me, the America's Cup campaign was simply an extension of the 29 companies I had in the Bond Corporation stable at the time — the challenge was as much a business as any of them, and I could see a profit at the end, win or lose.

My determination to win was also being driven by my fundamental belief in Australians, and Australia as a nation. I looked to old John Fitzhardinge, a friend and our first commodore of Yanchep Sun City Yacht Club, who regaled us with many stories about how he became a prisoner of war to the Japanese and survived the dreadful Changi prison camp. Those stories revealed the real guts and determination that were the very core of the Australian psyche. I was also driven by the fact that this was a way for Australia to emerge on the world stage and show what we were made of. We had the capacity and the skills to be leaders, and the technological know-how to win the Cup. With that win would come world recognition, particularly in America where they knew little about us. We saw that lack of knowledge about us when we first went to Newport in 1974. Most Americans thought we were little more than a bunch of cowboys who lived in the outback and survived by cooking food on barbecues. Winning the America's Cup would be the quickest and most effective way of changing that attitude.

However, as I started to put plans in place for the next campaign I came to realise that the mass of adverse press that came after the 1974 campaign had convinced everyone, particularly potential sponsors, that we wouldn't ever win the Cup. The papers gave us a terrible caning for being so badly beaten, even referring to us as a bunch of donkeys. As a result no sponsorship was forthcoming for 1977, and worse still for me, the crew from 1974 didn't believe they could win, so there was an enormous amount of motivation required on my part to get things back on track. The one positive aspect was that I believed in myself, just as I do today, and I say that unashamedly. I have proved over and over again that what many people see as being impossible can actually be achieved. It's that belief, as I have said, that led to a lot of people trying to bring me down or hinder my progress because they couldn't grasp my vision, believe in it or keep pace. Many people need encouragement to believe in themselves, to be told that they can do the impossible, and that was the main reason for us ultimately winning the Cup. The seed that is unseen below the ground needs to be nurtured daily until it springs into life and then bursts into bloom.

I'd kept my hand in the sailing scene by contesting the Admiral's Cup with a new design from Ben. But when it came to talking about going for the America's Cup in 1977 he too didn't want to know about it. He took the defeat in '74 very, very badly. For me it was a stepping-stone towards winning but Ben was hurt and essentially went away with his tail between his legs. Part of the problem was due to the fact that we had gone to Newport with a very positive attitude, something that we had to do, and the media picked up on that — they too became convinced that we would win. When everything backfired they gave us a horrible beating and Benny took it to heart. He couldn't cope, became very disenchanted and went into one of his bouts of depression where his only escape was to go to Europe and essentially hide. Everyone who knew him gave him his space, but after a while I knew I had to travel to see him, talk to him and get him to come back and get ready to go again in 1977. I had to help him get his confidence back. As far as he was concerned that second place in the Cup match was as good as coming second in boxing. I had to convince him that on his first attempt he had beaten yachts from three other nations to become challenger, a remarkable achievement.

Many sports people have difficulty coping with both success and failure. Quite often winning in sport does not deliver the euphoria you anticipated, especially when you consider the amount of time, effort and dedication that has gone into the victory. It can bring an emotional vacuum and it can take a lot of time to pick yourself up and go again. That's why motivating people is such an important part of today's world, and it was motivation that I had to apply to Benny. I had to encourage him to go the extra yard. He eventually realised that while we had been knocked down, we didn't get knocked out. I took him back to the house in Perth and set him up so he was again part of the family. It was to be a situation that would remain in place for much of the time through to 1983.

Once he was up and running again I had a young Dutchman, Johan Valentijn, join with him to develop the design of our 1977 Cup contender. Compared with *Southern Cross*, the new boat, which we named *Australia*, was conservative. It was smaller, had more sail and had no unusual features. To give us added strength on the ground I had Warren Jones, who was by then a director of Bond Corporation, come on board as team manager.

To get to the Cup match in '77 we had to beat another Australian yacht, *Gretel II* — which I'd sold — plus the French and the Swedes. But the closer we got to the main event the quicker we were running out of cash. We needed new sails and the money to cover general costs, but there was no sponsorship and Bond Corporation was financially stretched at the time, so I had none of those reserves to draw on. Outside of putting in as much of my own money as I could afford, I had one other alternative, to do a 'ring-around' to friends in big business and ask for financial support. This produced a much-appreciated $1 million, which with the $9 million I put in, covered the cost of the campaign.

We went on to dispose of the other challengers, beating the Swedes 4–0 in the final of the eliminations. We were then destined to meet the defender, my old mate Ted Turner, who was steering *Courageous*.

I'd switched to Noel Robins as helmsman because Jim Hardy had decided to try to put together his own challenge, which didn't happen. Noel was a very competitive yachtsman who had climbed to the top of the sport through great adversity. He had an attitude that I liked. He was classified as a walking quadriplegic after suffering a severe back injury in a car crash in Perth in the 1950s, yet he had not let this stop him. I felt that he had a special inner strength and a determination to prove a lot of things to himself; he wanted to do what any other man could do in the sport and it was this determination that I was out to harness. I had always felt that determined people could overcome being handicapped. Noel was one of those very people. Sadly this great sailor and human being died after being knocked down by a car in Perth in May 2003.

While *Australia* did win through the eliminations to become challenger the same boat and crew proved to be no match for the very talented Ted and his team.

From the business side, our 4–0 loss to *Courageous* in 1977 delivered distinct benefits for Bond Corporation and me — thanks in no small way to Ted. His nickname was 'The Mouth from the South' and the doddery old establishment at the New York Yacht Club hated the thought of him defending their Cup, especially after they had twice refused his application to join. But Ted, who was one of the best yachtsmen in America at the time, was always good for an outlandish quote, so the media loved him. That meant that the America's Cup was enjoying unprecedented media exposure in America and around the world, and with Australia being the challenger, 'Alan Bond' became even better known, something that opened more corporate doors for me. Ted's greatest moment with the media came after the final race when he arrived at the press conference well under the weather following heavy victory celebrations on the dock with his crew and adoring fans. By then Ted's southern drawl sounded as though someone had pressed his slow motion button, but that didn't stop him from firing from the lip at the conference. Somehow he managed to dish out a powerful verbal serve aimed directly at the New York Yacht Club establishment, but his *pièce de résistance* came when the alcohol really kicked in and he fell off his chair. He didn't care because he was the winner and the media loved it. He had saved the New York Yacht Club's bacon.

I left Newport that year in no doubt that we were getting closer to winning the Cup so immediately announced that we would challenge again in 1980. The plan was to get Ben to modify the existing yacht because I felt we hadn't got the boat to its full speed in '77. And by updating the existing hull we would have more time to concentrate on the sail development program and crew training, all because we would get more time on the water. Jim Hardy returned as skipper and we went back to Newport that year with what we believed was a pretty potent package. *Australia* was a much better yacht and the nucleus of the crew was becoming increasingly experienced in America's Cup racing. To get to be challenger we had to beat yachts from Britain, Sweden and France, and we did just that despite all of them having improved significantly since the 1977 campaign.

Our only casualty along the way was Ben, who broke his wrist, not sailing, but on shore. He thought that I was going to replace him with John Bertrand as tactician aboard *Australia* and he blew up. He went back into our office and saw a photograph of John on the wall, so smashed his fist through it — the photo *and* the wall. Ben, who had only two years of formal schooling, admitted that John, who went through university in Melbourne and then MIT in Boston, always frustrated him.

During the challenger eliminations the Brits produced a radical bendy mast that gave us a real fright, and gave us something to think about as we prepared for our meeting with the Americans. When the top section of this mast was bent to its maximum and fitted with a special sail, the British yacht got a 10 per cent increase in unmeasured sail area, a significant gain in a 12-metre class yacht. The difference it made to their speed in light winds was remarkable — they went from a situation where we were beating them by up to 15 minutes to where they were almost able to match *Australia's* speed. It was like fitting a turbo charger when the wind was light. But for us to change a winning yacht, as *Australia* was, just weeks before the Cup match and fit a mast unlike anything we'd ever used before, was an enormous gamble, and it was up to me to decide if we should do it. After consulting with everyone who mattered, and letting my theory about *nothing ventured, nothing gained* come to the fore, I decided it had to be done. Ben set about designing it and arranging for a fibreglass expert to come across from Sydney to build it. The plan was to cut up an old aluminium mast from the 1977 campaign and fit it with the new bendy top.

The work had to be done in total secrecy so that the Americans didn't catch on. Incredibly, the only place we could find to rent as a workshop was an inconspicuous old fish-packing shed just metres from the waterfront base of the defending yacht, *Freedom*. When the mast was built we had to have it measured, and we even managed to keep our secret from the measurers. Our fear was that they probably would have told the Americans if they realised what we had done, so our guys painted the fibreglass top of the mast white so that it matched the lower section. They also had to make sure it didn't bend when the measurers lifted it up to weigh it. Everything went fine until it came time to get the mast to the yacht. There was only one way we could do it — carry it. So with everything ready to go the entire team assembled at the shed early one morning, before the town had woken up, and literally carried this 30-metre long mast through the streets of Newport. It was an amazing sight ... a giant human centipede crawling through town to the dock. After a day-long effort, the mast was stepped aboard the yacht just before sunset, and with *Australia* docked almost alongside *Freedom,* our team couldn't resist the opportunity to show the Americans and the world what we'd done. As darkness fell the crew tensioned the rigging so that the mast bent like a giant fishing rod, then with a spotlight, they illuminated our secret weapon — the one we had built right under their noses.

The crew couldn't believe the improvement in the yacht's speed in light winds during the pre-Cup trials. We went into the match against *Freedom,* which was being skippered by the now legendary Dennis Conner, feeling that at last we had a boat that could beat the Americans, especially if the wind was soft.

History shows that we lost the 1980 match 4–1 in the best-of-seven series. What it doesn't say is that we could have, and should have, won the America's Cup that year. We had the weapon needed to beat the Americans but yet again we couldn't match their experience in this league, and we made some expensive mistakes. Conner had steering problems in the first race but we made enough tactical blunders to let him off the hook. In Race Two though the world saw what we had when the new rig aboard *Australia* came into its own. We hit the front in that race only to be beaten by the clock; there was a five hour and 15 minutes time limit imposed and we couldn't complete the course in time. The rescheduled Race Two was to be our day: *Australia* beat *Freedom* by 28 seconds to become the first yacht in a decade to take a race from the defenders. We should have won the fourth race but didn't, primarily because of the decision not to use our largest mainsail due to a forecast for strengthening winds, which didn't eventuate. It was a result from which we were not able to recover psychologically, and the Americans went out and won the two remaining races in a comfortable fashion.

I was disappointed but not disillusioned. This was the closest we had come to beating the Americans and I was convinced more than ever that they could be beaten. What the series had shown me was that with the same level of experience as the Americans, and greater innovation, we would win. I wanted Ben to design two boats for the next campaign — one along conventional lines and the other where he would start with a clean sheet of paper and let his imagination run wild. The conventional boat would be the benchmark and a back up if the wild card didn't work.

I jumped aboard *Australia* from our support boat as soon as they finished the last race and congratulated the crew on a fine effort, an effort that took us a big step towards the ultimate goal. I then announced to them that we would be back in three years, and with Jim Hardy retiring as skipper, John Bertrand would take the helm. For the crew, the news was the next best thing to winning the Cup because they too now believed we could win.

CHAPTER FIVE
TAKING CARE OF BUSINESS

While we didn't win the America's Cup in our first three attempts we came home winners in so many ways. Every time we challenged for the Cup it became increasingly obvious how great the benefits were. We were winners because in beating yachts from other countries we were getting headlines like 'Australia does it' and 'Australia wins' across America and in the international media. It was being recognised that this small nation from the other side of the world was fighting against the odds and, through determination and technological advancements, was making an impression — incredibly valuable global awareness for the benefit of all Australia, for me and for my companies. That was the case even after the supposed drubbing we received in 1974, as was illustrated when a friend from Europe came up to me and said that there were two things everyone remembered about Australia and the America's Cup — one was Alan Bond, and they weren't quite sure what the second one was.

As Australians we must accept the fact that our profile on the world stage is not grand, and that it is sport, not politics, that will enhance that awareness. With no disrespect to the Prime Minister, I'm sure more people around the world today know who Ian Thorpe and Cathy Freeman are and where they're from than know the name of the Australian Prime Minister. In recent times, as a consequence of the war in Iraq, our Prime Minister's international profile has lifted, but only time will tell if this will be a positive or negative for Australia.

Logic says that the government should support something as beneficial to the nation as a serious challenge for the America's Cup simply because of the enormous benefits it can bring for the entire nation, win or lose. But such support might be interpreted in some sectors of the media and the electorate as wasting money on a supposed elitist sport, and for that reason it is a no-go zone. But look at what I achieved for Australia and my business activities as a result of my four challenges, and in particular with the win in 1983. The benefits to my companies were considerable, and so they should have been because I was the one carrying the enormous financial burden across the decade of effort.

While gaining great recognition for Australia through the early Cup campaigns it pleased me even more to be getting recognition for Western Australian companies, which for so long had been generally ignored by the federal and state governments based on the other side of the continent. They more often than not thought it would get them more votes by bringing foreign companies in for major projects instead of looking for local talent. The politicians wanted the electorate to believe that foreign interest in a project meant that the state was hitting the international big time when in fact nothing could be further from the truth. I found it most distressing to see foreign companies getting a better reception from politicians than local ones. Western Australian companies in particular were thought to be too small for big jobs. No one believed they had the ability to do it. I proved this way of thinking to be very wrong, time after time. We were always more Australian in our attitudes to business development than the government of the day.

■ ■ ■

As challenger for the America's Cup I met people who were global in their business thinking. I was a guest at lunches and dinners where I met the presidents of banks and huge corporations, as well as people like the Rockefellers, the Bass family and many more of America's most influential citizens.

I first met Perry Bass after the 1974 challenge. He was a great yachting navigator who had inherited $100 million in 1930 — an incredible amount of money back then — from the family's oil business. He took me down to the family farm in Corpus Christi, Texas, for a week. It was a very enlightening experience for me because he told me all about the oil business. He said: 'Alan, you've got to get into oil. There have got to be big opportunities in Australia. If you find one small puddle of oil then it's like dog shit; you find lots of droppings all around you. It doesn't come in just one pool. What you want to do is get into acreage in Australia where they've already made a discovery and you'll find a lot more.'

The conversation made a big impression on me and when I got back home I had already decided to go into the oil business. The opportunity to do just that came soon after when Burmah Oil got into trouble and wanted to get out of its Santos oil and gas project in South Australia's Cooper Basin. Burmah had lost a bucketload of money on their international shipping business and was faced with having to sell their fleet. They were in desperate financial straits, but no one wanted to look at buying Santos from them because the company hadn't made a profit. The problem was they weren't getting much money for the gas they were recovering. They had found some puddles of oil — they had proved reserves of about 35 million barrels — but there hadn't been sufficient drilling done to prove there was more. Even though geological expectations indicated there would be, they faced one other big problem. They needed to build a 1300-kilometre pipeline to deliver the product.

On paper it looked as though there was no way to finance the project so it could be developed to its full extent; it was difficult to justify the economics based on the limited reserves that had been defined to date. And then there was the South Australian government, which held sovereignty over the reserves and contracted those reserves to the company, as is the case for all oil reserves in Australia. The South Australian government believed that sovereignty gave it a bigger stick, one that allowed it to hold control over anything that Santos might want to do, because the company was required to have development approval from the government for every aspect of the venture, even though the government didn't hold any shares in Santos. It was an interesting loop because at the same time, the government was indirectly tied to the development of the project as it had a long-term agreement with AGL for the purchase of gas, and AGL in turn had an agreement with Santos. This meant the state was economically tied in to the development of the Cooper Basin.

Soon after I heard Santos was for sale I flew to London to meet the Burmah Oil people. At the same time I had David Tremain, who was working for me and knew a lot more about the oil and gas business than I did, have a look at the project. Burmah Oil had 45 per cent of the company, the rest being spread widely through a public company that wasn't trading very well. All I could think about was the huge acreage the company held and the fact that Perry Bass had said that if there was one puddle of oil then there would be more. I was as keen as hot mustard to buy Santos, it was a deal I had to have, but there was one small problem — I didn't have any money because the credit squeeze was having a massive impact on land sales and, because of that and other influences, Bond Corporation at the time was facing tough times financially.

Still, I was undeterred, so I flew off to London where I met with Campbell Anderson, an Australian working for Burmah Oil who had been running the operations in Australia. He was prepared to give me a hearing, so when I walked into his office I told him that I wanted to negotiate a deal to buy them out. Campbell asked me if I had any money, to which I replied: 'Don't worry about the money. Let's get to the deal.'

He was surprised, to say the least, and while he didn't take me very seriously he was prepared to discuss a deal. After a few days of negotiation we arrived at a price of $27 million, which sounded reasonable to me. They then thought they'd get rid of me by putting the pressure on, thinking that I didn't even have $1 million for a deposit. And they were right. Their proposal to me was that I had to put up a $1 million deposit, pay half the outstanding money in 90 days and the rest in a year. And if I didn't pay the first instalment in 90 days I lost the million. All that mattered to me at that stage was that I had a deal; after that I just had to work out how to arrange the finance.

While the discussions had been going on I realised I didn't know enough about Santos as a tangible asset. All I really knew was that the deal meant I was buying a package — 45 per cent of Santos and 80 per cent of both Reef Oil and Basin Oil. I decided that the only way I could get the information I needed to satisfy me that it was a worthwhile proposition was to get my employee David Tremain to have a look at it on the ground. I had him telephone people at Santos and say he was doing a thesis on oil and gas exploration in the Cooper Basin. David was a university graduate, so knew what he was doing. They agreed that he could visit, so two days later he flew into the Cooper Basin and was given a tour. He had a good look over the project and was told all about what they were doing and what they expected in the future, based on the geological assessments they had. David rang me in London even before he left Cooper Basin to say, 'I think it's worth going for', adding that he thought there would be a lot more oil to be found. The Santos people never knew that I'd done this, but it meant that I had information not available to any other potential purchaser, information that I think should have been freely available but which, fortunately for me, wasn't. I think the reason behind this information not being made available to any others was because they were only selling the share block, and behind the scenes the Santos board was trying to find their own tame purchaser or purchasers. They wanted to keep the price down so it was easier for local companies to buy in. Basically this meant that there was a failure by the Santos chairman, John Bonython, and the Santos board at that time to cooperate with their major shareholder, Burmah Oil, to ensure that they obtained the best price in selling their position. It was obvious to me that some members of the board did not want to swap one major shareholder for another major shareholder, unless it was somebody substantial like BHP or Western Mining. They didn't like the thought of being controlled from outside the state and wanted to keep the control in South Australia. Tough luck for them, as I was coming in as the major shareholder and on top of that I was buying a foreign-owned company back for Australia.

I was convinced I had a good deal but I still didn't have the $1 million deposit and, worse still, I didn't know how I was going to raise the rest of the money. But when I started going through the company's balance sheet things began to fall into place. I saw that there was about $4 million paid annually in insurance premiums as part of the cost of operations. I immediately called Brian Coppin, our insurance broker at Western Underwriters in Perth, a man who I had backed with all our insurance within three weeks of him starting business in Perth. I ended up staying with him for 30 years. The conversation went something like this:

> AB: 'There is a $4 million insurance deal for you here if I can win this deal, but I need a million. If you can crank a million for me for the deposit and I get the deal you get the insurance business.'
> BC: 'Oh Jesus, Alan, are you going to lose the million if the deal doesn't happen?'
> AB: 'I think we'll be alright, Brian. I'm sure we'll get the rest of the money. I'm not sure how yet, but I think we'll get it.'

Next I spoke to Bruce Jackson, a stockbroker I knew well and whom I had done deals with: 'If I can get this deal, do you think you can do a share issue in Bond Corporation so we can raise some capital?' He said yes, he believed he could raise the money. So there we were, things were falling into place, and soon after that the board of Bond Corporation approved the deal.

Brian sent the $1 million over to London and I strode into the Burmah Oil office: 'Here's the cheque for the deposit.' They were taken aback but, to the full credit of Campbell Anderson, it happened. He said to his board: 'Look, I think this guy will either get the money, or he'll walk away and lose his million dollars. He's brash enough to get the money, so let's give him a go.' They were so engrossed in their big shipping problems involving hundreds of millions of dollars that they had little hesitation in accepting my deal. Still, it was Anderson who really propelled the decision to give me a shot at the project, and I will be eternally grateful to him for that. Incredibly both Western Mining and BHP, who had the money to write a cheque on the spot and buy the company, had knocked it back. I don't think they saw the opportunity in the deal.

Once the media hooked onto the story that I was looking at buying Santos the publicity was generally negative, partly because they knew Bond Corporation was cash-strapped. They knew all the major players, including Western Mining and BHP, had rejected the deal, then suddenly we appear on the scene like a bunch of upstarts from Western Australia. The media decided that the only way to get an angle on us for their story was to go to BHP and get their view on what we were doing. 'Is this a real deal from Bond Corporation and will it go through?'

BHP responded along the lines of: 'Well, we've knocked it back because we don't think it's any bloody good; it's a dud deal. How, and why, is he going to pay $27 million for a dud deal?'

So as we finalised negotiations the media had reached its own conclusion: 'It's a dud deal for Bond Corporation', without actually knowing what we intended to do, or what we were capable of doing. It was a different story when I got back to Australia and announced the deal was done for Bond Corporation and what some of our intentions were. Our share price doubled. As a result Bruce Jackson had little trouble raising somewhere between $10 and $12 million to help meet the 90-day deadline. We subsequently found the other few million we needed without a problem.

With that initial part of the deal done I moved onto the Santos board, my priorities being to investigate the strategic direction of the company, how we could increase the cash flow, and how to work towards a development plan aimed at bringing the oil into production. This oil aspect necessitated the borrowing of an additional $600 million, a task made more difficult by the fact that the balance sheet for Santos showed a net worth of only $25 million. I did the rounds of every Australian bank and was knocked back. I went to banks in America, Canada and Germany and I think I had more than 40 knock-backs. But three banks did decide to back me — the Republic National Bank of Dallas, the Canadian Imperial Bank of Commerce and the International Energy Bank in London. They agreed to sign up for a consortium worth $600 million.

I had the money. Next I had to work out how I was going to develop it into being a viable project. My first thought was: 'Now you've got to build a 1300-kilometre pipeline. There's nothing unusual about that. Just build one.' It looked pretty straightforward until the experts told me that the pipeline would take three and a half years to build — twice as long as I could afford. I wouldn't accept their proposal so working with the engineers we came up with a unique plan where we could build it within two years.

With 35 million barrels of oil in reserve the project was only just economic, but most importantly there was great long-term potential. We went into expansion mode and the operation grew to where a refinery was built which, directly and indirectly, resulted in the employment of thousands of people. Gradually more oil was found and I believe there's still a lot more to be found. It seems every time they drill a hole they get some liquids and oil.

The Santos share price started to rise as we progressed with the pipeline and that made things easier. But to make the project economically viable I wanted to get a world price for the gas — something we were entitled to under the major contracts we held with AGL and in turn the South Australian government. They were 25-year contracts that provided for price increases and also a review of the market. At the time we were being paid 45 cents per gigajoule for the gas while the market rate was much higher. So we asked for $1.50, expecting that we'd negotiate down to $0.90. Regrettably the South Australian Energy Minister, Hugh Hudson, was a socialist of the worst kind, and he believed that individuals should control nothing while the state controlled everything. Paranoia seemed to set in because all the state could see was the price of gas being doubled, and that would be passed onto consumers. They didn't even consider negotiations. The cry went out in the state government to 'Stop Bond ... somehow'. Their theory was 'if this guy controls this project through price rises then he controls the state economy'. They feared we would hold the state to ransom, but what they didn't do was read the contract and realise that we could only do what the contract stated. There was no way we could hold the state to ransom. Unfortunately, we handled the public relations from our side very poorly. At one stage a photograph of our Managing Director, Peter Beckwith, was published in a newspaper under the title of 'The public face of capitalism'. The whole thing turned quite nasty.

We had no option but to go through the arbitration court where it was decided that the matter should be resolved using procedures laid down in the gas sales contract. Some time later, in consultation with Bonython and one other director of Santos, the government introduced a new agenda — to eliminate a major shareholder in Santos by enacting legislation that would limit any shareholder to owning no more than 15 per cent of the company. For the first time in Australian corporate history the government brought together the two houses of parliament over a weekend to make its move — to pass the *Santos Limited (Regulation of Shareholdings) Act* and force us to sell down our shareholding. This was an abhorrent move, passing such legislation affecting one public company. It continues to be a blight on the democratic processes in Australia and all I can say is that no company should consider investing in South Australia until this punitive legislation is repealed. If they can do it to Santos then it can be done to others.

Quite incredibly we were ordered to sell our shareholding in Santos in just 30 days or the government would assume ownership of those shares and sell them at its discretion. But we were able to keep Reef Oil and Basin Oil because the government couldn't legislate against them as they didn't have any gas contracts. We were sufficiently disgusted with the way that we'd been treated to decide that we'd had enough of South Australia and we'd get right out of everything to do with Santos. The big plus side to all this was that over the two and a half years that we had Santos, we turned our $27 million investment into $500 million for Bond Corporation — a bonus also for all other shareholders in Santos because they too shared in that growth of value. But had the Santos board not worked against the interests of the major shareholder, Bond Corporation, in initiating this move with the government then the long-term result would have been ten times this figure.

There was another direct benefit for Bond Corporation out of all this. Shell was also interested in buying Santos, but didn't get into the race because I concluded my deal before they had the opportunity to finalise their purchase approval within the company. As a consequence Dr John Jackson, who was then head of Shell Exploration and who had been with the company for 18 years, came to see me and I ended up employing him because he knew so much about the project. He stayed with me for 20 years.

The biggest mistake I made during all this was that I left John Bonython as chairman of Santos. I had control of the company and I should have chucked him out. He'd been chairman since 1954 and I'm certain that he and some of the other directors in South Australia undermined us. That they did nothing to oppose the government's move was, to me, evidence that they were determined to work in collusion with the government to *Get Bond*. While the government had an obligation to act in the interest of all shareholders they went after Bond Corporation because of the single agenda they held — to have control of Santos maintained in South Australia.

With a 30-day time frame on the share sale, I quickly looked at my options and decided that Rupert Murdoch and Sir Peter Abeles were the logical ones to approach to buy the 30 per cent I was being forced to sell by the government. My thought process said: 'You might be getting rid of me, but I'm going to leave you a legacy —

two other strong individuals who you won't be able to push around. I get the last laugh on this one.'

There was another reason for going to Rupert. He owned the major newspaper in South Australia and I thought that this would stop the government doing other ridiculous things around the project. In turn the price of the shares would go up and I'd make more money on the remaining 15 per cent I held. I said to both Rupert and Sir Peter: 'I've got to sell these shares and I need to do a deal. This is the price, and as soon as the deal is done you'll make a lot of money.' They agreed, and in two days the deal was done. They bought the whole lot and paid me cash. As I promised them, this turned out to be an astute investment for Murdoch and Abeles as they virtually doubled their money in only a few months.

Today the wealth of Santos is measured in billions of dollars, yet still this stupid 15 per cent shareholding rule is holding it back and preventing the generation of real wealth for all the other shareholders and the state. If the government were to remove the 15 per cent rule then the stock would substantially increase in value, as there would then be a takeover premium on the company. I think that the best proposition would be for Santos to merge with Woodside and create a really strong Australian corporation. I almost bought Woodside from Burmah as well, as it was offered to me, and this was going to be my next purchase had things proceeded as planned with Santos.

It has been suggested many times over the years, particularly when we were rapidly growing the business, that I never feared failure, but while it may have appeared that way from the outside I don't see it as being true. The fact is that I could always rationalise and accept a position on any deal because I had knowledge of all the facts, while outsiders didn't. Those outsiders could only make assumptions on where we were heading and what we were doing. In developing the company we knew what we had, what our goal was, how we were going to get there and how the project fitted into our 20 to 50-year plan for the company.

At the same time others, without the full knowledge of all the circumstances, could easily reach a different conclusion, and that was what happened so often, particularly in the media.

A perfect example was the Yanchep development. It was perceived by many to be a total disaster for me while in fact it was quite the opposite. Certainly we had to fight to survive through the financial crisis facing the company in the early 1970s, and also cope with the fact that the government for a long time would not let us sell our entire shareholding to our partners, Tokyu Corporation. But our saviour arrived in 1977 with a change of government and the sale was approved. The result on Yanchep was another milestone for the company in that it delivered our biggest profit to date. Tokyu paid us an additional $15 million for our share and took over the outstanding debts of $13.5 million. When you add that to the $19.5 million we'd already received it meant we got $33 million out of Yanchep for an initial $1.9 million investment. Land sales had covered the money we had spent on the early stages of development and also paid for the 1974 America's Cup challenge. It proved to be a great investment for us.

The question of fear of failure doesn't enter into the equation for me. There was never any anticipation of failure with the Yanchep project or any other that we undertook. However, from time to time mistakes are made and circumstances outside your control can impact on the final result, and that's when it's quite arguable and acceptable to say that you should always be prepared for the storm that might come along. Such a plan is important for business and life in general. One has to plan ahead. We certainly did plan for a worldwide stock market collapse in 1987 and as a result we survived it, and I still have no doubt that Bond Corporation could have, and should have, survived its eventual collapse. One thing that no one saw coming, or could have predicted, was banks charging interest rates as high as 22 per cent around that time. No one was prepared for such enormous swings in interest rates. I'd not seen anything like that in my business career and we, like most others, were not prepared for it.

Often what some people might have interpreted as failure I could only see as a progressive step where nothing more than a simplistic approach was needed to progress along a path to success. For example, while we were lampooned by many people after our first attempt at winning the America's Cup, I looked at the project as if it was a company that had failed but which, if given the opportunity, still had the potential to go on and be successful. I knew that the talented people within that 'company', and the assets it held, represented the potential to recover. So while plenty of outsiders proclaimed that we would never win the Cup I knew from all the information I had available to me from within the organisation that we could and more than likely, would, win it. I believe that too many people give up too easily in life. When you hit a brick wall you must work at getting over it or around it. Learn from what you have done in the past and go on from there. It's amazing what humans can achieve if the personal motivation is there. Few people ever reach anywhere near their upper level of excellence in life. In trying to achieve the ultimate goal I have often looked to that famous quote: 'Yes, of course in hindsight I would have done it differently', and I can certainly say that today, but that's all part of the learning process. I have tried wherever possible to give people a second or third chance for the reason that while they might appear to have failed, they in fact still have the capacity to achieve their goal.

In 1982 Bond Corporation was recognised as Western Australia's largest company, not that it meant much to us because our long-term goals were way beyond that. And besides, such a status didn't matter to us because it didn't reflect the true value of the company — we were never able to use the potential of the capital markets to increase the capital base of the company. I'm sure this was because of parochial attitudes in Australia. Bond Corporation was out of Western Australia, had many arms to it and had Dallhold holding a 51 per cent share, a situation that led to institutions, from the east in particular, not wanting to invest despite the company being run successfully by a very effective team in Peter Beckwith, Tony Oates, Peter Mitchell and me. They were reluctant to look at investing in a company with such a broad base; they couldn't understand how I could oversee everything that was going on within the company at the time and retain effective control. The convention with institutions was that if they wanted to invest in brewing they did just that, and those that wanted to invest in media went to that market. It was a long-held approach to the markets and accordingly the institutions certainly didn't want to be investing in media and then find out they also owned an oil well, were exploring for oil offshore in Western Australia, or constructing a building in New York. We were seen to be a conglomerate that was too diversified, an attitude that we actually concurred with, and subsequently we mapped out a strategic plan that would see us eventually separate the assets into single-purpose entities and float them on the stock market. While others talked about strategic plans we went out and got on with it, and institutions didn't necessarily understand this approach at that stage.

My first venture into goldmining was when we established a mine not far from Kalgoorlie for Windsor Resources, a company controlled by my family company, Dallhold, which was involved in various mining and exploration activities, specifically gold and nickel. I purposely developed Dallhold with three prongs over the years so that if one of the arms experienced a downturn then the other two arms could continue to support the company.

From this small beginning with Windsor Resources, Dallhold's goldmining interests grew to enormous proportions during the 1980s. It culminated with us making two significant purchases in 1987, St Joe Gold Corporation and Gold Mines of Kalgoorlie. St Joe, which we paid $700 million for, was one of America's largest goldminers with significant international interests. The purchase of Gold Mines of Kalgoorlie for $375 million reinforced Dallhold's position as the major player in goldmining in Australia.

It was the Kalgoorlie gold deal that really got me interested in that industry, and the opportunities that were out there to be taken. During one of my initial visits to Kalgoorlie in the early '80s I was amazed by what they called the Golden Mile, the strip close to the city where masses of shafts had been dug in search of gold. The history of the place intrigued me so much that I went to the local museum and found a book written by the British born and South African based visionary, Cecil Rhodes, the man whose name went onto the Rhodes Scholarship. He had written that if the Kalgoorlie mines ever became one mine it would be the richest mine in the world. That got me thinking, especially after what I'd seen through the early days with Lang Hancock and our own Robe River project where they mined millions of tonnes of material to make things viable. I went back to Perth and said to the guys: 'Let's have a look at who owns all the companies on the Golden Mile and see if we can bring them together,' and before very long I had bought control of all the major mines on the Golden Mile. The plan was to get enough money together to create an open cut pit because underground mining was becoming uneconomic. It was becoming just too costly to get the stuff to the surface, and because of this demise of underground mining, the city was entering quite a depressed state. Thousands of miners were being laid off.

My designers and engineers then started drawing up a plan for an open cut pit in 1984/85, and when I saw it I had only one comment: 'Make it bigger; make it five times the size, and we'll call it a Super Pit, a pit where we'll mine all of the ore bodies in an open cut operation.'

I was told: 'Hell, Alan, you'd have to move 50 million tonnes of material a year, and no one's ever done that in goldmining.'

'Well,' I said, 'they move 50 million tonnes of iron ore a year in the Pilbara in the north of the state, so what's stopping us here? Let's do it. And think about this — we'll mine it for 100 years, and when we've finished Kalgoorlie could be the greatest resort town in Western Australia because the pit will become a massive lake where you can sail yachts. That's how big this will be when we're finished. It will be fantastic.'

I convinced one of the leading gold banks, Standard Chartered, to put up the $500 million we needed to get the project started. This became the foundation of Bond International Gold, or B.I.G., as it became known. We built one giant processing plant that required us to put millions of tonnes through annually to make it financially viable. I employed contractors to operate the big 50-tonne trucks and remove the material as quickly as it could be carved out of the ground. The fact that we were removing so much dirt meant we recovered a lower grade ore, but the volume made it work because eventually we were recovering more than one million ounces of gold annually. Our plan was to take the hole down to 300 metres, making it one of the deepest open cut pits in the world, a real engineering feat that set new standards in the world of open cut mining.

The success of this project, and the addition of mines in America and Chile, led to me floating Bond International Gold on the New York Stock Exchange for $600 million. Two years after it was listed it was taken over for about $1 billion, making this a very profitable deal for Dallhold. The Super Pit is still going today and remains one of the most successful mining operations in Australia. It is so large it is one feature in Australia that can be seen from outer space. But even more satisfying for me, this project saved the historic city of Kalgoorlie.

In developing our mining assets in the 80s, in particular our goldmining projects, there was an associated high profile in the media, and I guess it was that profile that made us fair game for a classic con job. It started when two guys came into my office one day and said: 'We've found this enormous gold nugget. It's shaped like Texas, the map of Texas. It's the largest nugget ever found.' I'd already heard about these blokes and the nugget, which they called the *Yellow Rose of Texas,* and that they were out to sell it. It was a huge thing that was presented in a leather case, and it had a certificate with it confirming it to be gold. It was certainly impressive and looked to be the genuine thing, so much so that I bought it for a few hundred thousand dollars, a price that put a 100 per cent premium on the true gold price because of its uniqueness. But as I would find out some time later, the only unique thing about it was that it was a fake. These guys had formed the nugget in a workshop using a block of foam for a mould. They had cut out a rough shape of the state of Texas in the foam, sprinkled some sand in it to give it the right sort of finish, and then poured in the gold.

We were ignorant of the fact that this 'nugget' was a fake until the police came and told us some time later. It turned out they were searching premises one day when they found some photographs of some guys showing off their handiwork, holding the nugget and the mould. They thought they were protecting themselves by being photographed from the waist down, but they'd forgotten about the shoes they were wearing, and that's what gave them away. The culprits were nailed for fraud, and I sold the *Yellow Rose of Texas* to a mint to be melted down.

There was another very public gold story where we were on the receiving end of a dud deal at what was called the Rabbit Warren prospect in Western Australia. A chap named Danny Hill came to me, produced a lot of nuggets and said that they had come from an open cut mine on the site. After some investigation I bought the permit from him for $4 million. I then organised for our machinery to go in there and start digging, but we didn't find any nuggets.

These bitter experiences only proved that all that glitters is not necessarily gold, but they were valuable lessons learnt, experiences I carried with me for my later ventures into mining projects around the world.

Soccer was my game before I came to Australia and once I became a local I played rugby, but I always struggled to comprehend the intricacies, skills and appeal of what cynics called 'aerial ping pong' — Australian Rules Football, which was to the vast majority of the population in Perth, Adelaide and Melbourne 'the only game'. Eventually I did bow to the sheer weight of numbers around me and became interested in *the game*, that interest being sparked by Bill Hughes, Eileen's father, who was the president of the South Fremantle Football Club. Before long I was helping with the club finances, and then our company became a major corporate sponsor to the degree where the club was able to buy some good players, strengthen the team and climb all the way from the bottom of the ladder to the top.

It was that relationship with South Fremantle over the years that contributed to me later becoming president of Richmond Football Club in Melbourne, a club that drew many players from our club in the west and which also sent players to us; we were like sister clubs. Through this association I got to know some of the hierarchy from Richmond and later, when they hit financial trouble, they came to me to ask if I would become president of their club and help solve their problems. I agreed, but as a result I can lay claim to one of the shortest presidencies ever — just a few months in 1987. I quickly discovered that my idea of what a president did was the exact opposite of theirs. For me, a president had to make decisions, decisions for which that president was responsible, but the Richmond committee held the view that I should simply supply a lot of money and be there in name only. They wanted to continue running the club their way, as if nothing had changed. We did put some money in to stop the club going bankrupt, and in doing so we were naturally looking for some form of direct return for the brewing interests we then owned. There were big beer marketing battles going on then so we wanted to profile our own Swan Beer through the club. That would give us another shot at the big Carlton and United Brewery and its chief, John Elliott, who was also chairman of Carlton Football Club. But the Richmond people also reacted adversely to the Swan side of the deal, so I had no option but to announce to the committee: 'I'm either going to be here, take responsibility and do things my way or I'm not here at all.' It was immediately evident that there was no real reason for me to be there at all, so I quit.

My exit actually worked out well for the club because as a consequence they found themselves heading for deep water once more. Their realisation then was: 'Oh, hang on, we now understand where Bond was coming from.' They then adopted a totally different attitude for the new people who came in to help and the club survived.

Our corporate support of Richmond was a small part of an extensive national sponsorship program that we had put in place during the mid-80s, primarily through our brewing interests. At one stage we were the principal sponsors of rugby league across Australia and the sponsor of major horseracing carnivals in New South Wales, Western Australia and Queensland. We were spending millions of dollars on sponsorship to raise our profile and our profits. For me it was all part of taking care of business.

CHAPTER SIX
THE DAY WE STOPPED THE NATION

What was the intrigue with the America's Cup for me? Well, apart from the distinct international commercial benefits it offered, it was the fact that the Cup was something that no one had taken away from the Americans. For well over a century it had sat in the clutches of the New York Yacht Club, and not since they won the very first contest against the Brits in 1851 had anyone been able to get near it. It was the longest winning streak in history, and the Cup itself is the oldest trophy in sport. It was first contested way before soccer and tennis were developed and well before the modern Olympics started.

In every one of the 24 matches prior to our 1983 campaign the Americans had done everything possible, fair and foul, to keep the Cup, so it was an incredible feeling for me to be in Newport that year with a yacht and a team that had a real chance of changing the course of sporting history. We had reached that position through tenacity and our determination to learn from our three previous campaigns. We had been punched on the nose and knocked down more than once, but then we got up and kept coming back. I also kept coming back because Ben Lexcen had as much determination to win as I did.

I reminded myself of the missed opportunities in 1980 and how, after we fitted the bendy mast, we found ourselves genuinely knocking on the door. We just had to find the breakthrough.

Everyone who had been part of our three previous campaigns could take pride in the fact that they had contributed towards us being there with *Australia II* and being a real threat. Those earlier efforts were just challenges, but in 1983 it became a war against America and its technology. We knew by then how to manage the syndicate, how to train the crew, and we also knew we had a clear superiority over the technical mind of America in the form of the yacht. By that year we had moulded a great team, a team built from a strong nucleus that had come with me over the years. And I'd stuck with the same team behind the scenes, like Steve Ward as the yacht builder, and a host of others, including John Bertrand. I nominated him as skipper immediately after the 1980 challenge because I liked his coolness and general demeanour, and I liked the fact that he had a technical brain. On top of that he was a bloody good helmsman, an Olympic yachtsman who had been through tough competition. He was an intelligent man who was a great sailor, and for this campaign it was important to have a helmsman who was prepared to understand and work with us on developing new technology and new sail designs. While John was quite young at the time he was very mature in his outlook; he had the intellect to grasp that we had to develop something different that could win us the Cup. If he had a shortcoming it was that he internalised the pressure and he wasn't able to get rid of it by stamping his foot, shouting or blowing a fuse like Benny could ... or me on the odd occasion. I looked at this team as the perfect formula to finally take the Cup away from the Americans.

We built two yachts for this campaign, one conventional and the other radical. Our hopes were pinned on the radical boat, but we needed the other as a safety net. Ben drew the conventional boat first, and it looked to be a very sweet yacht, a logical development from our 1980 challenger. Then he went away with a clean sheet of paper and let his mind go wild. He went back to the lateral approach that he was so famous for, and he analysed every aspect of America's Cup racing and the 12-metre class design rule, and then started putting pen to paper. Ben had John Bertrand work with him on the analysis of the concept and its speed potential.

It wasn't long before Ben was convinced he was onto something so he and John flew to Perth to convince me he was right. I was mentally prepared for something substantially different, so when they rolled the plans out in front of me there was no element of shock, more an appreciation of Benny's genius. This design was a quantum leap — it was an amazing looking yacht, small, yet with masses of sail. The now legendary winged keel looked like it was fitted to the hull upside down. But it made sense because that shape put the heaviest part of the keel at the very bottom, and that meant the yacht had enormous stability when it came to counter-balancing the power of the sails. Benny's enthusiasm for this design was right out there. He told me that this yacht had the potential to beat the Americans to the first windward mark by three minutes — an incredible margin. It was like putting the Concorde up against a Boeing 747. But knowing Benny as I did, I had to temper his enthusiasm with a commonsense approach. Over the next few hours I had Ben and John walk me through every feature of the design and discuss what was needed to develop it. At that moment it was simply a theory that needed to be proved, and I was the one who had to make the decision on whether or not to invest millions of dollars to prove it. If such a radical proposal was wrong then our chances of winning the Cup would, at best, be only a little better than they were in 1980 because we would have to use the conventional boat. Gnawing away at me all the time, while I was considering the options, was my firm belief that we had to be more technologically advanced than the Americans if we were to beat them. I reminded myself of the analysis of the 1980 effort — it was unrealistic to think that we could field a better crew than the Americans and gain an advantage, and it was unrealistic to think that we would have a better match-racing helmsman because Dennis Conner was very, very good. It was also unrealistic to think that we would have better sails. On all three points we could only hope to match the opposition and therefore we had to take an enormous gamble if we were to win, but it could be a calculated gamble, and pushing that argument was the Alan Bond approach — dare to be different! Go with your gut feeling!

It didn't take long for me to come to the conclusion that we had to build this yacht. But I also decided we would build the other design as our backstop.

Ben started to put the finishing touches on the design and at the same time booked us into the Netherlands Ship Model Basin in Holland where he could tank test large models of the yacht and get the most accurate indication as to its potential. In all, 12 models, each one a different version of the concept, were built and tested. I went to Holland twice during the testing program to see first hand what was happening and how things were shaping up. Each time I came away feeling more confident that Ben might be onto something. And by the end of the tank-testing session, which had cost me $1 million, we all believed that we had a breakthrough yacht.

Steve Ward built both this yacht and the conventional boat in total secrecy in Perth. Following some preliminary trials off Fremantle, I decided it was all or nothing for our challenge with what would be *Australia II*, so I opted to sell the conventional design to a Victorian-based syndicate. It was named *Challenge 12*, but unfortunately the syndicate behind it collapsed early in the piece. Luckily, I was fortunate enough to get one of Australia's richest men, Dick Pratt, from Melbourne, to come aboard and salvage the campaign.

We shipped both boats to Melbourne for trials before going to America, and *Challenge 12* gave us a real fright. The conventional yacht, which was being steered by Jim Hardy — who had been knighted after the 1980 Cup challenge to become Sir James Hardy — beat us on plenty of occasions. We were soon to realise, however, that the problem wasn't with the design, but with how John Bertrand was steering it. *Australia II* was so different in the way it tacked and tracked that it required a totally different approach in handling if it was to reach its potential. It was twitchy and flighty and John was yet to learn the required technique.

While *Australia II* was breaking new ground, the series in Melbourne revealed to the public for the first time something that would become an Australian icon — the boxing kangaroo flag — today a symbol of Australian sporting supremacy. It came about as a consequence of a bet I had in England two years earlier, prior to the Admiral's Cup. We were preparing for the series in Cowes when an English friend, Peter de Savary, and I decided we should have a match-racing series between our two yachts. We decided that the loser would pay the winner in gold coins, and it was to be a substantial amount. We won, and as a result a long-standing crewman of mine, John 'Chink' Longley, got together with our tactician and sailmaker, Hugh Treharne, to come up with something that would rub salt into the British wounds — a battle flag we would fly from our yacht showing a kangaroo wearing boxing gloves standing over a dazed and bandaged British bulldog. It was a big hit so around a year later, as the 1983 America's Cup challenge developed, 'Chink' decided that the boxing kangaroo should become a symbol for *Australia II*. After having a graphic artist in Sydney come up with the profile of the boxing kangaroo, Chink again went to Hugh to put the flag together. Hugh outlined the kangaroo's profile in black ink on a large white flag and after that a signwriter filled in the colours, including the piercing red eyes and red boxing gloves. It's wonderful to think that from such a simple beginning the boxing kangaroo has become as symbolic for Australians at international sporting events as our national flag.

Democracy doesn't work in an event like the America's Cup — somebody has to make the decisions and stand by them right or wrong. And accordingly one of the great misconceptions about the 1983 challenge was my role in the entire operation. While Warren Jones was a very effective shore manager and media manager I was the syndicate head and team captain — the commander of the ship. I wasn't just the fun guy signing the cheques so that everyone could have a good time. I was the driving force, the one making the decisions that mattered, because it was my money and my reputation that was on the line. I underwrote each campaign either personally, through our private family company, Dallhold, or through Bond Corporation. By 1983 the cost of the challenge had risen to a lot more than $10 million, and of that less than 10 per cent came through sponsorship. I worked alongside Ben during the design stage, giving him every encouragement and opportunity he needed to come up with the right yacht. From the outset I was the one making the calls. There was input from a lot of people, but I decided on the design team, the sail making, and the bulk of the crew selection — all the things that mattered. But before making those final decisions I always consulted the likes of John Bertrand, sailmaker Tom Schnackenberg, Ben, Warren Jones and Jim Hardy, who were the back-up in our team. Sometimes I had to make some very tough decisions, but as unpopular as they might have been, they had to be made. My sole intent was to get the best person for every job, something made even more important when we decided to go to America with the smallest possible team so that we could achieve maximum effort with minimum distractions. Every one had a job to do and everyone did their job extremely well.

For me running this campaign was no different from running a business. It needed a critical path and a business plan, starting with the hierarchy and working from there. You have your finance arm, your design team, boat builders, sailmakers, crew, management, sailing program. The list goes on. Most importantly you have to consider human relations, how people will work together in an enclosed environment on the other side of the world for at least six months of what was a three-year campaign. Lives get bound up in these things and I'm not just talking about team members, but also their families, whose support was vital. It's never a party. It's a job requiring total commitment from everyone because the team that wins the America's Cup is the one that makes the fewest mistakes. You will never be perfect, but you have to strive to be as close to perfect as possible — better than 90 per cent in every department.

Even though we were convinced that we really did have something going for us with the winged keel, it was imperative that we kept it under wraps and away from prying American eyes. The last thing we needed was for the Americans to get wind of what we were doing and rush off to copy it. *Australia II* always had a skirt around the hull when it was out of the water, and to make aerial observations of the keel difficult when the yacht was sailing we camouflaged the shape with paint so that it looked like a conventional appendage. When we arrived in Newport, Rhode Island, we set up our waterfront base so that the hull could be lifted from the water and remain concealed behind a green and blue plastic shroud. Fortunately for us the Americans remained unperturbed, their attitude being 'isn't it nice to see the Aussies trying to psych us out, but really, who cares'. We liked that, and we also liked it when New York Yacht Club representatives didn't come and look at the yacht when the match officials were measuring it, as they were entitled to do. It was measured as a legal 12-metre class yacht.

With so much interest and so many challengers lining up for the 1983 match, Louis Vuitton came in as a sponsor of the challenger elimination event and created the Louis Vuitton Cup as the prize for the yacht that won the right to face the American defender. Winning that trophy was our first goal, but to do that we had to beat two other Australian yachts, *Challenge 12* and Syd Fischer's *Advance*, plus contenders from France, England — which had Peter de Savary as the backer — Canada and Italy. *Australia II* struggled somewhat in the early stages of the round robin racing, which in a way was a blessing because it helped keep the heat off us as far as interest from the Americans was concerned. Our two biggest problems were our sailing technique and our downwind sails, the spinnakers. The sails improved dramatically as the summer progressed, thanks in no small way to the incredible ability of New Zealander Tom Schnackenberg, a man who was to sailmaking what Ben was to yacht design. Our racing tactician, Hugh Treharne, and navigator Grant Simmer backed him up, and between them they gave us some of the best sails ever seen on a 12-metre. Tom actually pioneered an entirely new style of headsail on *Australia II* using the first ever fully computer-generated design, a sail that made a dramatic improvement to the yacht's speed.

By the time we got to the end of the challenger selection series we had won the Louis Vuitton Cup with a score of 48 wins and six losses, and in doing so I had kept intact my unblemished record for becoming the Cup challenger. One of the losses we suffered came when we had to forfeit a race to the Canadians after one of our crewmen was badly injured out on the course. Scotty McAllister was working at the top of the mast trying to clear some jammed rigging when an aluminium strut on the masthead buckled, crushed his arm and broke it.

Scotty's arm was pinned against the mast and he was being hurled around so badly that he was knocked unconscious. Worse still, it became evident that he might lose his arm. The only option was for a crewman, Colin Beashel, to be hoisted to the masthead, free Scotty and bring him back to the deck. It was an incredible feat considering the wind was blowing at more than 20 knots and the seas were quite rough. Sadly, Scotty's injuries were bad enough for him to be forced out of the team, but he was replaced by an equally talented bowman, Damien 'Knuckle' Fewster, from *Challenge 12*, which had been eliminated. He was a very good and likeable young chap out of Victoria. This opportunity resulted in him becoming recognised as one of the best bowmen in the world, and as a consequence of his involvement with the campaign he met my daughter, Jody, and is now my son-in-law.

Throughout the summer in Newport there is another side to the America's Cup that is very rarely recorded, and that is the social scene for the upper echelons of American society. In this particular society, most people are so wealthy they never have to consider working, they just manage their money. They live in amazing mansions on tree-lined streets adjacent to the oceanfront, and coming to Newport each summer is simply what they do. To be invited into their inner sanctum as an outsider was an enormous honour, and that's just what happened to Eileen and me. The garden and dinner parties we attended were incredible affairs where waiters and servants were dressed to suit the theme of the occasion. We were also invited to become members of the very exclusive Bailey's Beach Club for tennis and to dine, and on one occasion attended a Presidential fundraising dinner in one of the mansions. Their high regard for Eileen and me brought an acceptance of our challenge among people who counted, people who, as well as introducing me to some of the most powerful business organisations in America, could lean on the New York Yacht Club hierarchy when they challenged the legality of *Australia II* and say: 'You must know that we like these Australians and we don't think it's proper that you are trying to throw them out of the race.'

This was an attitude also reflected among those members of the American populace who knew of the America's Cup. Outside of the New York Yacht Club there was an undercurrent of support for the Aussie underdog.

As *Australia II*'s wins accumulated towards the end of the Louis Vuitton Cup, so did the concerns of the New York Yacht Club. There was a feeling in the air that for the first time there was a serious contender that might take the Cup away, and for someone else to win the Cup just wasn't the done thing. That's why no one had taken it away from them in 132 years, even though they put on this façade about being fair in competition. What they were doing in each campaign over the years involved them smiling nicely and making you feel welcome: 'We have this lovely sailing event called the America's Cup so please come on over here and we'll have a good race where the best team will win', when in fact what they were really saying was: 'We've got this yacht race for the America's Cup. It's our Cup but please feel free to come over and race so we can beat the arse off you, make ourselves feel good and send you home empty-handed. We'll thank you for coming and giving us another opportunity to have a nice summer in Newport . . . and again satisfy ourselves that we're the best in the world.'

So you can understand why, when they thought there was someone who might spoil their party and win *their* Cup, that the bullying and dirty tricks campaign started in earnest, a campaign that was well documented at the time. Suddenly they decided our yacht was illegal because of the winged keel, and because of that they did not want to race us in the America's Cup match. Warren and I had numerous heated meetings with the New York Yacht Club officials, and just to confuse them we had great fun swapping roles each time — one day he was the bad guy and I was the good guy, then at the next meeting we would do a role reversal. The meetings never got us anywhere and the club remained ruthless in their efforts to produce evidence that the keel did not fit within the rules. They were effectively calling Benny a cheat and that was something that he could not cope with. Their harassment of him and the team would soon prove too much for Ben and he suffered a mild heart attack. Still, that didn't stop him. He bounded back more determined than ever to see his radical yacht beat the Americans.

There was a wonderful level of maturity and an unprecedented will to win within the 1983 team and we held a very definite attitude towards social functions. Whereas in previous campaigns the crew occasionally had a big night out on the town, this time it was different. This was a very close-knit group, like a team of commandos totally focused on the mission, probably due in part to the fact that they knew that Benny had given them a yacht capable of creating history. And most importantly, Warren and I deflected the New York Yacht Club and their efforts to create controversy so that the team was able to concentrate on their task.

One of our best pieces of ammunition against the New York Yacht Club was the media, and we did everything possible to fire up international sentiment against what were seen as the old fuddy-duddies from the club's hierarchy. That way we kept them busy while we got on with our preparations. One day the media was pounding their beat outside our office, waiting for the next development. Nothing was happening, but it was an opportunity too good to be missed, so I went out and told the media that we were so disgusted by the New York Yacht Club's smear campaign that we were going to force them to front the International Yacht Racing Union (IYRU) under some rule number that I just pulled out of my head. I told them the rule related to bad sportsmanship. There was no such rule under that number in the IYRU's regulations but the media had their story and off they went with it. One other thing in our favour came when we gained the support of America's most famous modern-day America's Cup yacht designer, Olin Stephens. He went on record backing us, saying there was nothing fair about the New York Yacht Club trying to remove *Australia II* from the competition just because it was too fast. Eventually the pressure to get on with the racing and decide the event on the water became so strong that the club capitulated, and in mid-September 1983 the racing began. We had just won our first big battle on the road to the Cup. *Australia II* would race Dennis Conner's red-hulled *Liberty*, a far more conventional yacht than ours.

You'd expect that the morning of the first race would be full of excitement and anticipation. But no, our crew showed the benefit of all their years of experience in America's Cup competition by going about their jobs on that first day after the usual breakfast and my motivational speech to them in their usual business-like manner. They knew what they had to do. Comfortable in the knowledge that we could do no more to prepare for the challenge, I joined a small group of key syndicate people, including Benny, Warren and Jim Hardy, to watch the race from *Black Swan*, our support launch that towed the yacht to and from the race course each day. During each race *Black Swan* had the additional role of being the nerve centre for all our race analysis computers, which collected data from the yacht and plotted *Australia II*'s performance against the Americans.

The result of Race One left us in no doubt we could win the Cup — but we didn't win the race. Despite some tactical blunders, *Australia II* was right on *Liberty*'s stern with little more than one leg of the race to go and looking as though she could win. But then John Bertrand turned the yacht through a tight manoeuvre and broke the steering in the process. It wasn't his fault, the fitting should not have failed, but as a consequence some of my worst fears were realised. After the race, which we lost by little more than a minute, John and Ben had another of their great clashes, John claimed that Ben's engineering on the yacht was not good enough, that the steering fitting should never have failed. While John was technically correct he didn't take into account the 44 races we had sailed to become the challenger and that wear and tear were a natural occurrence. As an engineer he was the one person in a perfect position to eyeball the boat before the race if he had any concerns. All this blow-up did for me was confirm that John was physically and mentally exhausted, and as a result tensions were building within the team. It was decided that the best thing we could do for John as the series progressed was have him listen to motivational tapes to offset the stress. This helped up until the last two races when the pressure really came on strong.

In Race Two we suffered another fitting failure, this time at the masthead, and lost again. Then *Australia II* came back in Race Three, posting her first win that, much to my delight, was by a comfortable margin. Race Four was one we'd rather forget about because Conner came out in what we knew was a slower boat and gave *Australia II* a hiding. We were then 3–1 down and could not afford to lose another race.

I was a shattered man when I got back to the dock that night, but I couldn't let anyone know. What annoyed me more than anything was that I knew that after four races the Cup should have been in our hands — we had the boat that should have won 4–0, but I couldn't dwell on that and I couldn't get angry, I had to step up and be counted. I had to boost the morale of the entire team because I knew that we could still win. What made me even more determined was the thought that the Americans were already chilling their champagne and planning the dockside victory party, a sight that I'd not enjoyed seeing at three previous America's Cups.

At breakfast on the morning of Race Five I stood up and delivered what Jim Hardy would tell me later was one of the greatest motivational speeches he'd ever heard. I said to the guys:

> Listen, you're in the history books, you've won one race and the last page of the history book is still open for you guys to be on. If you really want to be remembered in history then now is your chance. Get out there and win some bloody races. It's up to you now — no one else. I've given you a boat that's capable of winning and you keep cocking it up. You have breakdowns, you stuff up on the bloody tactics and other things while you're out there. So it's not the boat any more, and it's not me any more. It's you guys, and you guys alone.

I impressed upon them that they were good enough to win, and more importantly, it wasn't only for them that they had to win. I reminded them that they had tens of millions of supporters both in Australia and around the world who wanted them to win, not just for the sake of the racing, but because they believed that Australia was as good as the Americans.

When we went out to the start of Race Five you could see the Americans making initial preparations for the celebrations. They were brimming with confidence because they'd retained the Cup on 24 previous occasions and in their minds this time around was going to be no different. I smiled to myself as I watched them get ready to party.

By the end of the day I was smiling even more because we had spoiled their party. They had to put all their champagne back on ice because *Australia II* had won the race by close to two minutes, making the score 3–2. However, this was a win that didn't come without dramas on our boat. The stress John was under as helmsman became obvious immediately after the start. Dennis and the team on *Liberty* walloped us in the pre-start manoeuvres and

Australia II trailed them by 30 seconds, a frightening margin in a match race. John literally threw his hands in the air in total desperation, convinced that this was the end of the campaign. One crew member flew at him, telling him to get back onto the helm and do his job, that there were 10 other crew on the boat determined to win the race. John cooled down and started concentrating. The result on that day confirmed yet again what a great crew we had, and what an exceptional yacht *Australia II* was.

It was now more obvious than ever that John had run the race of his life to this point and he was suffering from exhaustion and stress. If we were going to win this series then the rest of the crew had to play an even greater role than before.

The Americans' party preparations were underway again as we headed out for Race Six. We lost the start, but *Australia II* showed her comeback ability and sailed home a convincing winner by almost three and a half minutes ... and the Americans put the champagne back on ice again.

This was where the benefit of the experience gained in our three previous challenges really shone through. It was achieved through total dedication by the entire crew. And while the victory was exciting I remember the race because of one very special incident. Coming to the fifth and final turning mark, *Australia II* had the race won. Only a miracle could save Dennis Conner and *Liberty*. As *Australia II* turned that mark and the spinnaker was being set, Dennis deliberately sailed *Liberty* off the course and tried to target *Australia II* for a collision, his ploy being a last desperate effort to win the race by protest. I'd never seen Jim Hardy so incensed in all the years I'd known him. The New York Yacht Club's America's Cup Race Committee was right alongside us on their motor yacht, so Jim gave them both barrels, shouting that Dennis's act was the greatest display of bad sportsmanship he had ever seen. And while the Race Committee cringed at the verbal barrage they were copping, the crew on *Australia II* were letting the *Liberty* team know in no uncertain fashion what they thought of their tactics.

With *Australia II* doing so poorly at the start of most races, and the next day scheduled as a lay day, we decided that with the score at 3–3 we should try to help John and get him some starting practice. Dick Pratt had very kindly made *Challenge 12* and all his team's equipment available to us, so we organised for Irish yachtsman Harold Cudmore to sail that yacht against *Australia II* for some intense training. It's something we later wished we hadn't done because Harold, who had skippered the English contender in Newport that year and was a match-racing expert, literally tied John in knots. It did nothing for John's sagging confidence.

There are no certainties in yacht racing, something that was never more evident than when we went out for the final showdown with Conner and *Liberty*. There was no wind, and after hours of waiting the decision was to postpone the race for 24 hours, so we decided to again grab the opportunity to give John some more starting practice in a patch of light breeze near the harbour entrance. Again Cudmore and *Challenge 12* crushed John in the pre-start manoeuvres. We returned to the dock desperately hoping John could put it out of his mind.

The professionalism of the *Australia II* team was typified in their approach to the morning of the final race. Again nothing was any different from any other morning — we all had breakfast together, enjoyed a few laughs before I made my usual address, and then headed for the boat.

The atmosphere around the dock was incredible and there were now as many Australian flags flying as there were American. And for the first time Warren and I discussed what we would do 'after we win'. We decided to store a massive Australian flag on *Black Swan* that we would transfer to *Australia II* and fly from the mast after the finish.

When we started towing *Australia II* out towards the race course our battle song 'Down Under' by Men at Work was blasting out louder than ever from the big speakers mounted on the upper deck of *Black Swan*, and there was a cacophony of cheering, sirens and horns blaring from vessels docked around the harbour. While all this atmosphere was being generated around us I was feeling anguish and stress — here was my team going into the winner-take-all grand final event and I was the coach. My mind was running through every inch of the boat and then went through the entire crew, remembering all their idiosyncrasies and what might go right and what could go wrong. The main point to come out of it all was the fact that I knew if we could get a good start then we would be well on the way to winning. What concerned me most was the pressure that John was now desperately struggling to deal with. Once again the crew would be called upon to to support him.

As we moved out through the massive spectator fleet towards the starting line, it felt as though we were guiding a prize-fighter towards the ring. It was obvious that for the first time ever many of the Americans crammed onto spectator boats were starting to think the unthinkable — that they might lose the America's Cup. Still their attitude was that their heavyweight champion of the world, Dennis Conner, was better than John Bertrand, and he'd win it for them. Well, I was soon thinking they were right because we blew the start, and everyone knew that once you are behind at the start of an America's Cup race against Dennis Conner then it's bloody hard to get to the front. He doesn't give you any chances for recovery. Three-quarters of the way through that final race and it was becoming agonising to watch because *Australia II* was not making any impression. I could only think about the celebration champagne again being pulled out on the American dock back in Newport Harbor, and the excitement that would be mounting as they began their now well-rehearsed victory party preparations.

While we watched *Australia II* struggle and *Liberty* retain total control, all of us aboard *Black Swan* did what we could to put on a brave front, reminding each other that while we were still out there racing there was a chance. But when we were sailing upwind to the second-last mark and still trailing by near a minute I decided I couldn't watch any more. This was my boat that had victory in the America's Cup written all over it from the outset, the boat that represented every dream and aspiration you could ever want to have going into a Cup match. When we left the dock that day I was confident that we were going to win, but here we were so far behind and teetering on the edge of the precipice once more. A thumping stress headache started and I had to go below to lie down. Benny came below as well. He'd seen enough. I said to Benny at the time: 'We've tried so hard and we've had the backing of everyone in Australia, and we are going to let them down.' I could think of nothing else.

When *Australia II* rounded the mark she was trailing by 57 seconds and I heard someone call out from up on deck: 'We're around the mark and they're not covering us,' then a few seconds later: 'They're not covering us, they're not covering us,' and then he started shouting: 'They're still not covering us.' This was fantastic news. There was a window of opportunity opening for *Australia II*. Benny and I rushed back on deck to watch things unfold, and as history will tell you the *Australia II* crew spotted better breeze, cruised into it and sailed past *Liberty* under spinnaker then went to the last rounding mark with a 21-second advantage. Only an upwind leg to the finish stood between the Cup and us.

That final leg seemed as though it would never end. Conner pulled out the only card he had left and engaged *Australia II* in a fierce tacking duel, so fierce that at one stage both boats had lost so much speed they were virtually dead in the water. But our guys refused to let him escape their cover. It was sensational stuff — like two gladiators standing toe-to-toe, exhausted and unable to throw another punch at each other. Dennis would not give up, throwing in false tacks, trying to get some undisturbed wind by escaping the block that *Australia II* had established. It was so intense at one stage aboard *Australia II* that our tactician, Hugh Treharne, took the only option that would ensure the cover remained over *Liberty*. He grabbed the helm from John, stood in front of the wheel and faced the stern so he could look back at the Americans and match their every move. It was the quickest and most effective way to counter the American attack. Once *Liberty* had surrendered and stayed in phase with *Australia II* John took back the helm.

Still, I knew it wasn't over because *Australia II*'s equipment was built to the absolute minimum of tolerances to save weight. It was a delicate boat as we'd already seen in this series. It wasn't until our boys tacked *Australia II* for the last time and headed directly for the finish line with *Liberty* still trailing that I began to think we might win.

The gun went and unbelievable euphoria erupted aboard both *Australia II* and *Black Swan*. Benny, Warren and I rushed over to the yacht on an inflatable boat, climbed aboard and immediately everyone started hugging each other and cheering. It was a joyous moment as we began the long tow back into the harbour with the boxing kangaroo battle flag and the massive Australian flag flying proudly from the mast. It was a situation that I still struggle to comprehend — one of those heart-stopping times in your life that you know you will never capture again.

It was near dark as we arrived back at the dock surrounded by Coast Guard launches with their blue lights flashing. The noise, the atmosphere, was fantastic. We hadn't planned any victory party prior to the race because that would have taken our focus off winning, so we weren't sure what was going to happen that evening, but the scene at the dock was amazing, and that was enough. The American crew came by and saluted us while thousands of people crammed along our dock. Hundreds more were hanging from buildings and sitting on roofs and soon the chant went up, 'show us the keel, show us the keel'.

After a few moments of contemplation Jim Hardy urged me to do it, so I leapt up onto the back of *Black Swan*, threw my arms in the air and signalled for the curtains to be raised from around the keel. A roar went up from the crowd and within a few seconds our masterpiece was there for the world to see.

There were incredible scenes in Newport where tens of thousands of people crammed into the narrow streets, cheering wildly and wanting to share in our historic moment. We struggled to get through the crowd and into the press conference at the international media centre where one of our greatest supporters,

Rupert Murdoch, who had followed the race from our VIP vessel and was as excited about the win as I was, joined me.

Within two hours of coming ashore we were back at the crew house for celebratory drinks with about 50 friends and supporters. But it wasn't a party as such. The entire team was emotionally drained. Suddenly all the adrenaline was gone as we stood looking at each other in stunned disbelief. We couldn't celebrate if we tried. It was all too much. We were asking ourselves: 'What do we do now? What's going to happen? What have we done? Is this what taking the America's Cup away from America for the first time in 132 years really feels like?' Actually, when you think about it, if we weren't emotionally drained and totally exhausted that night it would have meant that we hadn't given it our all, that we'd held something back in reserve, and what we had held back could well have been the difference between winning and losing.

Most of the crew were in bed before midnight that night. I slept too, but not for long — long sleeps aren't part of my life.

Looking back on the human resources side, without John Bertrand and his detailed understanding of sail aerodynamics we would not have won the America's Cup. I also credit Sir James Hardy with much of our victory because he brought an extremely valuable America's Cup sailing experience to our team. He had a lot of pressure on him when he had to step in and take over the helm on *Australia II* during the Louis Vuitton Cup when John was unable to sail because of neck problems. And apart from Jim and John, other key members were John Longley, Hugh Treharne, Grant Simmer, Colin Beashel and Warren Jones, along with sailmaker Tom Schnackenberg. Special mention must go to my son-in-law and *Australia II* bowman Damien Fewster who managed to keep a smile on everyone's face even when we were looking to be down and out. And let's not forget Eileen for her important achievements on the social front. But highest on the pedestal of all is Benny. He was a god in the world of yacht design as well as a magnificent man.

Apart from some New York Yacht Club members who begrudged the victory, a surprising number of Americans were happy about

Australia's win. Their attitude was that if anyone was going to take it from them, then who better than the Aussies. Prior to us winning the Cup few of them knew anything about Australia, and many of them were actually confused between Austria and Australia. But suddenly they knew about us, and they liked us. On the other side of the coin though, the New York Yacht Club's antics in trying to prove *Australia II*'s keel was illegal so they could keep the Cup had done the American image a lot of harm around the world. They did themselves no favours either when it came to the official handing over of the trophy to the Royal Perth Yacht Club, the club *Australia II* was representing. The ceremony held on the verandah of one of the classic old homes in Newport was far from in keeping with the great history of the Cup. The club appeared far from gracious in defeat; in fact the way the trophy was presented was close to insulting. It was as though they were thinking: 'Hell, let's save ourselves any more embarrassment. Just give them the trophy and get them outta town.' It should have been a day of great celebration and camaraderie.

I must stress again that it wasn't all the membership of the New York Yacht Club that was anti-*Australia II*; some of their senior members were very, very honourable men who accepted that there were two sides to the story and ours was a better yacht. But even today there are some members who carry the grudge, adamant that *Australia II* was illegal, a preposterous claim from people who can only be called sore losers.

The feeling within New York Yacht Club after the loss was captured by Melissa H. Harrington when she wrote the official 150-year history of the club:

> The endless journey of the spectator fleet back to Newport from the 88th race for the America's Cup was, in reality, a funeral procession complete with grim faces and a sick feeling in the pit of the collective stomachs of members truly and deeply shocked by what had happened. No living person had ever known the world of the New York Yacht Club without the America's Cup; how could we act and feel now that it was gone except saddened and stunned?

During the summer, stories had appeared in the international media that likened the New York Yacht Club's attitude towards us to that of a street bully, something that didn't sit too well with much of the establishment in America. After the Cup there were obvious efforts to repair the damage, such as an invitation for our team to go to the White House in Washington for a Presidential reception in recognition of our win. It was seen as a way for America to mend some diplomatic bridges and rebuild the ties between Australia and the United States.

It was to be a day we'll never forget. We were in front of the world media in the Rose Garden at the White House. It was also a day I'll never forget because I unwittingly made a diplomatic *faux pas*. It started when President Reagan, standing at his lectern with the seal of the President of the United States of America on the front of it, made a wonderful speech congratulating us on our victory, and praising the determination and effort that had gone into the campaign. He was very gracious, saying something like: 'You guys did a great job and if we were ever going to lose this yacht race then we couldn't think of anybody better to lose it to than the Australians.'

Once he completed his speech I walked up to the lectern to respond. The President stepped aside and I took over the microphone. First up they weren't expecting me to respond, and secondly, as I was to find out later, no one but the President is supposed to stand at a lectern behind the President's seal and make an address. My speech was carried across the United States on prime-time television. If the people of America didn't know me before then, they certainly did after that.

On a personal note, I decided I should give each team member something very special in recognition of their achievement, so I had a Bermudan America's Cup gold coin specially struck for them. I presented one to each team member with a note of thanks attached. It was a small consolation prize in comparison to their great commitment and achievement. Unlike the America's Cup teams of today they were not financially remunerated.

The entire team became national heroes in Australia and they couldn't get home quickly enough to be with family and friends and share in the celebrations. They sensed something big was awaiting their return after their five tortuous months in Newport, but it wasn't until they flew across America to hook up with a special Qantas flight out of Los Angeles back to Sydney that they began to realise the enormity of the nation's reaction to their achievement. The flying kangaroo on the massive red tail of the jumbo jet they were to fly home on had been replaced by a giant boxing kangaroo. The flight turned into one massive mid-air party all the way across the Pacific to Sydney where the real partying started.

For me, my world had just turned upside down. While I was struggling to come to grips mentally with our history-making achievement and what it meant to Australia, my profile was rocketing up the ladder leading to the top of international business. My photograph even appeared on the cover of *Time* magazine, and Sean Connery, who was the other 'Bond', James Bond, even sent me a congratulatory telegram. So many banks and business organisations that didn't know me before certainly knew me then. The fact that we'd won the America's Cup meant that I was seen as a corporate door leading to Australia. Opportunities began to flood in, and I had to capitalise on the ones that mattered for Bond Corporation.

But just how close we'd all come to seeing none of this happen was evident the day after we won the Cup when we took *Australia II* out sailing for a promotional photo shoot. After just two tacks the headboard fitting at the top of the mast failed and the mainsail came fluttering down. Two more tacks on race day and we would not have won the America's Cup.

Winning the America's Cup in 1983 meant that we had to look towards defending it off Fremantle in 1987. But before we could even think about that we experienced one of the greatest periods of celebration that Australia had ever seen. The highlight for the entire team was the welcome we received when the Cup arrived in its new home city, Perth. More than 750 000 people turned out to cheer the crew and the Cup in a massive street parade. Our historic win made headlines across the country for weeks.

Once things settled down we had our first meeting with the Cup holders, Royal Perth Yacht Club, and from that moment we knew that we, and the Cup defence, were in trouble. The club's attitude from the outset was: 'Well, this is our Cup. We are the holders of it so now we have to go about running an event to defend it.' It was like they were saying to us: 'Thanks for coming. See you later.'

With that, they formed committees, got the government involved and employed marketing people. We were never invited to be part of it, even though we had the experience of four America's Cup campaigns behind us. Sure, staging a great regatta was a priority, but keeping the Cup was what mattered above everything else. But no, they knew better, and in a flash the club had secured around $10 million of sponsorship money for the event, a lot of which could have been better spent on the actual defence. While there were some great things done, like building the new outer harbour at Fremantle where the club established a new annexe, the club's focus was on the event and not the retention of the Cup. This could be seen in the number of 'research' trips taken by some of the hierarchy. Their focus was askew.

Royal Perth should have been like the New York Yacht Club in so many ways — brutal in their approach to the rules covering the defence — but they were too honest in interpreting the 'deed of gift' and therefore rejected any confrontation, especially with our international challengers. We tried to convince them otherwise but we couldn't get past first base. They just wanted to make sure it was a memorable occasion for everyone.

They certainly succeeded there because, as we all remember, Australia lost the Cup. That was the most memorable thing, and if there was a good thing about that for us it was that our syndicate was not part of the failed defence. I'll go to my grave saying that if the club had listened to us and made us part of the plan then Australia would have kept the Cup in 1987.

We put a plan to Royal Perth for the defence, based on the fact that *Australia II* had won the Cup and therefore we had the right to defend it, just as we are seeing in the event these days. We wanted to do a single defence so that we could concentrate every talent and every available dollar available in Australia on keeping the trophy. More than one defence syndicate would only dilute the effort.

Royal Perth didn't see our plan as being in the best interest of racing, the attitude being: 'It will be far more exciting to have a number of Australian syndicates fighting for the right to defend, and after all, the New York Yacht Club encouraged more than one defence syndicate, and they must be right.' What they didn't stop to think about was that the New York Yacht Club had just lost the Cup, and also that America had a far greater asset base than Australia so they could afford to have more than one syndicate if they wanted to.

The scenario to the Royal Perth Yacht Club approach was that as well as there being a syndicate from both Sydney and Adelaide there were two from Perth, and that was totally wrong. There were not enough people in Perth, let alone Australia, to create the best possible defence.

All the time we were planning our campaign for the defence, and yet again I met the millions of dollars needed for funding our own defence effort.

What the world saw in the end was the greatest-ever America's Cup regatta, and for that we must give the Royal Perth Yacht Club full credit. In just a few months Fremantle was transformed from being a sleepy little waterfront town at the entrance to the Swan River to being a thriving, exciting metropolis while retaining the character of all the old buildings. Coffee shops, restaurants with outside dining and bars, and new accommodation sprang up everywhere. It was a transformation that was well justified because apart from there being four Australian syndicates, there was an unprecedented 13 teams from six nations racing for the right to challenge. These teams spent millions of dollars just to be in Fremantle to race. The Italian syndicates even brought their own chefs and established restaurants locally, something that contributed enormously to the cosmopolitan atmosphere and the calibre of the food that was available across town. And all this contributed to hundreds of thousands of people from all over Australia and around the world descending on Perth and Fremantle to be part of the scene. It was a wonderful, wonderful time to be in the west.

The elimination series that the Royal Perth Yacht Club orchestrated to find the Australian defender was very controversial in its structure, but resulted in the two Western Australian syndicates, ours and one led by Kevin Parry, going into the final showdown. Our dilemma was that while we wanted to develop a yacht for the weather conditions that would be experienced off Fremantle at the time of the defence, we had to try to remain focused on beating Parry's yacht, *Kookaburra*, for the right to defend. The final result proved our original theory to be correct, that there should have been just one Australian group concentrating on retaining the Cup. It was because the conditions expected for the elimination final and those for the Cup match were going to be considerably different that we had to work on two different keel styles for our yacht, and that's what cost us the right to defend. It was madness. *Kookaburra* beat us 5–0 because we spent too much time working on defence keels and not keels for the elimination. In fact we got so messed up with the options that we had available to us we used the wrong keel on *Australia IV* in the final elimination race against *Kookaburra*. Then *Kookaburra* went out and lost the Cup to America in conditions that were very different from those experienced when they raced us.

All I could say to Parry at the final press conference of the Louis Vuitton elimination series was: 'I've won it. I hope you don't lose it.' His reply was memorable, but I won't elaborate. I knew from that very moment that *Kookaburra* wouldn't win.

Dennis Conner became the challenger and took the Cup back to San Diego with a score of 4–0 over *Kookaburra*. I know he was a very relieved man when he saw he was facing *Kookaburra* and not *Australia IV* — because we knew the America's Cup game.

Unlike the New York Yacht Club, Australia and the Royal Perth Yacht Club lost the Cup with dignity — they distinguished themselves by showing considerable grace as losers. The parties they staged were wonderful and the presentation of the Cup to Dennis Conner's group was done with a great show of true Australian sportsmanship.

Still, for our syndicate, seeing the Cup lost didn't hurt as much because we weren't the defenders. It was Kevin Parry of the Royal Perth Yacht Club who lost the America's Cup.

How the yacht club has changed since then! It can now be counted as an unwavering supporter of me in my difficult times and their presentation of the Cup memorabilia is outstanding.

The twentieth anniversary America's Cup Gala Ball was an exciting re-run of the huge ball held in Fremantle after the America's Cup win in 1983. The Royal Perth Yacht Club used it as an opportunity to honour all of the crew and those associated with the historic win — including acknowledgments of myself as the main person who brought the Cup to Australia. The ball was attended by several hundred people and videos re-lived the excitement of 1983. The atmosphere was just as moving for me as receiving the accolades back then.

CHAPTER SEVEN
RIDING THE WAVE

Just about everyone in Australia remembers where they were when we won the America's Cup. Because of the time difference between America's east coast and Australia — it was early on the morning of 27 September 1983 in Australia when we won — people had stayed up all night to watch the race on television or listen to it on the radio. The stories we heard the next day in Newport about people going to great lengths just to follow that final race and the Australia-wide celebrations were incredible. Someone told us about boundary riders and drovers in camps in outback Queensland travelling hundreds of kilometres to a homestead for an all-night party so they could follow *Australia II*'s progress. The only people disappointed that night were those who went to bed when we looked beaten going to the fourth turning mark. They'll never forgive themselves for not seeing one of the greatest comebacks ever.

There are millions of memories from that day, one of the most famous being our Prime Minister, Bob Hawke, at the Royal Perth Yacht Club where he'd watched the race, drenched in champagne after we won and announcing to the media that any Australian boss who sacked an employee for not turning up at work that day was 'a bum'. It was as good as declaring a national holiday.

Beating such great odds and defeating the Americans brought a new level of national pride. This was a great lesson to all — that we as individuals, as Australians, were as good as, or better, than anyone else. Since 1983 many people have told me how *Australia II* winning the America's Cup had been an inspiration for them. It showed what a person who started with nothing, but who had worked hard and stuck to his beliefs, could achieve. The win gave people a lot of hope and if you don't have hope, if there's nothing to aspire to even in a mundane job, then life is a pretty poor place. They realised that you should not fear your own personal development, and the development of your own technologies. If your belief and determination is strong enough you can add the skills needed to get you anywhere. In the corporate world, businesses were suddenly saying, 'Yeah, we can do this', and banks were more confident about dealing with Australian companies.

Banks from across Australia and around the world certainly showed that attitude towards me by showering money on Bond Corporation and Dallhold for investment. Their feeling was that if you could win the America's Cup then nothing was impossible. There was to be a period of five years where the money was there to do whatever project we wanted — loan money, long-term loan money, short-term loan money — you name it. The banks were knocking themselves over in the rush to make sure they had one of my companies in their portfolio.

The momentum that the America's Cup win brought to my life was quite remarkable. I felt as though I was about to break through the sound barrier. I could want for no more commercially and personally, yet I knew that the future was to be even more dynamic and exciting than I could ever imagine.

One of the first things to come my way was an invitation from the US State Department to become an international adviser to President Ronald Reagan. I joined a number of people from around the world on what they called the International Forum. Rupert Murdoch was the only other Australian member. The White House was becoming concerned that Americans generally weren't popular in the world, despite their massive programs to help under-developed countries. One of the big problems they faced was that the vast majority of Americans don't travel outside their own country, and that they are somewhat ignorant about what happens in the rest of the world. The President wanted an exchange of ideas from us, an influential cross-section of international society, and also wanted to be able to impress upon us what America was doing for the world. The desire was to destroy the *Big Ugly American* syndrome. They wanted thoughts on how they could better communicate with the world. I guess you could say they wanted to be liked. Nearly 20 years later, their worst fears came home to roost when terrorists attacked the World Trade Center in New York on 11 September, 2001. Becoming an international adviser to the President was one of many accolades that I was to receive in the ensuing years. And one of my greatest distinctions was the award of 'Entrepreneur of the Year' in 1985 from the prestigious Babson College in America. This major international award is made to only one individual each year.

In 1987 I received from Sir David Rowe-ham, Mayor of London, the key to the city of London. This was another acknowledgment of both my America's Cup and business successes. For a bloke from Western Australia it was all very special.

The year 1983 was remarkable on many fronts. As well as striking gold with the America's Cup victory I struck oil for Bond Corporation, or more specifically, Bond Petroleum.

When we sold out of Santos we were looking around for other opportunities in the oil business, so we decided to take up some offshore oil and gas exploration permits for an area near Varanus Island, a few hundred kilometres north of Perth. I went into it with the assistance of John Jackson, a great oilman who worked with me on the Santos project. We chose that area because it was close to the

Barrow Island oil fields and I always kept in mind what Perry Bass had told me: 'Go to a place where oil is found and you are likely to find more.' The only thing was that we had to drill to find it.

We put down eight dry holes costing $8 million each before we struck oil at what would become the Harriet Oilfield. Bond Petroleum went in there with other partners, including Australian Occidental but during the operation we bought them out, a deal that gave us in excess of 50 per cent of the entire project. Harriet became yet another very successful investment for us. In just two years we took it from discovery to production, a world record time, and in that period we built the offshore oil rig platform and a tank farm on the island. We established the sub-sea connections between the island and the platform and generally set up for full-scale production. It was the first time an Australian company had established its own oil field, bringing together the expertise needed to create and operate the oil field itself. The rise in our share price reflected our success.

We achieved what was considered unachievable in just 24 months because I was able to find the right people to do the job. One of my strengths in business has been my ability to go out and employ people who could do a particular job better than I could — people who could not do it by themselves, but who, with the enthusiasm and opportunity that I was able to provide, could rise above the limits of their own abilities. The classic example of this came with the construction of the oil platform, the likes of which had never been built by an Australian company. While some people told me otherwise, I could see no reason to look overseas for the platform. Instead I went to a heavy engineering company that I knew well in Perth, J. R. Cluff and Son, and offered them the job. They had the capability to build this massive structure but had never had the opportunity to prove themselves, so I gave them that chance. We financed the project and when the platform was complete we towed it up the coast to the oil field and put it in place.

The success of the Harriet Field saw even more recognition for Bond Corporation and the business opportunities being presented to us grew accordingly.

For most of the years that I was in business I felt that we were more often than not employing people not ready for the world of business. While they had the appropriate university qualifications, they really needed to learn about the practicalities of corporate life — they hadn't been prepared for the rough and tumble of the corporate world. Universities might argue that they are there only to teach students, to give them the broad education, and after that it is up to the individual to sink or swim. Obviously that attitude doesn't apply directly to the likes of medical doctors, but generally we found that when graduates came out of university with a degree they couldn't do anything that was directly beneficial to the company. They weren't free enterprise orientated, and didn't know how to go out and think a project through while fending for themselves. They were more encouraged to become employees; that was their lot in life. As far as I was concerned they weren't shown how they could develop their own personal entrepreneurial skills in whatever field they chose.

I guess I went to the 'University of the World' by being involved in international business from a very early age. But still I always appreciated the role a university played in society. I recognised the need for further education because it was instilled into me by my mother when I was young: 'Alan, you didn't finish school so you've got to go and do some night school to better yourself. You should never think you are too old to learn.'

I always saw universities as being a vital cog in the success of our society and that was why I created a proposal for a private university as part of my master plan in the Yanchep development. My thoughts on what type of university it should be, and how it should differ from the norm, were influenced in no small way by our experience in employing university graduates at Bond Corporation. It was company policy to get on board the brightest graduates and then move them on to external universities as part of the Bond Corporation Development Program. Even in the late 1970s we put graduates through Harvard and Stanford universities as part of this program.

From the early days of business I envisaged that one day I would establish Australia's first private university, my thought being that the private sector should have a university where the target curriculum would prepare graduates to go out and actually do something in the business world, whether it be in law, commerce, computer sciences, humanities or communications. No matter what degree a student was doing they would be able to walk out of this university and actually contribute to the business rather than have another two years of training within the organisation.

Because of the desire to establish such an institution I was forever gathering information. I visited the first private university in America, Harvard, during one of the America's Cup campaigns and also went to look at Cambridge and Oxford universities in England, just to see how they were built and how they operated.

My plans were continually frustrated by the fact that I couldn't get any support for the concept in Western Australia. All that did was make me more determined to succeed, because a private university was an important element in the 20- to 50-year plan that I was developing for the Bond Corporation of the future. I was trying to implement this plan to ensure the long-term success of the organisation as I believed that planning for a company's future is just as important as planning for life. Put simply, the minute a child comes into a family parents automatically implement a 25-year plan, a vision, for that child — primary school, secondary school, further education and then employment. I'm always amazed how many big companies don't have such a plan, and governments certainly don't employ such a vision for the state or the nation, primarily because they are up for re-election every three or four years, so they want to focus only on the short term to catch votes at the next election, rather than consider things that might bring a long-term benefit for the nation.

With a university at Yanchep now off the agenda, my attention turned to the other side of the continent, to the Gold Coast in the southeast corner of Queensland. I was approached by a group of Gold Coast business people and residents who were aware of my frustration in not being able to establish a university in the west.

They had been considering one for their region, but not necessarily a private one, so they decided to make contact. The Gold Coast was starting to show signs of dynamic growth, and after listening to them I decided we should take a serious look at what we could do. We already owned a number of pine forest plantations on the coast, and Bond Corporation had ownership of the Castlemaine-XXXX brewery. After our initial feasibility study it became apparent that the Burleigh Forest plantation, which we had jointly owned with Kerry Packer's Australian Consolidated Press (ACP), would be an ideal site for a private university. We had bought Kerry out of the property some time earlier when we originally proposed that it become a real estate development. His immediate response over the phone to me was that he didn't want to be in land development and that we should buy him out. Kerry is a straight talker, just the way I like it. I was in his office the next day to make the purchase.

We were fortunate at the time to have a Gold Coast local, Brian Orr, working with a division of Bond Corporation that was involved in the pine plantation business. He was very skilled in property development and project management, with particular emphasis on the architectural side of things. He liked the idea of the university so he came aboard as project manager and suddenly things began to roll.

After a lengthy study, Brian presented Peter Beckwith and myself with a report stating that the university was viable and recommending that it be established. He proposed that it be built in stages, the plan being to have 2500 students by the end of five years of development, and between 8000 and 10 000 by the end of 20 years. Student accommodation, both dormitory and townhouse style, were to be an integral part of the plan. There was also a plan for an industrial research park.

Peter and I assessed the report and on 3 July 1986 told our team to proceed, subject to support coming from the Queensland government. Ironically, that same day we were meeting with the Queensland Premier, Sir Joh Bjelke-Petersen, to discuss other projects, so we took the opportunity to tell him of our decision to build Australia's first private university. He welcomed our proposal with great enthusiasm and immediately asked if he could announce the project at his political party's national conference on the Gold Coast. I agreed, but then put the pressure on Brian Orr and his team by promising the Premier that we would have a large model of the university for display at the conference just two weeks later. Which we did in time!

While the Queensland government didn't financially support the project, Sir Joh Bjelke-Petersen sponsored the *Bond Corporation University Act* through the parliament and, in his typical style, made sure there were as few obstacles in our path as possible. The biggest challenge we faced was transport because the university could not exist without a suitable transportation system to get the students there. I explained to the Premier that the university needed a freeway coming to it down the coast from Brisbane, otherwise we weren't going to get enough people to come in. His answer was simple: 'Yes, we are already planning a freeway and I'll get Russ Hinze to see if he can accelerate its development.' And that's what they did. Hinze, a state minister, saw that the construction of the freeway was completed ahead of schedule and to the highest international standards. The attitude was a pleasant change from what we experienced when we proposed a university in the west. There all they did was put hurdles in front of our plans for Yanchep.

Also high on the agenda in the early days was a name for the university, and I can say most definitely that it certainly wasn't ego on my part that led to the decision. I had no say in it. There were numerous suggestions, including the Gold Coast University of Technology and the University of South East Queensland, but the university Advisory Council confirmed the name, Bond University, basing their decision on the grounds that I had provided the foresight, enthusiasm and funding sources to initiate the project. I was honoured.

My thinking on how I saw Bond University positioned in the academic world remained essentially unchanged from what I had been planning for Yanchep. It would have an emphasis on areas beyond what was happening in existing universities, especially in relation to extending the boundaries of learning. It also needed a special marketing hook, and there my intention was for the university to play an ambassadorial role for Australia. I was of the firm belief that Australia was falling short when it came to an understanding of the Asian region and what it had to offer us, so we as a university would look towards Asia for much of our student intake. The reverse benefit of this move would be that Asian students would get a complete understanding of our way of thinking and operating in the world of business. I'd always got along very, very well with Asians, recognising that in being neighbours it was vital to the well-being of our nation, and for Bond Corporation, that we developed a solid understanding of the various cultures throughout the region. It was something I certainly strived to do when I was young because I often found myself dealing with successful Asian businessmen 30 years older than me. I soon learnt that the best way to break down the barriers was to be invited into their homes, or to take them to my home, as this created an ideal foundation for a better understanding of each other ... and it nearly always led to successful negotiations. At the same time my approach gave me a valuable opportunity to learn so much from them because they were masters of business strategy and negotiations in the corporate world, and I was the beginner.

I could see the new university having a similar, very hospitable role bridging the gap between Australia and our Asian neighbours by bringing together the cultures of the entire region. My desire was for students from Singapore, Malaysia, India, Japan and China, along with others from the USA, Canada, South Africa and England, to make up 40 per cent of our student population while the remaining 60 per cent would be Australian. As a group they would integrate and benefit from the fact that many would return home to become leaders in business and politics over the next 30 or 40 years. And with the Bond University alumni spread throughout the world the way would be paved for better understanding and greater opportunities for both the individuals and for their countries.

One important objective was to eliminate the fear so many Australians held in doing business with other cultures. At the same time international students would have a better understanding of Australians and their way of life. The university could create a common bond — one where there could be an immediate comfort level in dealing with people from foreign lands. The last thing we need to do is be like a lot of Americans who have a reputation for not wanting to understand other cultures. They think the only way to do business is to walk up, pull out the contract, have it signed and then walk away, an attitude that is due in no small way to the fact that they think the world revolves around them. This is partly because Americans are always under great pressure to produce results each quarter — that's why they are always in a hurry. Australians are a little different in that we are more cautious, we want time to think about a deal because we have a fear of investing in a country where we do not understand business conditions. If, however, we have a better understanding of the people we are dealing with then things would be so much better all round.

While attracting students from the Asian nations was one of the parameters for the student intake plan, attracting Asian investment in the university was a personal goal for me in what was an international project. Having corporate involvement from Asia would help open doors for the university in target markets. That led to me going to Japan in July 1986 for meetings with the head of the EIE Corporation, Harunori Takahashi. EIE was one of the major players in property and tourism around the world, and a significant property holder in Australia. Takahashi-san liked the idea of the university so agreed to bring in some long-term money to support the project and agreed to purchase a 50 per cent interest. It was a move that I welcomed because, as well as there being financial aspects attached, it signalled significant support for what we were out to achieve. We also had the benefit of having Dr Bungo Ishizaki, a professor at the Osaka University of Commerce and an international adviser to Takahashi-san, join our university's Advisory Council.

My son John played a major role in the establishment of the university. He was a member of the Advisory Council, working particularly on the architecture, the development of the legal structure and curriculum. Of the many great initiatives offered by the university, the one that has held the greatest appeal for foreign students was a curriculum offering the opportunity for them to continue their studies during what would normally be a university holiday period. By doing this they were able to reduce the time taken to secure a degree by up to one-third.

Unfortunately, while all those plans for the university were falling into place we had unwarranted and unwanted hurdles to contend with at home. The fact that we were establishing the first private university in Australia didn't wash too well with some of the establishment in the world of academia, as well as some of the union movement and student unions. They didn't like the idea of university education moving away from the established path of government control, so much so that the then Federal Minister of Education, Susan Ryan, came out and labelled private education as elitist, stating that the government would in no way assist our project, and adding that our university would threaten the high international acclaim that the Australian university system enjoyed. The anti-Bond University sentiment was very vocal, but more frustrating for us was the fact that it was uninformed comment because the protagonists were oblivious to what we were out to achieve. Those against us initiated an often-spiteful media campaign that certainly had a negative impact on our early enrolments. As far as they were concerned you should never spoil a good story by referring to the facts, and they made sure their version of the news got out there even if it was terribly wrong. The knockers also told us that we couldn't get the university up and running within three years — it usually took that long just to plan the project, as was seen in the six years it took to get Stanford University in America operational. We responded by doing just what we said we would do: building the university in three years, despite the Gold Coast experiencing two of its wettest years on record. Today we sit back and smile, proud of the fact that Bond University is an extremely successful institution setting exceptional international standards that are recognised around the world. The ethos is right — the encouragement of the private enterprise approach, the will to go out and seek opportunities then achieve a goal, to try new lines of approach, and to think globally.

I have always maintained a close relationship with the university, and in recent times I have attended functions organised by the alumni in London where more than 100 Bond University law and commerce graduates are living. Even while I was in prison I received regular updates from the university on developments, including newsletters from the Head of the Law Faculty. One of the things that symbolised my close relationship with the university was their acceptance of a painting that I did while serving time in Casuarina Prison. I presented it to the Law Faculty and it's hanging there today. Quite ironically it's of a court scene where a senior counsel is seated while a young female lawyer is gesticulating over a point of law. While I was doing this painting the Western Australian Attorney-General, Peter Foss, visited the jail and came to talk to me about it. He commented on the fact that it seemed odd that I was painting a courtroom scene while I was in a maximum-security prison. It didn't cause me any concern because such a scene was still vivid in my mind.

During my incarceration I became extremely distressed when I learnt that a few people were trying to have the name of the university changed. It would have been a difficult move to complete because the title was designated by an act of parliament, but before that move could be made the power of the people came to the surface. There was a huge backlash from the students; they rose up and said they didn't want the name changed. Their reaction created a very special moment for me during my darkest times. The name Bond University is now recognised worldwide as an institution of the highest standard, while locally it is one of the Gold Coast's larger employers. It remains Australia's only privately funded university and is becoming increasingly recognised as one of the world's leading independent institutions of higher education. Today Bond University boasts six academic units: the School of Business, Health Sciences, Humanities and Social Sciences, Information Technology, Law, and the Institute for Learning Communities. One of many proposed expansions is the establishment of a Medical degree program in the Health Sciences unit.

Students from more than 60 countries attend Bond University and represent approximately half of the more than 2500 students on campus. The university offers its own English Language Institute that provides intensive English language courses so international students can prepare for university entrance.

In Brian Orr's book *Bond University, The Beginning, 1985–1991*, Sir Joh Bjelke-Petersen paid me a wonderful tribute, stating that the university project: 'required bold imagination, a grand vision, tremendous personal strength and generosity. All are qualities with which I identify and with which Alan Bond is well endowed.' On the subject of the campaign mounted against the establishment of the university he said: 'There is nothing worthwhile that is achieved without hardship, no dream that has been without "knockers", nothing new that has not been the subject of criticism.' Orr wrote that despite the personal and corporate problems I faced in the late 1980s and early 1990s, 'Bond University remains his greatest public achievement.'

Another contribution to Australia that I look back on with great pride is the *Endeavour* project. It came about essentially because I was ambushed in the nicest possible way by a journalist, Bruce Stannard, in the lead-up to the America's Cup defence in Fremantle in 1987. He was interviewing me for a television story and when the interview was over he seized on the opportunity to put in front of me his proposal for building a replica of Captain Cook's three-masted bark, *Endeavour*, the ship Cook sailed on his voyage of discovery along Australia's east coast and to New Zealand in 1770.

Building a replica of *Endeavour* had been Bruce's dream since childhood. It took its first step towards reality when his associates on the Founding Council of the Australian Maritime Museum agreed with his idea that the vessel would be an appropriate showpiece on the museum's docks. They then added that as it was his idea then he should go out and find the money.

He had just about every corporate door that mattered in Australia shut in his face, but he did a wonderful sales job on me. As he outlined his thoughts I could see that this project presented some special opportunities for my family and Bond Corporation — there was a nice link between Captain Cook, *Endeavour*, and my coming to Australia from England as a youngster to start a new life. Without hesitation I said: 'That's a great idea. Find out how much it will cost and I'll see if we can get this moving together. I'd like to make *Endeavour* my lasting gift to the people of Australia as part of the Australian Bicentennial celebrations next year.'

Bruce went to three of Australia's biggest shipbuilders and came back with similar quotes — around $10 million — and after considering all the options I decided the best thing to do was to build it in our own backyard. By doing the job in Fremantle I could keep an eye on its progress and probably build it for less than the quoted prices. I was sure we could assemble the talent for the job. For a start, the America's Cup defence facility we had on the edge of Fremantle Harbour was the perfect place to build it. All we needed to do was erect a shed big enough to house the ship while it was being built.

Once again this was a project I approached laterally. I didn't need shipbuilders as such. I needed people who could share my passion and vision for the project. One such person was John 'Chink' Longley, the long-standing member of my America's Cup campaign crew. He was a school teacher who I knew had the talent to take on the role of manager, but he didn't realise that when I approached him: 'Gee Alan, I'm a school teacher. I've never built a boat in my life.' I reminded him how we'd won the America's Cup after starting from nowhere, and that convinced him to think otherwise. He took on the role and did a fantastic job. Then, instead of going to a builder of classic ships to do the actual construction, I went to Steve Ward, a great local boat builder who put *Australia II* together for us: 'Steve, we've got this ship to build. Can it be done?'

'Well, I think so Alan, but I'm not sure that it will float. There isn't a lot to go on.'

'For Christ's sake Steve, if they could build this ship 200 years ago and Captain Cook could sail it here, surely we can get it to float.'

'You're right Alan.'

In reality, this project was a giant leap of faith, but I knew we could do it. I covered the $1.3 million needed to build the shed in Fremantle and then Bond Corporation contributed more than $7 million over the next two years. I was hoping that our commitment might lead to other people and companies wanting to contribute, but that wasn't to be the case.

It was exciting to see this massive wooden structure starting to take shape. It was something that looked like the rib cage of a giant wooden whale. Finding suitable timber locally was a real challenge. Jarrah was the preference, but it had to be well-seasoned so that it was as dry as possible. Timber from old bridges and buildings all over the state became our best supply source.

Construction of the hull had progressed well when the difficult times began to descend on Bond Corporation, Dallhold and me personally, and it soon became apparent that I was no longer in a position to fund the project. I had already put in around $7 million of a final budget that was expected to be $12 million. Fortunately the ship was well enough advanced for people to appreciate, and I hoped that this situation would make it easier for the management to secure the funds needed to finish the project. John Longley certainly picked up the ball and did everything possible to keep the project alive, even though sadly many of the boat builders, riggers and sailmakers on the staff had to be laid off. He also threw the ball back into Bruce Stannard's court, calling him and saying: 'Stannard, you started this, now you've got to finish it.'

Bruce set about forming the HM Bark *Endeavour* Foundation with Arthur Weller, a Scottish businessman who had been a master mariner and had served on the *Cutty Sark* Trust in London, as chairman. The board included some of the most astute business brains in Australia, and they worked towards getting the money to complete the project. Meanwhile Chink went to the Western Australian government for support, but he was knocked back.

Eventually Bruce found a favourable ear in Garfield 'Garry' Weston, chairman of British Associated Foods, and he wrote a cheque for £500 000, which equated to $1.16 million dollars back then. And finally, to get the project home, advertising guru John Singleton saw the big picture and pitched in $1 million of his own money. It must also be mentioned that school children from across Western Australia also made contributions through an education program based around the *Endeavour*.

Being forced to step back from such a wonderful and exciting project under stressful and highly publicised circumstances was extremely difficult for me, as was the fact that there was no longer any recognition of our contribution, or an invitation to the official launch. But you have to accept that in today's society. Regardless, I am more than comfortable in the knowledge that without my foresight and my money *Endeavour,* just like the America's Cup victory, would not have happened. But forget the money — it was the vision and my belief that created this ship, and that is really important to me.

I have been aboard the ship but not with an official invitation. Even so it was wonderful to absorb what it represented to me as well as to see the pleasure it was bringing to others. And I'm proud the ship has done two circumnavigations of the world carrying the Australian flag.

Fortunately, there are some people who have recognised my contribution to the *Endeavour* project. Bruce Stannard has gone on record saying: 'Alan Bond has copped a lot of flack over the years, but if there's one thing that he really ought to be given full credit for it is his willingness to embrace the *Endeavour* project. Alan Bond is the man who built Australia's flagship. He was the one who made it happen. If it hadn't been for Bond, the whole project would never ever have gone beyond being a fantasy in my head.'

Generally everyone's lifestyle is proportionate to their wealth, and believe me happiness does not necessarily come in the same proportion. Regardless, most people are fascinated by the lifestyles of the rich.

What was interesting for me was that as my world of business grew and grew it became increasingly difficult to define between what was personal lifestyle and what was business development. My daughter Susanne's wedding in 1985 was a classic example. It was an enormous affair, a function for more than 500 people, and apart from her family and friends, we had many of my business associates and politicians present. They weren't really friends per se but they were important people to me, and in turn the family. Susanne married a New York radiologist, Armand Leone, and like any proud father I went to every conceivable length to make this a very memorable day. She married where Eileen and I were wed, St Patrick's Catholic Church in Fremantle, and the reception was at home. No expense was spared on any aspect of the day. I even had a dance floor built out over the beach in front of the house and an orchestra installed on a floating pontoon alongside. The reception ended with a monstrous fireworks display, the finale being a flaming outline of the happy couple. People crammed aboard a fleet of small boats to watch the fireworks and listen to the music until the early hours of the morning.

Going to such an extreme is often difficult to comprehend for people who are looking in from the outside. It's seen as total extravagance. But your home is as much a business headquarters as your office in the city. For us to have an intimate dinner party at home for just a few friends was extremely rare. They were usually large dinners or garden parties for a lot of people, and to do that you needed a large garden with a swimming pool or a large and very plush dining room with nice furnishings and interesting artwork. While it might appear ostentatious, actually it goes with the job — it's the environment successful business people live and work in; it's a lifestyle you come to expect in those circles. Developing a comfortable working relationship with a business associate is very important, and more often than not this is done in the home. Deals are often done at home, as was the case when Dr Armand Hammer agreed to sell me his oil exploration company, Occidental Australia, over drinks around the piano at my home. The requirement to entertain at home was even more important for us living in Perth because there weren't a lot of restaurants you could take clients to and feel comfortable while you talked business.

The family recognised that our home was an important part of the business and to that end I must say I was extremely fortunate in having Eileen as the hostess. No one loved a party more than her. She thrived on organising parties and functions and always ensured that everyone had a memorable and enjoyable time.

Our home in Perth was quite large, about 250 squares spread over four levels — probably 10 times the size of the average home — with very large rooms. It was designed and built to be like the magnificent mansions that graced Ocean Drive in Newport, Rhode Island, that we saw during the America's Cup. They were the summer homes for some of America's wealthiest families and were built for entertainment as much as living. For us, the home we built in Perth was the one we could afford; I didn't need to borrow to build it because I had the money readily available.

If there was a significant difference between our home and the residences of many other very wealthy people, it was that ours was structured around the family. Bond Corporation and Dallhold had business operations in 23 countries so we were operational around the clock, but regardless of how busy I was I always made a concerted effort to have breakfast with the family whenever I was not travelling. I also encouraged the children to have their friends come over. It was always an open house at the Bonds', so it was not unusual for John, Craig, Susanne or Jody to have five or six friends over to the house at a time, and to hold their parties there.

Inevitably our lifestyle also led us to own many spectacular houses across Australia and overseas, yet the only place I ever considered to be home was our riverfront residence in Watkins Road, Perth. At every other residence I felt that we were just visiting.

My own lifestyle saw me enjoying plenty of social activity outside the home. For a long while the favourite place to gather for the young and high-powered business people in Perth was the

Mediterranean Restaurant, particularly on a Friday. This was the scene of many lunches that became legendary in some people's eyes. In reality, the big and memorable lunches rarely happened more than once a month; we were either out of town or too busy to do it more often than that. The Mediterranean was always a place where you'd catch up with everyone, including your own senior executives. In one afternoon, over some champagne or wine, I'd find out more about what was happening around Perth than I could anywhere else — who was doing what in business, what was selling and what wasn't. You would meet builders and developers, stockbrokers and the oil guys when they were in town. It was like a cross between a confession box and the bush telegraph. These were the high-flying 80s where everyone was making money, and spending it!

One of my more memorable lunches at the Mediterranean had to be the day I actually walked in as a patron and walked out as the owner. Craig had been in the hotel business and wanted to step into restaurants, so when I heard that it was up for sale I did a deal and bought it for him. I saw it as a fairly illogical step for Craig because anyone who's ever been in a restaurant knows how difficult it is to operate successfully. When you own it the level of pleasure you might previously have enjoyed as a patron quickly disappears. You can't sit back and enjoy the ambience when you have a financial investment in the place. You are forever looking around to see what's wrong, what's not running smoothly. Craig sold out two years later and soon after the Mediterranean closed down, so we all moved over to Coco's, an equally pleasant riverfront establishment on the ground level of a high-rise building in South Perth.

The scene at both the Mediterranean and Coco's was always enhanced by very attractive young women who were drawn to it like moths to a flame, all looking for champagne and a laugh. These were very exciting times that were filled with lots of fun. The young women were among the glamorous trappings of success, so it was not surprising that this environment led to many high-powered executives going through a period in their life where they believed they could have both their family life and some 'entertainment' on the side. I know that I fell into that category. It wasn't hard to go to the Mediterranean for lunch with three or four other guys then before long have six to eight girls around the table, all soaking up the atmosphere. There were many temptations and it wasn't difficult to find your way into a dalliance where one thing would lead to another. I look back and say: 'From a family sense I certainly stretched the boundaries a lot more than I should have.' But I stress this was not done with any malicious motive — it was a spontaneous reaction in an enjoyable environment.

Big boats and planes also came with success. They were important adjuncts to the business. Bond Corporation used both its boats and planes as part of the public relations effort to promote business worldwide. Being an international company operating out of such a remote part of the world, as Perth is, meant we needed the aircraft to be readily available to move us from business centre to business centre. It was also important to impress upon the market that we were an efficiently run organisation capable of responding rapidly to any situations or opportunities that might develop anywhere in the world.

I ventured into luxury motor yachts with the purchase of *Southern Cross II*, a 100-foot long vessel that I used as a VIP and corporate platform for my second America's Cup bid. She was a fabulous boat that I had built in Queensland.

By the time the America's Cup defence came around in Fremantle in 1987 I had moved up to the 170-foot *Southern Cross III*, because I needed to host dignitaries from around the world in the best possible environment. She then went to the Mediterranean where she became a business headquarters for our European operations and a base from which we could promote the company. *Southern Cross III* was built in Japan, the world's first vessel of this size to be constructed entirely out of carbon fibre. At the time of her launching she was considered to be one of the most spectacular and lavishly appointed vessels of this type in the world. She had a marvellous dining room with carved panelling throughout, and the quality went right through to having split marble on the walls of all the bathrooms. Being a business centre as well as a pleasure yacht meant business had to be able to be conducted around the clock, so *Southern Cross III* had a fully staffed office fitted with two of the most sophisticated satellite communications systems available. We could contact people anywhere in the world as quickly as you could call from any city office. Because this vessel was travelling in possibly dangerous international waters, like those around Indonesia and through the South China Sea, we also carried a complete armoury to protect us from pirates. It included shotguns, machine guns and handguns. And being built from carbon fibre the vessel was essentially bullet-proof.

As well as *Southern Cross III*, I also owned the magnificent 203-foot schooner *Jessica*, a three-masted yacht that was an absolute classic. I couldn't resist a name change for her — *Schooner XXXX*. She captured marvellous publicity in the Mediterranean when we were launching XXXX beer across Europe.

We had the leaders of many countries and some of the world's most influential people aboard these boats, including the Aga Khan, Prince Rainier and Prince Michael as well as movie stars, such as Joan Collins. The standard we maintained in both the presentation of each vessel and our hospitality only helped put the best possible light on Australia. We opened up opportunities for our companies and I'm sure we created the right image for a lot of other Australian companies looking to do business abroad.

Here again, people thought our boats were an extravagance where we lost money, but I can say categorically that we made money on every one of these luxury vessels. We built *Southern Cross II* for about $2 million and sold her for $3 million. We paid $6 million for *Jessica* and after three years sold her for $9 million. *Southern Cross III* was built for $12 million and we sold her for $18 million. It was because we knew what we were doing in the boat business that we were able to achieve these results. We didn't waste money.

We used our private Boeing 727 for our domestic and international air travel. It was probably the world's most luxuriously appointed aircraft of its type, not because we wanted it that way —

it was already like that when we bought it from an Arab sheikh. A passenger-configured 727 would carry up to 200 people, but we never had more than around 12 aboard. We paid $5 million for it when the décor alone, which was very much over the top, would have cost much more than that. It had strips of mirrors across the ceiling, hot showers and gold taps in the bathrooms, marble on the floors, and a full dining table with silver service for 18 people. It even had a private cabin with a double bed. And so business could be done at any time, it was fitted with offices and facilities for two secretaries who had access to every possible form of communication.

The importance of having the 727 was that we were able to fly safely anywhere in the world, especially into places like Chile. We had a team going there every month and it made sense to get our people there quickly on a plane that had sleeping facilities for everyone travelling. When we arrived in Chile we went through a security check on the ground and then immediately went under the umbrella of our own security guards. I had to have bodyguards all the time I was there and I was always driven around in a bullet-proof car — that's how dangerous it was. Everyone in our team lived under the constant threat of kidnapping.

Parties were almost an occupational hazard during the good times, and spontaneous ones were among the best. Probably one of the most memorable was when Susanne had a birthday while she was in London. On the spur of the moment I said: 'It's your birthday tomorrow so I'd like to take you to France for lunch. You can invite 12 friends and we'll fly over in the plane.' So off we went, flying from London to Paris where we went to the famous and lavishly decorated restaurant, Maxim's, for lunch. We were joined by a number of French bankers — it was always difficult to separate business from pleasure — so I could talk business with them. They enjoyed the celebrations and it turned into an unforgettable party where we drank wonderful wine and saw one guest finish up dancing on the tables. And when that was all over I went up the street and bought Susanne a diamond necklace as a birthday gift. We were back in London for the evening.

One of the most memorable parties we had at our home in Perth, and we had a lot of them, was when we had Neil Diamond come around for dinner and he then entertained us. And when it came to fun aboard *Southern Cross III*, the best dinner party was one night in Monaco Harbor, when Prince Rainier, Prince Michael and everyone else finished up around the grand piano singing until 3am.

But without doubt the grandest party Eileen and I were ever invited to was the 65th birthday celebration for American businessman Malcolm Forbes, the publisher of *Forbes* magazine, at the house in Tangiers where he and his partner at that time, Elizabeth Taylor, spent a lot of their time. There were 1000 guests from around the world, a who's who of international business. Just about everyone flew in on a private plane and absolutely everything, including your accommodation, was covered for the four days.

The celebrations started from the moment we arrived. The street approach to the house was lined with 4000 traditionally dressed women who were chanting while local men paraded on magnificent white horses.

In the grounds of the home there were three huge marquees resembling Arab tents that were set up for the party. Every breakfast, lunch and dinner was a special event with amazing entertainment, and each time you arrived for a function you picked out a card from a bowl and the number on that card was the table you were at for that particular event. You never knew who you were going to meet.

The setting was stunning with mountains forming a beautiful backdrop while the tents had Persian rugs covering the ground. Within five minutes of everyone being seated there was a massive 'boom' to signal the arrival of 1000 waiters bringing food and drinks.

The most stunning piece of entertainment was when 100 horsemen, all dressed in full regalia, suddenly came charging down the hill towards us, shooting their guns in the air and shouting at full voice, only to stop in a cloud of dust just a couple of metres in front of us. We all applauded and thought how impressive it was, but no sooner had they turned to retreat, another wave of horsemen came down until there were 1000 of them, guns in the air, charging around and around in a mock battle. Next thing more than 10 000 women emerged from the background, harmonising in a most haunting chant. It was some of the greatest theatre and the most extravagant party I've ever witnessed. Something very, very special.

Needless to say that over the years my own socialising put my marriage with Eileen under considerable stress. She couldn't help but be aware of what was happening, especially when something appeared in the newspapers about where I'd been seen and suggesting, rightly or wrongly, what I might have been doing. I was in the media spotlight and paid the price. This situation, and the fact that I was spending so little time at home anyway because of business, meant that Eileen was starting to live her own life with a wide circle of friends across Australia and overseas.

I can say that as well as Eileen, I have had two significant loves in my life, the most important one being Diana Bliss, who is now my wife.

Diana fascinated me from the first time I saw her. She was only 21 and we met in totally innocent circumstances at the Wentworth Hotel in Sydney. It was in the late 1970s and I was there having a drink with some of the Sydney-based contingent of my America's Cup team while she was there with a girlfriend. We had a chat for a few minutes and that was that, but I remembered her because she had a very bubbly personality and a delightful smile. Through sheer coincidence Diana decided about a year later that she would drive to Perth to see some girlfriends because she was having boyfriend problems in Sydney. Some time after that I bumped into her at a bar in Perth and we got acquainted again. The next time I saw her she was 25 and the maitre d' of the restaurant in the Parmelia Hotel in Perth. Her personality and her charm were still shining through and it was always a delight to see her there, chatting away to people in the restaurant.

After a few visits to the restaurant I knew I had to ask her out, but she knocked me back because I was a married man and she didn't want to get mixed up in that sort of situation. I understood, appreciating that she had very strong views on the subject, *and* her father was a minister of religion. However, I persisted and eventually we did get together on a couple of occasions and really enjoyed it. Our relationship remained very much a friendship, although it took an interesting twist when I offered Di the job as hostess on our corporate jet. She was perfect for the job and took to it with great enthusiasm.

Di was always very passionate about the theatre, something that may have been sparked by watching how theatrical her father was when in the pulpit, and while she had no formal training she remained a frustrated theatre producer. She invested in a production in Melbourne and then, after many visits to London during corporate flights she became engrossed in the theatre scene there. In 1986 she decided she would go there to live and jump into the deep end of producing. She did that for 10 years.

I saw Di on the odd occasion during my many visits to London.

My other love was Tracy Tyler, a delightful young lady whom I met after Di had gone to live in London. We enjoyed a serious relationship for about two years, but as time passed I came to realise that it was not going to mature into anything. Tracy was full of life and very energetic. She was much younger than me and was caught up in the atmosphere of the carefree 80s — always out to have fun at any time. I'm not quite sure what her motivation was in life, and I'm equally unsure about her feelings towards me, but I think she probably fell in love with the fascinating lifestyle more than the person.

This was when I realised that I wanted to go my own way in life. I was only married to Eileen in name, and divorce was inevitable. We had drifted apart and I knew I needed unbridled freedom to be able to re-establish myself emotionally. Eileen understood the situation and when it came about she simply said: 'It's best you go and do what you want to do in life.' This move for freedom was not with the intention of marrying Tracy or anyone else — I was destined to be a bachelor for more than two years. Fortunately, after the divorce I've been able to retain a wonderful relationship with Eileen — we are great friends, not enemies. Looking back I realised that in all our 37 years of marriage we only very occasionally had an argument. Our divorce wasn't based on malice; we both realised that we'd just gone down different paths. The friendship that we still retain was never better illustrated than when I was in prison. Eileen gave me every possible support.

When I later saw Di in London, something I had known deep down for a long time but wouldn't accept was triggered. Diana was sitting with me in a restaurant looking comfortable, confident and happy with her life and was enjoying success in business. I was impressed by her even more than when I first met her, and within moments I was saying to myself: 'Hello, I've made a mistake here. You're really the one I care about.' From that moment my relationship with Tracy was on the slide. My relationship with Diana had changed and she was emerging as a real friend. This was in the early 90s and she was fully aware of the problems I was facing, yet unlike so many other so-called friends, nothing seemed to change. I'd already been wrongfully imprisoned in Perth in 1992 and had been acquitted. Then I had to go to hospital for a heart operation. Without hesitation Diana said: 'Would you like me to come over and help you through the operation and look after you for a while?' and with the same lack of hesitation I told her: 'Oh, that would be wonderful', and that's what she did.

Her support during and after that operation confirmed what a wonderful person she is. And the fact that I had horrendous legal challenges to resolve did nothing to daunt her support of me. Di is a very special person, a giving soul. If someone comes up to her and compliments the jacket she is wearing, she will give them the jacket. Friends always surround her and she is very supportive of those in need, something that has stemmed from her religious upbringing.

I guess it was fate that brought her into my life full-time. It was when I needed a real friend, someone who could give me emotional support. Certainly my family was there in a very special way, but Di gave me the direct emotional strength I needed. I loved her for it then as I do now, but as most people discover with years, the definition of love changes — it's a different love as you get older. My first love as a young person, my true love, was Eileen, but that was very different from the emotion I now share with Di, a love based on warmth, companionship and friendship. That's what allows people to love each other. It's not like the passionate love affair that you have when you are young. When you're older the flame of passion is not as strong, even though it remains important in your relationship.

Regardless of this, my move towards proposing marriage to Di was full of romance — a moonlit night on Cottesloe Beach in Perth. I was concerned that she had never been married and while I knew that together we could share a wonderful life, commitment on my part was what was called for. However, I was also concerned that with the difficult times I was facing, marriage might not be her wish, that she might quite understandably reject my proposal. But in typical Di fashion she had no hesitation about becoming my wife.

One can realise how special she really is when you consider that during the first eight years of our marriage I was incarcerated for a total of three years and eight months. During that time she visited me every possible moment without any hesitation, even though at times she faced a possible strip-search before being admitted to the prison. She supported me emotionally throughout my ordeals; she was the one on the telephone to encourage me when I was experiencing my darkest hours.

At the time of our wedding in April 1995 I was facing an uncertain future, but notwithstanding this it was a marvellous, memorable affair. Diana had planned it as though it was her greatest stage production, and she had done the job so well that all I needed to do was arrive for the ceremony. Both the wedding and reception were at the Museum of Contemporary Art in The Rocks, in Sydney. She had used stage-setting techniques and backdrops to create a miniature chapel and the appropriate atmosphere, and she had a number of friends from the theatre provide the entertainment. Her family gave her wonderful support and, quite fittingly, the minister who performed the ceremony was a close colleague of her late father's. I was supported by two of my oldest and closest friends, Mike Lindsay and Murray Quartermaine.

The profile I was generating at the time through the battles to save the company, and my highly publicised court appearances, turned the wedding into a massive media circus. Photographs of the event appeared in newspapers, magazines and on television across Australia as well as in celebrity magazine *Hello* in Britain.

While our wedding was a modest affair, the same couldn't be said for those of my children. These wonderful celebrations came at a time of considerable prosperity for me, so quite rightly they were impressive in every way. The only exception was Susanne's second marriage, to Dr John Edwards, which was very much a close-knit gathering of family and friends at the Upp Hall, the family's 500-year-old country estate in Hertfordshire, just north of London.

All other marriages in the family quite appropriately took place at the church we call home — St Patrick's Catholic Church in Fremantle, and it was Eileen's brother, Father Don Hughes, who conducted each ceremony.

John and Gemma were the first to marry and today they have four adult children — Jeremy, Laura, Emerald and Banjo. I'm proud to say all have done extremely well scholastically and in artistic endeavours.

Craig's marriage did not stand the test of time, but today he is extremely happy in his relationship with Dianne Beaman. They have twin baby boys, Gabriel and Dylan.

Jody and Damien enjoyed yet another spectacular family wedding, and in early 2003 they presented me with another grandchild, Dashiel.

The entire family is living in Perth and today I look at each one of them with great delight. I can honestly say that now, with Diana in my life and Eileen remaining a true friend, I have the support of two wonderful women. I am a lucky man who is very content and happy with the way his new life is evolving.

CHAPTER EIGHT
DARK CLOUDS

Throughout the 1980s brewing became an increasingly important part of Bond Corporation.

It was the sale of Santos that provided us with the funds to make our first move into the industry by buying Swan Brewery, the brewers of Swan Lager, in Perth in 1981. The decision for the purchase was based on the realisation within the company that we needed to have a business that gave us a reliable cash flow. The brewery was one of the few large businesses in Western Australia that had international aspirations and also fitted the category, television stations possibly being the only other. The decision to buy Swan was also influenced by what Baron Bich had impressed upon me about owning strong brands, so getting into the brewery seemed to be the logical thing to do. There were a number of big hitters in the industry on the east coast while Swan had the west to itself. And making the Swan deal more appealing was that the company was stable and had significant land holdings in its asset base.

When we went ahead with the purchase I paid the $162 million personally. The reason I bought Swan as an individual was that the deal was not subject to the takeover provisions set out in corporations law. Obviously when those laws were drawn up it was never anticipated that an individual could bid that sort of money, but I did and subsequently on-sold the brewery to Bond Corporation for the same price. And because Bond Corporation was buying the brewery from an individual the takeover provision did not apply then either.

We weren't in the business for long before realising that we could not stand alone long term and survive without a far greater market share. Swan had 90 per cent of the Western Australian market so the obvious target for significant gains would have to be the east coast, but parochial attitudes made it extremely difficult for Swan to get a foothold in that market. On the other side of the coin, the east coast boys were so powerful they could afford to dump beer in Western Australia and claim an immediate market share, and that meant *we* were vulnerable, not them. Our only options were get bigger or get out. This meant we either had to become a national entity in the industry and buy Castlemaine-Tooheys, the brewers of XXXX in Queensland that also had strong brands in New South Wales, or we had to sell Swan Brewery. Our investigations revealed great potential in the industry so we decided that we didn't want to sell. That meant that XXXX was the way to go if we were to become a national player. It would eventually give us the strength and opportunity to compete against the market leader, Fosters. The XXXX deal would also be enhanced by the fact that we already owned the Channel Nine television station in Brisbane and there could be a good cross-pollination between the two when it came to promotion.

While the Castlemaine-Tooheys people, along with much of the financial press, didn't think we could raise the money to make the takeover we knew we still had some of the cash left over from the Santos deal as well as lines of credit with a number of banks, so we knew we were in a position to buy. In August 1985 the Castlemaine-Tooheys deal became the biggest takeover in Australian corporate history, $1200 million and, while it had its moments of difficulty, it was well worthwhile because when it was combined with Swan Brewery we had 45 per cent of the national market.

The more we got into the brewing business the more we liked what we saw, especially on the cash flow side, and that led us to think about further expansion, but we knew if we were serious it would have to be overseas. Export was an option but that was something that had already been tried without any real success — there was no money in it because freight and marketing absorbed any profit margin.

So we went overseas in search of brewery acquisitions that would deliver greater markets.

At the same time we decided we should bring the two brewing assets in Australia together, so we hired a guy from Tooheys to plan it. His theory was that we weren't getting the message across to the public that all the breweries were part of Bond Brewing, and Bond Brewing was a company that was going to have a worldwide brand name, just like Fosters. All we had at the time were various product names but no direct identification with the parent organisation. This so-called marketing expert and his team then advised us that we ought to bring it all under one name, Bond Brewing. We did just that, and what we ended up with was one of the biggest marketing blunders of all time.

The decision meant putting the name Bond Brewing on the cans alongside the name XXXX in Queensland. We also replaced the illuminated Castlemaine-Tooheys sign on top of the brewery in Brisbane with a big sign reading Bond Brewing. Such changes would not have mattered in Western Australia because we had the dominant position there and could control it, but in Queensland it was like a declaration of war. As far as Queenslanders were concerned it wasn't a Queensland company any more, it was Western Australian, all because we used the words Bond Brewing on the can. Nothing else had changed, the same people were running the place, but as far as the Queenslanders were concerned the sky had fallen in on their beloved XXXX. It was a marketing disaster that cost us dearly, because as well as affecting the public attitude to the product it opened the door for Powers Brewery to emerge — it gave them a kick-start in the market because they played the 'Queensland-owned' card. What was the bloody difference? Queensland owned, Australian owned — it wouldn't have mattered anywhere else but in Queensland, God love 'em. The Powers' people very cleverly took one of our brewers who knew the XXXX recipes and quickly claimed a very valuable 10 per cent of the local market.

It was a marketing decision I wasn't directly involved with, and had I been I probably wouldn't have endorsed it because it went against what Kurt Lessheim had told me when I was a teenager, a view endorsed by Baron Bich — don't monkey with a successful brand. I guess that with Fosters being an international brand the experts thought they could do the same with Bond Brewing. How wrong they were.

We also inherited an unfortunate problem in this Castlemaine-Tooheys deal that led to a lot of drama with many of the publicans operating in our hotels. The brewery owned the freehold of hotels, and what rights we owned had already been established. The question was: 'Were the leaseholders entitled to any goodwill associated with the business?'

One of the issues in this saga involved what beer brands could be sold in these pubs. Some of the publicans in hotels we owned were selling our opponents' beer, and while we couldn't actually stop that under trade practices law we did have the option of taking back control of these pubs when the lease expired. That would allow us to put our own managers in and then give ourselves every chance of making sales of our product the priority. As a result we decided to exercise this option when leases fell due and run the hotels ourselves to protect our market.

Inevitably, a major dispute erupted over the value of the goodwill in each business. The legal argument in a nutshell was: 'You lease premises from us, you have it for the 20 years, the lease runs out, we're not going to extend the lease, so what rights do you then have?' It was a commercial argument that had to be determined in court and the final decision was that the publicans were entitled to certain things, while we were entitled to others.

If ever you want a lesson in bad public relations then this was it. Our brewery guys in Queensland and New South Wales handled it very poorly, particularly through the media. Instead of actually getting around a table and sorting it out with the publicans they became confrontational, and before we knew it the damage was done. The plus side was that the matter was eventually resolved, but not before much drama on both sides had been played out.

We pursued our overseas brewing investments and entered the American market with the acquisition of the small Pittsburgh Brewing Company for $35 million. This was soon followed by a big one — the $1.2 billion purchase of Heileman Brewing Company in late 1987, a huge organisation that had 10 breweries in nine states. The financing was done with the help of Drexel Burnham Lambert, an American bond-issuing house that I became acquainted with during the 1977 America's Cup. We were able to obtain 20-year finance unsecured with an interest rate of 12 per cent, something not available in Australia even though the rates were comparable at the time. What this financing deal did was give us access to the long-term finance needed in the brewing business. In hindsight though, we should have taken half of the deal in debt and half in equity. The final arrangement was that Bond Corporation put in $500 million cash, borrowed $500 million, and short-term funded $200 million, something we covered by selling some Heileman assets soon after we took over.

We based our decision to buy Heileman on the premise that if we were going to be serious about expanding our brewing business internationally then we had to be serious about a purchase, but this one turned into a bitter-sweet experience. In fact, it was a deal that we really shouldn't have done. Instead we should have turned our attention to another American brewer, the larger Millers, to get to where we wanted to be. It would have been much better for us. Hindsight again.

Regardless of this, the Heileman purchase had some real pluses going for it. For our $1.2 billion we got $4 billion worth of hard assets in plant and equipment, plus the business. Better still, it had one fantastic asset, La Croix Mineral Water, a product that we pushed to the stage where it captured almost 10 per cent of the United States market. That alone justified the $1.2 billion buying price. And, if you looked at the big picture, Heileman was a good business because, like La Croix, there were other parts of it that were worth every penny we paid; we bought it at 25 cents in the dollar for their assets. This brewery had the capacity to brew five times the amount of beer than they were producing, so to capitalise on this we had to further develop the market. However, this was to be a challenge much bigger than we had anticipated.

While the company had other valuable non-core assets, the fact of the matter was that we were only really interested in Heileman's beer brewing because we were in the global beer business. Our big plan was to put all our brewing assets into one group, Bond Brewing, within three years and float it on the American market so we could re-capitalise. It had all the hallmarks of being a hugely successful project.

Interestingly, the initial reaction of the Bond Corporation board on the Heileman deal was to knock it back, and that thinking was based on a report from my son, Craig. This happened when I was primarily operating overseas and had Peter Beckwith, Tony Oates and Peter Mitchell running operations, including Bond Brewing, in Australia. As we were unsure about the viability of purchasing Heileman, I decided that before we did anything we should send Craig to America to investigate and report back. He was well qualified for the task as he had a degree in international marketing from the London Business School and was working in the brewing operation of Castlemaine. Craig came back and presented a written report to the board stating that because the brewing side of Heileman was in decline, and with Anheuser-Busch dominating the marketplace, that we shouldn't buy it. His report said in essence that only five of Heileman's 64 brands were profitable and that Anheuser-Busch was in a position to absolutely destroy Heileman with marketing dollars. There was no way up. On the strength of that report the decision was deferred.

Subsequently, the managing director, Peter Beckwith, decided that Craig's report was too narrow in its scope and as Craig was not a board member he thought he should go and have a look himself — which he did, with the support of the board. He went right through the Heileman organisation, including the distribution network where he discovered that Heileman products were selling from the bottom shelf of most outlets. Commonsense says that sales improve in proportion to how high a product is on the shelves — sales are best when a product is at eye level. This is a basic marketing strategy.

Peter came back to the board and said that he disagreed with Craig's view on Heileman, adding: 'All we've got to do to stop the declining market share is to cultivate all the distributors, and we'll do that by putting more dollars into advertising. That way we will get them on side and they will move the products back to eye level. That's all we need to do to increase market share.'

He was very convincing, and his argument was reinforced by the opinions of marketing people from Bond Brewing.

This was completely against Craig's view, which we now know was right. Peter Beckwith and the others in the brewery side of the company, were wrong. I don't take any blame for this because I didn't actually do any research. I sat on the board and supported what the people in that part of the business thought was right. The discussion was: 'Yes, we want to expand in the US but is this the company we should buy, or shall we go and get the $2 billion needed to buy Millers, which is also on the market?' The decision to buy Heileman was based on Peter's report, even though Millers was sitting out there and available. One other thing about Heileman not considered by the board before deciding to proceed was that all the Heileman brands were localised — they didn't have a national brand like Millers, and a national brand would make it easier for us to achieve our goal. The other thing was that with Heileman we became the world's fifth largest brewer, but by spending an additional $800 000 million, which wasn't out of the question, we could have bought Millers, had a national brand and been the world's second or third largest brewer. It was the deal that made commercial sense.

Unfortunately for us there was another thing Craig had pointed out that Peter did not take into account in his assessment of the Heileman market — the big boys in the brewing business in America, Anheuser-Busch, were not going to let this little Australian brewing group get any significant foothold in their territory. Their immediate response once Peter's strategy of spending more money on advertising was implemented was to 'out-advertise' us. For every $1 we spent they spent $10, and we spent tens of millions of dollars. It was like being in a battle where for every rocket you fired at the enemy you copped ten rockets back. We just didn't give the opposition enough credit and as a result weren't prepared for the war. I think we could possibly have recovered in the long term by finding the right marketing strategy, but we also compounded our problems early in the piece by sending an Australian guy over there to be in charge of the marketing, a good guy who not only struggled to compete with the big guns but also had to deal with the learning curve he faced in America. As we were the new kids on the block I'm sure we were making mistakes that Anheuser-Busch had learnt from decades before.

We weren't alone in finding it difficult to read and penetrate the American market from foreign shores. The National Australia Bank and BHP also lost a few billion dollars through bad deals. I found it interesting to note these losses, especially when nothing happened to the directors who were responsible for losing those billions besides a rap over the knuckles — even though these losses eventuated because of bad decisions. Essentially, they were forgiven while I wasn't. I wonder why?

The frustrating thing for me in all this is that while the dramatic expansion of our brewing interests was happening, the rats were starting to eat away at Bond Corporation and it was starting to crumble. This is another example of why we should have a

Chapter 11 safety net for Australian business. Given another 12 months we could have floated this brewing interest to the American market and corrected the imbalance of debt to equity. We already knew what we had to do to fix Heileman, and more importantly we were at an advanced stage in our discussions to buy Millers, not that it was known in Australia at the time. With both Heileman and Millers we would have been in basically a duopoly situation and been able to consolidate the business by better utilising the brewing capacity, a move that would have strengthened our brands across America. We would also have sold off some assets and when the entire process was complete we would probably have been the world's largest brewer — a great position to be in for a float. It was all part of our strategy in restructuring the company that would soon prove to be our biggest Achilles heel in the eventual collapse of the Bond Corporation, Bell Resources.

Our pursuit of market share in America was important for investors, particularly international investors because, as I said before, brewing was becoming a business where you either got big or got out. It wasn't a business where you could stay still. If you did you were gobbled up. For us to have our desired place in international brewing we had to be big enough to compete with Anheuser-Busch, a company that would pay $1 million for a television ad at the Super Bowl.

While we were focused on America we took our eye off the ball in Australia and came under attack in our home market. One of the good things about Swan Brewing when we bought it was that it was virtually a monopoly in the Western Australian market but when we turned our backs Fosters got under our guard and grabbed a market share in the west. They didn't actually attack us in the true sense — we just opened the door for them and let them in, all because we didn't tie together our activities in America as quickly as we thought we could. Even so, the Castlemaine-Tooheys-Swan combination gave us a national market share of around 45 per cent while Fosters had just 2 per cent more. This position showed the benefits of a duopoly in a market, a situation where size really does count because the bigger you get, the lower the margin you can operate on and the better you can service the consumer. And satisfied consumers means better market share.

One of the most notable products developed by Bond Brewing was Swan Light no-alcohol beer. It was created under the guidance of Murray Quartermaine specifically for the Saudi Arabian market. He did a fantastic job for the launch. Being a linguist of some note he learnt to converse in and write Arabic in just six weeks, and to make sure he adapted to the environment there as quickly as possible he dressed in traditional robes. The product proved to be very successful for us.

It was about the same time in 1987 when we purchased the Heileman business, that Bond Corporation made our big leap into television in Australia by buying the majority of the National Nine Network.

The company had already stepped into the world of television in a small way with the purchase of the Channel Nine network in Western Australia in 1984. We considered it to be a worthwhile business that, in the long term, would generate substantial returns. Another important factor influencing the purchase was that investors liked media stocks because they were considered solid. As I mentioned earlier, we also liked television ownership as we saw a strong opportunity for cross-pollination between all our media and brewing assets in particular. It made commercial sense to use the media outlets for the promotion of our beer products. But as was the case with the brewing investments, we knew we had to significantly expand the business in Australia and internationally if we were to see true benefits. Buying Channel Nine Queensland had been part of this strategy.

The major stations in the Nine Network, Sydney and Melbourne, were owned by Australia's richest man, Kerry Packer, so a significant part of our operating costs went towards buying national programs from his organisation, something we were obliged to do as part of the network to maintain our required Australian content. Seeing this money going out the door in large lumps led us to review our position in the industry in Australia, and it quickly became obvious that there had to be one group controlling the entire network. So, there was only one thing to do — arrange a meeting with Kerry Packer. We met in my suite at the Wentworth Hotel in Sydney.

We both knew there was only one thing on the agenda, and Kerry announced it as he came into the room: 'We know what we are here for. Before we leave this meeting you're either going to sell your stations to me, or you are going to buy mine, and I don't really want to sell. So let's start from there. What are you prepared to offer me? It will have to be a very good price because we've had the network for a long time, it's like part of the family, and I don't really want to sell it.'

The fact was that he did want to sell it. He certainly didn't want to buy my two stations.

> AB: 'I want $400 million for my two stations.'
> KP: 'I want a billion for mine then.'
> AB: 'So you'll sell for a billion, will you?'
> KP: 'Yes, but it's got to be cash, cash, cash,' (he said, thumping the table hard each time he mentioned the word 'cash').
> AB: 'Hang on. We've got two stations worth $400 million, and while you have two bigger stations they can't be worth anymore than $800 million.'
> KP: 'Well, I might give you credit for the other $200 million. But you haven't got that sort of money anyway.'
> AB: 'Well, I think I can get it.'

Kerry showed me that the network would earn $60 million that year, and there were projections to $120 million. I left the room to discuss it with my advisers and we agreed that on those figures we could justify buying the stations for $1 billion. But they weren't the full audited accounts — just a few pages of figures followed by his assurance: 'It's a great cash business, a great cash generator. I shouldn't be selling it to you.'

When I returned to my suite I picked up the telephone and called Don Argus, the boss of the National Australia Bank. I explained that I was negotiating with Kerry to buy his two stations in the network and asked if it would be possible to arrange a loan of $800 million to complete the purchase. Bond Corporation was flying high at that stage and I didn't expect it to be a problem. I also explained to Argus that our plan was to establish a separate media company within Bond Corporation, Bond Media, and that we would put our two existing TV stations in there for $400 million, we'd then raise $400 million from the public in share capital and carry about $400 million debt. I explained that Kerry would leave $200 million in for a couple of years on a promissory note and then we would pay him back. In closing I just added that there were two other banks interested in doing the financing.

Don said there and then that the deal looked fine by him, but he would need to discuss it with his board before giving me the final go ahead within 24 hours:

> AB: 'It looks like I've got the cash. It's a deal,' (I said to Kerry as soon as I hung up). 'It's only subject to confirmation from the bank tomorrow.'
> KP: 'Okay, but 30 days is all you've got. I have to know the cash is there in 30 days.'

The next day, when the bank confirmed the loan, there was one condition. They insisted that their stockbroker A.C. Goode handle the initial public offering and that they be the sole lender of all funds until that time. I called Kerry and told him the deal was on. We then arranged for Peter Mitchell and his team to meet with Kerry's representative, Malcolm Turnbull, over the next couple of weeks to complete the documentation. But when the pair met it became more like a pub brawl than a negotiation. Peter started querying all sorts of things in the accounts to such an extent that Turnbull blew up and said in very definite terms: 'Listen here, I'm telling you that's the position of the company. You bought the stations. You told Kerry Packer that you have bought the stations, and that's the deal, so don't ask any more questions.'

Obviously Turnbull was under strict instructions from Kerry not to enter into any discussions on the figures. As far as he was concerned it was already a done deal.

Two days before settlement I became concerned about not having seen any documentation from the bank about the loan. I called Don Argus and told him that the documents hadn't emerged and settlement was only 48 hours away. That wasn't a problem for the bank: 'I'll tell you what we'll do; the bank will draft up a letter for you that will say that you'll sign all the relevant documents. Just sign that letter and that'll be good enough for us. You can go ahead and arrange a bank cheque.' I couldn't believe my eyes when the letter arrived. It was just one paragraph relating to a $1 billion deal. So I just signed it, sent it back to the bank and had a bank cheque for $800 million delivered to Kerry.

It quickly became obvious that we had moved too quickly in snapping up the entire network because Packer's two stations were not producing the cash flow that we were led to believe they were. They weren't actually losing money, but they certainly weren't producing the profit that Kerry had suggested.

This was further exacerbated because we had based part of our valuation of his business on the percentages we were achieving at Channel Nine in Perth. It turned out that our revenues and returns, proportionately, were far greater than what Packer's side of the network was achieving.

As time would prove for us, we had paid Packer top dollar. The reality of the situation was that I had the benefit of seeing what media assets were selling for around the world, and based on the profit projections supplied, along with our future projections, the value should have been okay. While we didn't realise the profitability that we expected in the initial stages of our ownership it would have been only a matter of time before we had turned the situation around. That was to be the case a couple of years later when the network was producing the right profit, but unfortunately for us we were no longer the owners.

In taking over the network I did make one mistake — putting Warren Jones in as executive chairman over Sam Chisholm, who was managing director. I thought Warren had a way with people but he certainly couldn't get along with Sam. There was a lot of confrontation between the two of them.

The first move we made after buying Channel Nine in Western Australia — after fully realising the extent of Kerry Packer's control over us through network program supply — was to decide that we should work towards becoming the master of our own destiny as soon as possible. Buying the entire network wasn't an option at that time, so after a great deal of research we decided that we could develop the first satellite sporting channel across Australia — Sky Channel.

It was to give us an Australian footprint and its success was excellent in proportion to the cost. It was also a valuable experience, so much so that when the British government decided to call for tenders for a satellite licence in the UK we were in a position to bid for it. We established a company where we held the major shareholding and took in two other British media groups as partners. And apart from putting money on the table we also delivered the expertise we had gained in creating Sky Channel.

Simultaneously, Rupert Murdoch was developing a similar satellite service across Europe, but our British Satellite Broadcasting — B-Sky-B — was the first to go to air. This was achieved by launching our own $US160 million satellite, which projected the first footprint over the UK and much of Europe. This by itself was a huge risk but a magnificent pioneering achievement for our media division.

This business was again one where projections developed from feasibility studies were poles apart from the reality. It was going to take a lot longer than expected to achieve profitability. Satellite dishes were being installed at a frantic rate even though there were technical delays that proved more costly to resolve than was expected. Nevertheless we claimed the first one million subscribers. Today the number of subscribers for B-Sky-B is in excess of six million.

For us there was also the Murdoch factor in the equation. There was really only room for one operator and we knew he would be tough opposition. So it didn't take me long to work out that we should merge with Murdoch, a logical conclusion that suddenly became complicated because one of our own partners, the *Financial Times* newspaper group, didn't want to have anything to do with Rupert Murdoch.

I decided to go into private discussions with Rupert and there I suggested that seeing we were both losing money we should get together. He agreed, partly because it was very important for him to access the UK footprint that we controlled. The two groups had already put about £500 million into the trough and only just touched the bottom. Another £500 million was required. The eventual wash-up was Rupert took a substantial shareholding in B-Sky-B. It proved to be another enormously valuable venture for us as our original holding of 33 per cent, for which we had put in £150 million, was eventually sold at a profit. However, this profit was nothing like the amount that could have been realised if we had been able to stay as a shareholder when B-Sky-B became capitalised at £15 billion and went on to become very profitable some time later. Full marks to Rupert on this one.

Our other international push into television came through Bond Corporation International in Hong Kong, which bought around 40 per cent of Hong Kong TVB, the main TV channel there. We went in there because it was a logical stepping-stone into China, where there was a huge market to be captured. TVB was the dominant media interest in Hong Kong, and the only one that was getting into China.

Bond Corporation International was planned as a separate entity that would allow us to raise money in yet another capital base. As well as the local TV group being part of it, there was a significant property portfolio that included the landmark Bond Centre on Hong Kong Island. The Chile Telephone Company and our Rome property development were also part of this company.

I acquired Channel Nine in Brisbane from the Sydney-based communications company, AWA, around 1985 and in the process of doing due diligence it was found that one of the liabilities was a writ, initiated by the Queensland Premier, Sir Joh Bjelke-Petersen, against the station over the content of a story the station aired in 1983. The boss of AWA told me that it was questionable whether it was a true story and that the station believed the writ was a genuine liability. He added that we didn't need to worry because any payout would be covered by insurance. He added that the maximum payment would be no more than $1.2 million. My response was: 'Well insurance companies fall over from time to time so I'll take that $1.2 million off the purchase price.' They agreed.

Not long after I bought the station, Sir Joh, seeing the opportunity to advance his cause through the change of ownership, called me into his office and he said words to the effect: 'Alan, do you know I'm suing that station for $1.2 million. They really defamed me. I've been maligned, seriously maligned and I want my money. I'm entitled to it and seeing you're the new owner of the station get off your arse and do something about getting it fixed.'

'I don't know much about it Joh, but I'll see what I can do,' I replied.

Our legal people subsequently told me that the matter was in the hands of the insurers, so I asked that it be tidied up as quickly as possible. This was at the time that I was doing quite a bit of business in Queensland. I owned Castlemaine-Tooheys, was in the process of setting up Bond University, and was establishing the export scheme for Queensland Nickel.

I then reported back to Joh what I knew of the status of the writ and told him we would do what we could to get the insurance company to deal with it. Then at a subsequent meeting between the Premier and myself it was discussed again. It was suggested that he would be satisfied with $400 000 to settle the matter. With that knowledge I then asked our general manager of communications, David Aspinall, to finalise the issue.

Little did I know that this decision would later cause such controversy. At the time I looked on it as no more than a commercial deal where I had already gained $1.2 million by having that amount removed from the purchase price of the station, and then with the settlement completed, there would be an extra $800 000 for our shareholders. Subsequently there were some discussions with the insurance company, and I believe that these discussions led to us getting back some of the amount involved in the settlement from that company. Our insurance broker, Brian Coppin, handled the matter. I can honestly say that I may have been naïve in how this issue was handled but it was not with any intent other than to resolve an outstanding issue that was not of our making.

Unfortunately that wasn't the end of it. The deal with Joh blew up again in 1988 when I did an interview on Channel Nine with Jana Wendt, two years after we had settled with Joh. It led to the Australian Broadcasting Tribunal announcing an inquiry into my comments in the interview relating to us paying Joh the $400 000. Was it a bribe, and was I a fit person to hold television licences? It dragged on for nine months, and from the outset I sensed we were in trouble because of the very left-wing attitudes of the woman who was heading the inquiry. It was never proved that the payment was a bribe, but there was enough innuendo flying around for things to go against us and, sure enough, despite Joh and me doing our best to convince the tribunal that we had acted properly in settling the defamation case, the tribunal found otherwise. As it turned out, fate, in the form of financial problems, set the course in this affair before it could reach a conclusion via another confident appeal on our part.

■ ■ ■

We had formed Bond Media by this time, a company that included television and radio interests across Australia and in some international centres, including the UK and Hong Kong, and if our television licence was removed there would be a $1 billion asset at risk. Again it was the ugly and rapid rise in interest rates that was beginning to cripple this media arm because of the debt load, including the lack of the $200 million that we were due to pay Kerry Packer as final settlement on the Nine Network deal. The share price was also on a rapid decline. It soon became apparent, as the domino principle of financial dilemmas began to spread across the entire Bond group, that we would have to sell Bond Media, including the Nine Network. It was our first public setback, and the first major sell-off we would have to make in a bid to stop the rot.

There weren't many potential buyers in the market so I soon found myself having meetings with Kerry Packer and Malcolm Turnbull at Kerry's home. It turned into another classic Kerry Packer negotiation:

> *KP*: 'You owe me $200 million. Where is the $200 million?'
> *AB*: 'Well, right now things are a little bit difficult, Kerry and I don't quite know how Bond Media is going to find the money just yet. There are a number of people who could buy the company, but they'd have to put in another $200 million to pay you back.'
> *KP*: 'No, I don't want that. I'm prepared to take it back. I'll take it off your hands.'

The consequence of that 'chat' was that we agreed on a final figure for Kerry to resume ownership of the Network, plus all of Bond Media.

Now this is where the history books relating to the buy-back need to be corrected, because Kerry Packer didn't buy the stations back for just $200 million, as everyone believed. There was the $200 million promissory note of his own in the deal that had not been paid out, and he had to pay the bank debt within the company, which was another $300 million. Then there was what he paid us for the shares. Once you put all the pieces together you'll find that the final figure he paid for Bond Media was probably more like $500 or $600 million. Then you must consider that after we amalgamated the Queensland and Western Australian stations into our original purchase of the network we, Bond Corporation, were paid $320 million for those, and we'd only paid out $70 million for them; so there was another $250 million for us. Kerry Packer said, 'you only get one Alan Bond in your lifetime,' because he got the network back for less than we paid for it, and he ended up with two more stations plus the rest of Bond Media. It was not as bad a deal for us as everybody was led to believe, but there is no doubt that Kerry got the deal of a lifetime.

Bond Corporation International was established as a public company in Hong Kong and much of its income derived from entities based outside that domicile, which meant that under their law we paid almost no tax on that income.

Establishing such tax-effective domiciles in various places around the world was an important part of our expansion towards becoming a truly global company. The scale of benefits that could be gained for the company is reflected in the fact that there were about 500 subsidiary companies in Bond Corporation and another 400 in Bell Group worldwide, so the more tax efficient we became the better it was for the company.

Our own internal tax department developed our programs to minimise, not to avoid, our tax liabilities, particularly on the international front. Because we had taxation commitments around the world we, like so many other international corporations, set up companies in the Cook Islands, the Netherlands, Chile and numerous other domiciles where, if the assets weren't there and you weren't therefore making money in those particular countries, then there was a zero or extremely low tax rate. By doing this we were able to plough the maximum amount of money back into the development of the corporation while also paying dividends to shareholders. Tax rates in Australia at that time were 42 per cent annually, and that amount, along with the annual dividend to shareholders, made it very difficult for Australian companies to have sufficient capital left to reinvest. The substantial proportion of all the wealth created from Bond Corporation was reinvested back into the business. In later years, when the shutters were coming down, it was obvious that we didn't move quickly enough to raise capital through worldwide stock markets rather than raising debt. What we should have been doing was restructuring so that we reduced our control position and brought in other shareholders — more equity, less debt. That was also our plan for Heileman Breweries in America where we had commenced a structure to allow the brewing interests to be refloated as a separate entity on the American market. However, we did not have the time to advance this before disaster struck.

Bond Corporation was always very interested in any business opportunity involving new technology. I'd always tried to impress upon people that they should never be frightened to try something new, just as we were the first in the world to brew no-alcohol beer, and had pioneered satellite television.

In 1984 our search for new technology took us to Airship Industries in the UK, a fledgling company that had some great ideas but no money. We were always impressed by the airships that had been used as high impact advertising platforms at the America's Cup. It was obvious that they had considerable potential for many applications, including aerial surveillance.

It was when I became an honorary International Advisor to President Reagan after the 1983 Cup that my interest in airships was really sparked; I learnt at one of the meetings at the White House that the US government was planning to offer a $6 billion contract for a fleet of airships to be used mainly for coastal drug surveillance. The big appeal for them was that they had the ability to remain airborne for a week or more, and they were extremely cost-effective to operate. Beyond this deal there was also the possibility of another order from America for a massive airship for passenger transport. I started thinking airships and in doing so realised that we could also use one as part of the America's Cup defence in Fremantle in 1987.

Consequently, we had a good look at Airship Industries and decided that if we were to literally get it 'up and flying' we would need some government assistance, and that was where I called in an offer from Britain's Prime Minister, Margaret Thatcher.

Bond Corporation was already strong in the UK through our brewing business, property development and B-Sky-B television, and because of this I had been invited by the Prime Minister on two occasions to dinner parties at No. 10 Downing Street. I was actually sitting next to her at one of these dinners before we bought Airship Industries when she said something along the lines of: 'I've heard that you are interested in the airship business. Let me know if there's anything I can do to help; come and see me if need be.'

So I made an appointment to see her and the minister whose portfolio covered the airship industry and told them that to establish the business in the UK I needed an order for at least one airship from them, and that I needed to be able to buy an old abandoned airport that was for sale at Cardington, in Bedfordshire, England, so I had a base for operations: 'Oh,' she said, 'well if that's what you want then I suppose I will have to consider putting the airport up for tender.'

'Well, while you're putting it up for tender I'll be moving the business to Italy. Britain won't get it at all.'

'What do you mean by that?' she asked. 'I only said that I would consider putting it up for tender. I didn't say I was going to do it.'

'And I'm saying that if you put it up for tender we won't be establishing the industry in the UK. I'm prepared to pay £1 million for the airport, and that's it.'

We were arguing back and forth and at times it became quite heated. I convinced myself that was the way she operated, and I wasn't going to back down. I'm sure she was waiting for me to give in, but I just stuck to what I wanted, and if I didn't get that then I was definitely going to take the business somewhere else. Italy was certainly a possibility, and we had a very positive offer from America to base the business there.

The meeting ended with Maggie saying: 'Well, I'll speak to my minister about it and we'll let you know.'

The minister walked me out of the meeting and once we were out of the Prime Minister's earshot he said: 'Look, I know you're from the colonies, but you just don't argue with Margaret Thatcher, the Prime Minister of England. You can't argue with her. It was the wrong way to handle the meeting.'

'So I suppose that means the deal's dead,' I replied.

'It's not up to me to say, but I wouldn't be holding my breath.'

'Oh, don't worry about it then. I'll go somewhere else.'

A week later a letter arrived from the minister saying: 'We agree to your proposal to purchase the airport which will assist the establishment of Airship Industries in the UK.' At a later date the government also agreed to a development grant of £4 million from the Ministry of Defence to assist with the research and development of the first two airships.

After buying 47 per cent of the company we injected, over time, a further $50 million and then, as we planned our approach to the pending US contract, we decided a smart move would be to have American investment aboard. We went to Westinghouse, which would be supplying all the technical equipment that the ships would carry, and went into a joint venture with them. I also put two US admirals on the board of Airship Industries.

The future was looking great. The British government was behind us and Westinghouse was in there battling with the US government for the contract. But suddenly, for some still unexplained reason, the US government went cold on the idea of airships. It was as if someone had woken up one morning and said: 'Airships aren't in the budget and we've got too many other projects on the go, so no airships.'

They changed their mind as quickly as you turn off a tap, and without a major defence contract Airship Industries was unlikely to be viable. That was where our long-term market was, not England and Europe at that time.

We did build 12 of the ships, magnificent big flying machines that were filled with helium; they were an incredible flying experience. We brought one to Australia and used it very effectively for aerial advertising of Swan Beer at America's Cup defence time. But despite our research showing us endless opportunities for airships beyond this application, Airship Industries was doomed. The share price crashed and with that Bond Corporation decided not to inject more money and sold its interest. The company's airship designer and engineer, Roger Munk, continued with the development of airship technology and has recently floated a new company to continue where we left off.

Being as prominent as it was in the 1980s, Bond Corporation not surprisingly had an incredibly large and diverse number of business opportunities presented to it and its associated companies. One such case was with the Walton's retail business in Sydney, an operation that we bought a 56 per cent shareholding in, not through a desire to get into retail but because of an affinity with the Walton family. It was a purchase based more on emotion than commonsense.

I'd known John Walton through sailing friends for some time and the company, which owned a large site in the heart of Sydney diagonally opposite the Town Hall, was under financial pressure and facing the threat of a takeover. John came to me and said: 'Alan, we've got this financial problem that we are struggling to fix. Will you come on board?'

We bought in and then I had my people do their investigations into what direction the company should take. The finding was that there was little, if any, future for Walton's as a department store: the industry was in a decline because the pattern of retailing had changed towards the discount retailers like Coles and Woolworths. It was also evident that this was an industry that we had entered far too late. Our only option was to consider developing a multi-faceted retail operation on what was a prime site in the centre of the city. In the meantime, knowing that Walton's could not succeed as a department store standing alone, we bought a large swag of shares in rival retailer Grace Brothers in a bid to try to reinforce our position. It all turned out to be too hard and once we took a serious look at our position we got out.

Business for me and Bond Corporation was never going to be all smooth sailing — that's just how it is in the business world. But I had no idea how tough things were going to become.

CHAPTER NINE
THE TIDE TURNS

As well as my parents' prompting, it was my interest in art at school that led to me becoming an apprentice signwriter, and I guess my first attempt at being an artist came with my painting of the Resurrection of Christ at St Patrick's Church in Fremantle when I was a teenager. By the late 1960s this 'interest' had grown and I was already becoming a true collector, having purchased a number of Australian works. By the early 1970s my collection had become a passion. In order to justify my decision to invest heavily in art I did considerable research on the subject, something that led to me teaming up with one of the best art advisers in the world, Lady Angela Nevill.

Angela is a godchild to Queen Elizabeth and the daughter of the late Lord Rupert Nevill who was Treasurer to the Duke of Edinburgh. She lived in London where she had the Nevill Keating Pictures and from there she consulted and acted for some of the world's greatest art collectors, including royalty.

'Ange' advised me on my entire international art purchases, particularly in the French Impressionist area where I purchased paintings by the likes of Monet, Renoir, Manet and Toulouse-Lautrec. They proved to be exceptional investments, increasing in value on average by at least 12 per cent per annum. But I wasn't buying to make a quick profit — being a true collector I found great difficulty in parting with any painting. In fact, when my collection was at its peak it would have been worth around $150 million.

By far my most famous purchase on the international market was Van Gogh's *Irises,* a deal that came with controversy and much speculation.

The painting was offered for sale in 1987 through the Sotheby's auction house in New York, and I was given a private viewing of it while it was on exhibition in London. I had been passionate about Van Gogh's work for a long time, and I had decided to buy one for my collection. However, my first move failed when I was the under-bidder to a Japanese buyer for *Sunflowers*. Sotheby's then came to me and asked if I was a serious bidder for *Irises*, and I said: 'Well, I would be a serious bidder but I've got a lot of financial commitments on my plate at the moment. But if we could do it on the basis that I pay 50 per cent down and the balance in a year then I'm very interested.' They took up the matter with the owner of the painting and quickly agreed that if I was the successful bidder, then the terms were half down and the balance in one year.

The purchase arrangement fitted perfectly with me because I was building my new gallery on top of the 50-storey Bond Building in Perth. It was designed to house the major part of my collection, and it wasn't going to be ready for about a year. My plan was that if I were the successful bidder for *Irises* then I would open the gallery with it as the centrepiece. The timing was perfect.

Part of my agreement with Sotheby's was that if I was the successful buyer then I wanted to remain anonymous until I announced that I was the owner at the time of the gallery opening. They agreed, so I had Angela act as my purchasing agent at the auction while I made my bids to her via telephone. The bidding was very spirited and exciting. *Irises* was finally knocked down to me for $US52 million plus a 5 per cent agent's commission for Angela — a world record price for a painting, but a price I was sure was justified. I made my initial payment of 50 per cent of the purchase price through a Hong Kong-based company that was controlled by Dallhold.

Once it became known I was the purchaser a controversy erupted in Australia, the suggestion being that the payment schedule meant I couldn't afford it — that I had to go deeper into debt. That was not the case at all. We made the final payment as scheduled and took delivery on the due date.

I just loved *Irises*. To own a masterpiece, a Van Gogh painted in 1889, was a wonderful, almost indescribable experience. You could sense the history. Whenever I could take a quiet moment for myself I'd go and look at the painting and touch it. It was a therapeutic release from a tumultuous world. I could feel Van Gogh's brush strokes, beautiful brush strokes that captured a freedom of expression, even though the subject was flowers. The strength of the colours was magnificent, and the thickness of his paint on the canvas was quite astounding — he seemed to trowel it on, and that's what created the aura that the painting holds for me.

As well as giving me considerable personal satisfaction, my collection proved to be extremely valuable to both Dallhold and Bond Corporation when it came to dealing with the heads of large international corporations, particularly those from Japan, because the Japanese were taking a significant interest in art, so much so that they were primarily responsible for pushing prices to crazy highs in the 1980s. I displayed many of my French impressionist paintings in Dallhold's boardroom and dining room for our guests to appreciate. These paintings brought great prestige and credibility to our companies.

When things got difficult for me about two years after I bought *Irises*, I arranged to sell the painting to the J. Paul Getty Museum in California. The general belief was that the sale price was about as much as I had paid for it. I was mocked for this, the supposed experts saying that the price was clear evidence that I had paid too much for it originally, and that I really didn't know what I was doing in the world of art. What these people didn't know was that the

LEFT: My father, Frank Bond, started working underground in coalmines in South Wales when he was twelve. At sixteen, he decided to join the army.

BELOW: Frank and my mother, Kathleen (*below centre*), married in 1934. My sister Geraldine (*below left*) was born in 1936, and on 22 April 1938 I arrived on the scene.

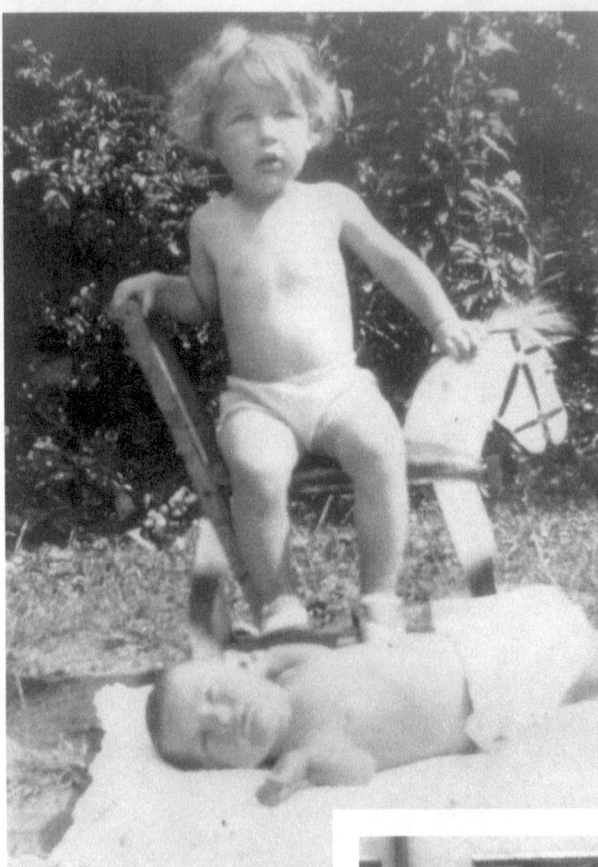

ABOVE: Big sister Geraldine keeps an eye on me as a baby.

RIGHT: One of mother's favourite photographs — me in my church choir outfit standing outside our London home.

ABOVE: The fawn coloured Ford Prefect four-door sedan that mother bought for us to take to Australia. It was the family's first-ever car.

LEFT: 'My Godfather, where am I?' Geraldine, my mother and I arrive at Fremantle as 'Ten Pound Poms' in 1950. It was February and hellishly hot — more than 100° Fahrenheit (38° Celsius).

ABOVE: My parents (*right*) showed great affection towards Geraldine and me, but their own relationship seemed very Victorian. I never saw them show any affection towards each other and I've no idea what their personal life was like.

LEFT: Marrying Eileen was a huge step for a 18-year-old and I was a little nervous, but outweighing that was the fact we were very much in love and excited about our future together.

LEFT: A proud father. I always made a concerted effort to spend as much time with the family as I could whenever I was not travelling. Here I am with (*left to right*) John, Jody, Susanne and Craig.

BELOW: The Duke of Edinburgh (*second from left*) joins me (*third from left*) aboard *Southern Cross* off Yanchep soon after the yacht was launched for our first America's Cup challenge in 1974.

TOP LEFT: Eileen and me out on the town in 1974.

TOP RIGHT AND ABOVE: My friendship with Lang Hancock (*with black-rimmed glasses*), the man who founded the iron ore industry in Western Australia, influenced my enthusiasm for the Robe River iron ore project. He gave me a strong insight into the mining industry.

TOP: I was named Australian of the Year in 1978 and appeared with Eileen, my mother, Kathleen, and my children, (*back row, left to right*) Jody, Craig, John and Susanne, on the television show 'This is Your Life'.

ABOVE: The race that stopped the nation: *Australia II* beating *Liberty* in the 1983 America's Cup. It was one of those heart-stopping times in your life that you know you will never capture again.

TOP: The America's Cup was far more than just another yacht race: it was a race against the might of America with rules that were made to be broken by them and not by us. After three earlier challenges, *Australia II* won the Cup in 1983. Here I am on deck steering the boat back to the dock with (*left to right*) Skip Lissiman, Hugh Treharne and John Bertrand.

ABOVE: *Australia II*'s designer Ben Lexcen (*centre*), skipper John Bertrand (*right*) and me at the presentation of the America's Cup in Newport in September 1983. The ceremony, on the verandah of one of the classic old homes in Newport, wasn't in keeping with the great history of the Cup as far as I was concerned — and the New York Yacht Club hierarchy appeared far from gracious in defeat.

ABOVE: *Australia II* in action during the America's Cup. The entire team became national heroes in Australia.

RIGHT: America's Cup 1983 — *Australia II* crosses the finish line ahead of *Liberty*.

ABOVE: While Eileen and I enjoyed the huge 'Welcome Home' parade in Perth after the America's Cup victory I was struggling to come to grips with our history-making achievement and what it meant to Australia, and me. My profile was rocketing ahead. My photograph appeared on the cover of *Time* magazine, business opportunities began to flood in, and I had to capitalise on the ones that mattered for Bond Corporation.

RIGHT: A day I'll never forget — meeting Ronald Reagan and committing a diplomatic faux pas on the lawn of the White House. After Reagan's wonderful speech congratulating us on our America's Cup victory, I walked up to the lectern, the President stepped aside and I took over the microphone. I was later told that no one but the President is supposed to stand at a lectern behind the President's seal and make an address. My speech went across the United States on prime time television.

LEFT: Parties were almost an occupational hazard during the good times. Eileen excelled in her role as a hostess for the business dinners and parties we had at our homes in Perth, Sydney and London, and while travelling around the world. No one loved a party more than Eileen — she was invaluable when it came to organising special functions, her challenge always being to ensure that everyone had a most enjoyable time.

ABOVE: Like a typical proud father I went to every conceivable length for all my children. My daughter Susanne's wedding in 1985 was a very memorable day. It was an enormous affair with more than 500 guests, and no expense was spared on any aspect of the day. The dance floor was built out over the beach in front of the house, the orchestra was installed on a floating pontoon alongside, and the finale was a monstrous fireworks display that ended with a flaming outline of the happy couple.

TOP: The expansion of our international gold mining projects took us into Chile in 1987 and inevitably I was to meet the President, General Augusto Pinochet, a man accused of human rights atrocities and persecutions. It was during one of these meetings that I agreed to have my photograph taken with him, and as a result unwittingly became a political pawn. The photograph was sent around the world with a caption suggesting that I supported the Pinochet regime. It was total propaganda on Pinochet's part.

ABOVE: Eileen (*not pictured*) and I were invited to a private audience with Pope John Paul II during his visit to Australia in 1986. It was one of the most fantastic moments of my life. You could feel an aura when he entered the room; you really felt that you were as close as you were ever going to be to God on earth.

TOP: *Endeavour* now proudly sailing the world's oceans under the Australian flag. Here she is in Doubtful Sound, South Island of New Zealand, in 1996.

ABOVE: I saw my contribution to the *Endeavour* project, the building of a replica of Captain Cook's three-masted bark, as a gift to Australia and a wonderful way to showcase the nation. Here I am dressed for the occasion of the launch of the project with the Prime Minister, Bob Hawke.

TOP LEFT AND MIDDLE: At the site of the project of which I am most proud, Bond University in Queensland, Australia's first private university. In 100 years, when I am long gone, Bond University will still be there making outstanding contributions to Australian society and the world.

RIGHT: Our magnificent 203ft schooner *Jessica*, a three-masted yacht that was an absolute classic. I couldn't resist a name change for her — *Schooner XXXX* in recognition of our XXXX beer. We had the leaders of many countries and some of the world's most influential people join us aboard our boats, such as the Aga Khan, Prince Rainier and Prince Michael as well as movie stars, including Joan Collins.

Diana Bliss (*above and left*) fascinated me from the first time I saw her when she was only 21. By the time of our wedding in April 1995 I was facing an uncertain future, but notwithstanding this it was a marvellous and memorable occasion. The emotion I now share with Di is a love based on warmth, companionship and friendship.

TOP: In Karnet Prison I spent every spare moment I had available to me painting. It took my mind outside the prison and kept me occupied.
This copy of Renoir's *The Boating Party* was painted by me in a six foot by nine foot room at the prison. Of all the paintings I did whilst in prison, this was my favourite; and yes, I did a number of copies of *Irises* that I later gave away to friends.

ABOVE: What matters today is that I am a happy man with new values in life. When I look back my greatest pride rests with my family. All I want now is to spend time with Di (*right*), my family and close friends.

museum traded in two very important paintings as part of this deal, and they were pre-sold by Sotheby's, a deal that made the total consideration for *Irises* $US74 million. It wasn't a bad investment at all. Soon after the sale of *Irises* the liquidators moved into Dallhold, took much of my collection and auctioned it off.

Australian art from the early 1800s was another area I concentrated on and I was considered to be a serious investor in Australian art for quite some time, owning nearly 50 very special works. I found it fascinating that many of the artists were convicts transported from England; there was some wonderful talent among them.

One of the most famous paintings in the collection, *Portrait of Captain Cook*, became the centre of considerable debate with the Bond Corporation liquidators. I never actually owned it although I had possession of it for some time. I know that it went overseas and eventually came back to Australia, but I don't know any of the details of how Richard England, the liquidator of Bond Corporation, managed to obtain it. There were suggestions that my friend, Jurg Bollag, was involved, but I was unable to confirm this. The National Portrait Gallery in Canberra subsequently acquired it.

My association with Angela Nevill led to me being invited to her parents' residence at St James's Palace. One of these occasions was a private Christmas party, which was attended by the Queen, Princess Margaret and other members of the royal family. There were about 50 guests in total. It was a wonderful and very memorable evening where I was fortunate enough to have a long chat with the Queen. She impressed me immensely with her knowledge of the America's Cup.

The highlight of the party was the singing of Christmas carols by London's famous Bach Choir, which was assembled in the palace courtyard. I had the pleasure of escorting Princess Margaret to the courtyard, which we reached by going down the stairs from the residence and out through the kitchen. Quite unusual I thought.

We were all standing in a group enjoying the singing when Princess Margaret turned to me and said, 'Can you lend me a fiver?' She wanted to contribute to the choir's collection box, so I pulled out a £5 note and gave it to her.

Once we were back upstairs Princess Margaret reminded me that she owed me £5, then suggested that instead of repaying me, she'd take me to lunch.

I responded: 'I would really enjoy that, and I just happen to have my jet here in London, so why don't we fly over to Maxim's in Paris and do lunch there?'

My suggestion brought a sardonic response: 'It's not necessary to do that. There are plenty of good restaurants in London.'

We left it at that and a few days later her secretary rang me to organise the lunch. Unfortunately, it was scheduled for a day when I was already booked up with meetings that I could not cancel. I returned to Australia £5 the poorer and minus a lunch with Princess Margaret.

I've always believed that you should put back into the community what you get out of it, and because of that both Eileen and I were great believers in philanthropy. We held a strong and religious belief in helping others less fortunate than ourselves. If you don't do that then you are not really balancing your own life, not getting the maximum out of it. It's good to give.

In the five years before the collapse of our business world we were putting around $5 million annually into charities, hospitals and the community. Some charities had received support from us for more than 20 years. Our donations were no different to those from people who support charities with a dollar or two — we gave what we could afford, or what we felt was justified. We made donations of $250 000, and in the case of the Ash Wednesday bushfires in Victoria, we provided 10 brand new brick homes. One of the reasons I was moved to do this was that I saw those people as battlers, just as I had been. I wanted to help them.

There was a great deal of personal satisfaction that came through our charitable activities, however it was disappointing to note how few beneficiaries and charities came forward with any message of support when I was facing my toughest times. No, I didn't want them to feel obliged to do so, but if they were as compassionate as they always made out they were when they came to me looking for a donation then you'd think they would have at least been able to say something like, 'sorry you're experiencing tough times'. I see this as one of the problems that charities generally have in Australia — they don't recognise that the contributions people make are a matter of choice, and they don't seem to care about you once they have received your donation.

There was one notable exception. I was a supporter of the Prince of Wales Youth fund in England, and a member of the Prince of Wales Trust, and when things went really bad and I was shipped off to prison it was the Trust's Angus Ogilvy, the Queen's cousin, who wrote to me on his official letterhead to say: 'We recognise that you've done a lot for us and we want you to know we haven't forgotten you. We are thinking of you and you will always be welcome in our group. Please do not hesitate to let us know if there is anything we can do for you.'

That was very special.

I have always found the Catholic Church to be a wonderful community where there's an unselfish attitude towards giving and sharing.

Over a number of years I got to know the hierarchy of the Church both in Australia and Rome. Locally I was often asked to advise on land purchases in Western Australia that were being considered by the church, and I was also happy to be able to make a number of significant charitable contributions to support Church projects, such as building a swimming pool for a particular group, or supporting a school.

In Rome my introduction to the Church came via Eileen's brother, Father Don Hughes and the Oblate Order to which he belonged, and through the fact that the Church had a vested interest in a major property development I was putting together there.

It was because of these relationships and my having made a financial contribution to Pope John Paul II's visit to Australia in 1986 that Eileen and I were invited to a private audience with His Holiness during his stopover in Perth. It was one of the most fantastic moments of my life, as I am sure it would have been for anyone else, no matter what their religious belief.

The meeting took place at the Archbishop's private residence where Pope John Paul II was staying, and there were only eight of us who had been invited. The moment he appeared on the stairs leading down to where we were standing, there was an aura that entered the room. You could feel it — you really felt that you were as close as you were ever going to be to God on earth. The man just radiated holiness.

Still, it was an extremely relaxed environment to be in — very informal and friendly and we chatted away for about half an hour on a number of subjects. He is such a wonderful man of great knowledge who exudes warmth and caring. It was an experience that strengthened my faith.

The property project in Rome that I referred to also came about in 1986 and involved the development of some 270 hectares within 12 kilometres of the Vatican. It was located inside what was called the Ring Road of the city of Rome, sitting there like vacant farmland right in the middle of the city, surrounded by 10-storey buildings. Its ownership and development had been in hot dispute between a number of families for many years. And yet again it was my profile from winning the America's Cup and the subsequent business contacts that I made in Italy, including meeting the Oblate Fathers of the Catholic Church, that led to me being asked if I might be interested in buying the property and completing a development.

I decided to look at it and, as I expected, it turned out to be a real mess. It even involved banks claiming ownership over some sections of the site. But there were opportunities and, with Bond Corporation already involved in developments in Europe, this seemed to be a logical extension of that business. If I could sort out the mess.

I had my motor yacht, *Southern Cross III*, moored in the south of France at the time, so I decided it was the perfect neutral territory for the commencement of negotiations between the warring parties. I flew the principal players down to the boat, including the bankers and some of the owners, and sat them down to a relaxed lunch. Things started to happen and after two more such lunches, along with three months of behind the scenes work on my part to get everything settled between the owners and beneficiaries, the result was that I agreed to buy the entire property. But I didn't just buy it on a whim. During the same three months of negotiations I developed my own ideas on what I could do with the site if I did decide to buy.

We established a Bond Corporation subsidiary company in Rome under the management of Neil Gillan to get things rolling then set about planning an initial development of 1.25 million square feet. It was designed to include many types of businesses: retail, warehouse distribution centres and car parking. The profit numbers on it looked fantastic.

Before we could go any further we needed to get the proposed development approved by the city council and the Mayor of Rome, and through my contacts within the Oblate Order of the Church, another door opened for me. Through them I was introduced to one of Rome's most high profile and powerful families, the Borgheses, and after telling them of my plans they said that they would organise a small dinner at their home and invite a few people who might be able to make things happen.

I was the guest of honour at their *little* dinner, and among the 20 other guests were three cardinals and the new Lord Mayor of the City of Rome. It was a beautiful evening and red wine flowed freely. At the appropriate time one of the cardinals next to me stood up and directed a speech to the Mayor:

Now look, Alan is a friend of ours, and he's a friend of the Church, and we would like you to really help him get this development through. Remember, we got you into the job as Lord Mayor, and you know we've supported you all along, so now we want you to get this thing sorted out, and make sure there are no delays in getting this planning through.

The result? My development proposals got onto all the right agendas at the City Council in rapid time, and it wasn't long before the project was approved.

I also met the high-profile politician and leader of the Christian Democrats political party, Giulio Andreotti, whom I'd met previously in Australia, to discuss the development, but more importantly to brief him on what effect our plans might have on the roads in the area. He became another ally, directing me towards the right financial organisations and contractors to deal with. My long-term plan was to add another five million square feet to the development after Stage One, an expansion that would mainly involve the building of apartment blocks.

Our own business structure saw us establish two companies around the venture and subsequently we sold 50 per cent interest to our Hong Kong company, Bond Corporation International. Everybody involved did very well out of it because the shares went up considerably.

My problem was that I had virtually all the approvals and was ready to go with the project, but the battle to save Bond Corporation and Dallhold in Australia had already started, and that warranted my full attention. So I reluctantly sold it, only because we didn't want to take on the cost of putting up a few hundred million dollars to develop the site when interest rates in Australia were around 20 per cent, even though there was a medium-term profit in it for Bond Corporation of $1.25 billion. We still did okay though, buying the site for just under $50 million and selling it less than two years later for $250 million. This project was sold as part of our disposal of Bond Corporation International to a Taiwanese group.

THE TIDE TURNS

■ ■ ■

My private company, Dallhold, controlled all the goldmining projects within the overall group. The expansion of our international goldmining projects took us into Chile in 1985 when we purchased 90 per cent of the El Indio mine from the American firm, Fluor Daniel, during a tender process that included Western Mining, BHP and Anglo-American. Before making our bid I did what I always tried to do prior to making any significant purchase, and that was to meet with the government and talk about what type of economic and social climate we might expect to find if we were the successful purchaser. I believed it was always best to get things out on the table early.

In Chile I met with the Treasurer and Minister of Mines, and subsequently the President, General Augusto Pinochet, who told me: 'We're welcoming foreign investment into the country because it's important for our economy. Coming from Australia you understand mining, so providing you look after the employees, and pay your taxes, you'll have no problem with the government.'

I also went to inspect the mine 14 000 feet up in the Andes mountains, and while it was obvious that it needed some improvements it was producing enough copper and gold to deliver a $US80 or $US90 million a year profit. I agreed with our mining engineers who'd already said they wanted to buy it, so the next move was to contact the Hong Kong and Shanghai Banking Corporation where I received approval to draw between $500 million and $600 million against the $1 billion facility they set up for me so we could tender.

I knew that in being up against the likes of Western Mining, which was backed by the ANZ Bank, and BHP in the bidding process the only way that I was going to get to buy El Indio was to negotiate a deal before the close of tenders. There was no way I was going to beat them in the tender process because they were playing hardball via a high-profile public relations exercise in Chile as part of their lobbying during the lead-up to the decision.

There was also no doubt that they had the backing of the Australian government.

We did our homework on the mine and then I had a meeting in Chile with the chief executive of Fluor Daniel, from New York, saying to him: 'Look we're really not keen to tender, so why don't you sell it to us now?'

He replied along the lines of: 'Oh, I can't do that. We've got all these tenders coming in, like Western Mining who have the ANZ bank directors in Chile now to support them. They're a really big company and you're small fry compared to them, so they wouldn't be very happy if we were to abandon the tender process.'

'Well I'm here right now. I'm prepared to purchase all the shares in St Joe Minerals [the company that owned the mine], including your 90 per cent. But I'm only prepared to buy it tonight. I'm not going to tender. I've got too much on my plate, too many opportunities, so I'm not going to frig around. If you want me to buy it, I'll buy it.'

He was a bit taken aback, but I was getting through to him:

Chief Executive: 'We don't know exactly what the figure would be, but it would have to be in excess of $500 million.'
AB: 'Okay, so why don't you agree on a figure with me and I'll buy it.'
CE: 'Oh. But you'll want more due diligence, and then there will be conditions, and all that sort of stuff.'
AB: 'There won't be any conditions on the deal. I've seen the government and discussed it with them, so I'll do the deal with no conditions.'
CE: 'What about conditions of finance?'
AB: 'No conditions. I'll pay you in 30 days.'
CE: 'What happens if you don't pay in 30 days and I've lost all my tenders? I'll have to call the chairman now to discuss it.'

The agony continued until the second bottle of red wine when I pulled out my chequebook and said: 'I'll give you $500 million. Here's my cheque for a 10 per cent deposit now.' He wouldn't say 'yes', so I just ignored him while I wrote out a cheque for $50 million: 'There it is. I've bought the mine.'

I told him that I'd buy 90 per cent of the shares in the listed company and would settle with him in 30 days. I then asked him to sign a piece of paper acknowledging the deal. 'I don't want to sign that,' he responded. 'I will have to ring the chairman and get his okay,' he continued. 'Go on, sign it,' I said.

He ummed and aaaahed after he returned to the table until we had a second bottle of wine. Then he pulled out his pen and signed it.

He took the cheque, only to be told by his company's lawyers the next day that I'd never settle. On hearing that I rang Willie Purves, the chairman of the Hong Kong and Shanghai Banking Corporation and said: 'Look, I've just given a cheque for $50 million, and we're going to pay the balance of $450 million in 30 days.'

After I also explained to him what our total plan for our gold investments were, and how I would refinance the debt, Purves told me it was okay and to go ahead.

So I had in place yet another part of the plan to put all our international gold assets into one parcel under the banner of Bond International Gold and then list it on the main board of the New York Stock Exchange. The plan was to get our money back and do a long-term debt restructure, and that led to Purves reminding me at the time: 'Don't forget we've got the right to do the long-term debt', and I acknowledged that fact.

Within 30 days of agreeing to proceed with the purchase we saw the 1987 worldwide stock market crash, and as a consequence expectations that I wouldn't be able to settle were even greater, but the due date came and I was ready. There was, however, one big problem — the bank didn't seem to be ready. Just 48 hours out from settlement the bank went incommunicado and we couldn't get any of the documentation we needed to conclude the deal. I couldn't contact anyone from the Hong Kong and Shanghai Banking Corporation, and I was relying on them for the money that had been promised. I had open access to Willie Purves, so tried calling him, but there was no response. Everyone was off the air, and suddenly I realised why — because of the crash they were having their little bank huddles, reconsidering whether or not they'd let me have the money for El Indio.

Then a call came from the chairman: 'Sorry Alan. We've been terribly busy, and a few people here wanted to have a bit of a discussion about your deal. But I gave you my word on it so you go ahead and draw the cheque.' I did just that and, much to the relief of the people at Fluor Daniel, they were paid. In fact they were so relieved they gave me $5 million worth of paintings as a 'thank you', telling me at the time of the presentation that I'd become a folk hero within their organisation and was welcome to do business with them at any time. I heard later that people in New York had been betting we wouldn't settle.

My team and I leapt into the project, very quickly striking a deal with the unions to introduce new programs and increase exploration. One of the initiatives was to finance skilled workers at the mine who wanted to buy a house. We guaranteed the required $4000 deposit, and they in turn agreed to work with the company for a set period. It was an extremely successful scheme because no one had ever treated these miners so well. More than 500 of them took advantage of the offer. This had the effect of improving relations with the workers and reducing work stoppages in the mine.

The unions and the government were impressed by our effort to help the workers, and this led to the creation of one of the most successful projects that Bond Corporation ever undertook, one that remains hugely successful today — the Chile Telephone Company, or more specifically, the Compañía de Teléfonos de Chile.

This project brought me a lot of personal pleasure as it pioneered the mass use of satellite communications in the world by making the telephone available across the country. Unfortunately though, our dealings with Chile also brought great controversy in Australia because we were seen to be supporting a powerful dictator, General Augusto Pinochet, a man accused of human rights atrocities and persecutions. It was a controversy that resulted in there being a number of protests, especially in Western Australia, claiming Bond Corporation supported Pinochet and his military regime. The protesters, who were camped outside my house and our offices, were misguided — they couldn't understand that what we were doing was taking private enterprise in communications into Chile, something that would result in there being greater public awareness of just what was happening in the country. We were opening the door for the world to hear what was happening. We certainly weren't supporting General Pinochet and his regime.

The first of two meetings I had with Pinochet were at the imposing Presidential Palace and we were scheduled to discuss our plans for the El Indio goldmine. My first impression of this much-feared man came from his eyes. They were a steely light blue and surprisingly, had a charismatic twinkle. They were eyes that didn't seem to match his reputation. Still, he was obviously a man who was very much in control.

It was during one of these meetings that I made one big mistake — I agreed to have my photograph taken with him, and as a result I unwittingly became a political pawn. The photograph was sent around the world with a caption suggesting that I supported the Pinochet regime. It was total propaganda on Pinochet's part, a blatant effort by him to try to prove to the world that he wasn't such a bad bloke after all.

As well as discussing the El Indio mine we talked about what other developments were taking place in Chile. Pinochet had said that they were going to privatise some companies and open the doors so foreign investment could come in. I was thinking of other mines so I asked what they were considering for privatisation and that was when he mentioned the telephone company. Straight up I asked him what he wanted for that.

> *Pinochet:* 'Well, it's a public company. The government owns 55 per cent and we will be offering these shares for sale. I suppose it must be worth about $100 million, something like that.'
> *AB:* 'Oh look, I'll buy it from you for that and take it off your hands.'
> *Pinochet:* 'That's a nice offer Alan, but I can't sell it to you; we have established a tender process and you're most welcome to bid for it.'

It was to be the first privatisation of a company in Chile, and it was a company that operated 96 per cent of the domestic telephone service there. It was a beautiful monopoly that was already making

$30 million a year, so the thought of buying it had instant appeal for me because I knew it would fit perfectly with Bond Corporation's plan to have direct involvement in the communications industry worldwide as an adjunct to our existing electronic media business. It was also a generator of cash.

Pinochet said that selling the company was an important part of his plan to 'free up' industry in Chile and help the economy. He encouraged me to make a bid for the company. I asked how the tender process was going to be decided, and he answered: 'The highest price, together with the confirmation that you have the capacity to expand the services that we badly need in Chile. So if you want it you'd better bid the highest price.'

I decided I should bat hard from the outset so I got hold of a tender document then met with Chile's Minister of Communications and Finance to discuss the deal:

> AB: 'I will give you a sealed bid on the understanding that it is not to be opened until after all others are opened.'
> Minister: 'What will that do?'
> AB: 'It'll just say that my bid is $5 million more than the highest bid.'
> Minister: 'No, we can't do that. It will have to be opened in public and read out.'

The minister also confirmed that apart from actually bidding, the plans to develop the business had to also be revealed. On that front we had something in our favour — we had an office already established there through our mining operation. It was clearly evident that we planned to be in Chile for the long haul.

Then came the crunch line for me from the minister: 'Tenders will be open for 90 days from next week'.

I exclaimed: 'Ninety days! I can't stay here for 90 days. Look, you can do one thing, and it'll be the same for everybody. Just reduce the tender time down to 30 days. Let's get on with it.'

The minister agreed and in so doing potentially eliminated a lot of the contenders. In the end there were nine tenders.

It was full marks to David Aspinall on this occasion because I got him down to Chile where he orchestrated a fantastic tender presentation. When we went in to present our offer, each of the government's key players was given a large leather book and when they opened it there was a coloured telephone inside. All they needed to do to get details of our offer was to pick up the receiver and listen. It was totally professional with music and words. The offer was also outlined on pages in the book. It was very impressive, but above all it was the tender price that mattered.

Prior to putting our tender together, Peter Mitchell, David Aspinall and I met in London and agreed that it would have leaked out that we had a figure of $105 million on the table because that was what I had suggested to Pinochet and the minister, so inevitably somebody was going to bid up from where we were. We eventually came up with a figure of $125 million, and for luck we threw another $2 million on top.

We won the tender by $2 million.

There was an enormous backlog of applications for telephones with a waiting time of around five years. We tackled that straight away and in a very short time we had considerably reduced the waiting list. In our first full year of operation we installed some 200 000 lines and more than doubled that figure the next year. When we took over the business they were still using plug and pull telephone switchboards, but in the two years that we had the company we made it one of the most efficient communications companies in the world through the application of new technology, including satellite mobile phones that were selling for $US3000 each. In a very short time the company was earning substantial money.

One thing we found when we got in there was that the government had 50 000 lines tapped — so we untapped them. We also offered free lines to the headquarters of the various political parties in Chile.

There were assertions far and wide of payola being associated with the deal when we originally bought into the company, but I can say categorically that the only thing I ever received from Pinochet was a cup of coffee, and he got nothing from me. Pinochet went to great lengths to keep it very proper.

We held the business for two years but we were never given the chance to realise its full potential because with the collapse of Bond Corporation imminent we were forced by the bank backing its loans to sell out in just 21 days. For our shareholders this was another deal that could have made a significant contribution towards preventing the downfall of Bond Corporation. When the problems for Bond Corporation started, the telephone company was debt free and sat in Bond Corporation International in Hong Kong. That was when the Hong Kong and Shanghai Banking Corporation came along and told us that because it held a high exposure to Bond Corporation in Australia, we were to sell the asset and send the money to Australia. At the same time the government in Chile was pleading with us not to sell because the growth of the company was indicating our shares would be worth more than $1 billion within six months. I tried to renegotiate with the bank but was confronted by a brick wall. All they were concerned about was getting a large repayment within 30 days, and if I wanted their support for Bond Corporation then I had better get on with the sale of the telephone company, even though at this point of time there was no legal security given to the bank over this asset. As an asset it was fully protected, the shares being held by Bond Corporation International Hong Kong.

My high pressure search for a buyer led me to a French lawyer I knew who in turn discussed the possible purchase of the telephone company with the chairman of the Spanish telephone company, which had been the under-bidder in the original tender process. Arrangements were made for me to meet that chairman over a meal at Harry's Bar in London with the intention of concluding a deal. I sold the 55 per cent shareholding to him for around $500 million.

Today our share of the Chile Telephone Company would be worth in excess of $10 billion.

I have maintained very good relations with the government in Chile. It was very satisfying for me to see that their contact didn't stop when I was in prison. Messages were brought to me via the Chilean Ambassador out of Canberra saying I'd be most welcome in Chile at any time and that I should consider going back there to do more business. They actually referred to me as a 'political prisoner', saying in essence in one message: 'We understand your problems in Australia are politically motivated.'

Going hand in hand with the collapse of Bond Corporation and Dallhold have been accusations that I siphoned billions of dollars from the companies and hid it all, primarily offshore, for my benefit. I'm sure those same people are expecting me to say here and now that there is no money hidden anywhere, so I won't disappoint them. *There is no money hidden. I did not illegally channel money out of the company and out of the country.*

Did I give significant amounts of money to my wife and children? Yes, of course I did, right from the very, very early days of business. It started more than 30 years prior to the collapse, and I did it because I wanted them to be independent. And as a consequence of the kick-start in life I was able to give the children they have been able to go on and become financially secure. They are continuing today to work hard and be successful. And of course Eileen, as my wife, received jewellery and other significant gifts from me. If you are a billionaire, as I was, and you can afford a $1 million dollar necklace, ring, or whatever else that amount of money can buy for your wife, then you give it to her. I could afford it, and she deserved it, just as the children deserved everything I gave them. We were travelling incredibly well in business, there were no suggestions that we were going to go bust, and like any other considerate father and husband, I wanted to give my family everything possible. It's all relative, rich or poor — you should always do everything you can to support your family and to make them happy.

The name Jurg Bollag has always been associated with the claims of the hidden millions. It's been said that he was my 'Swiss banker', the man who mapped out and manipulated a money trail for me.

Now it's time to put the record straight. Jurg was in fact a family friend and business associate over many years, a man with whom I had significant dealings prior to the Queensland Nickel project that we were both part of in 1983. I met him when he was a banker with Dow Chemical Bank. He was the director of the bank in Switzerland and Dallhold had some loan deals with the bank. I continued to deal with him when he left the bank and established his own business.

Bond Corporation gained Queensland Nickel in 1983 through a purchase of assets belonging to Mid-East Minerals but had to on-sell it because it had a billion dollars of debt in the company that would have had to be consolidated into Bond Corporation's accounts. It was also making substantial losses at the time. I agreed to purchase the company through Dallhold for $3 million, including the debt that was within the company.

I hoped I could salvage the company, float it and subsequently retire any debt that it retained. That was the path we were progressing along very nicely until the collapse of Bond Corporation and later Dallhold. But what made the result of the Queensland Nickel deal extremely difficult to swallow was that had I been able to see it through to the end it would have contributed significantly to the rescue of Dallhold and helped Bond Corporation survive.

This nickel investment fitted nicely into my plans to have a diversified portfolio of business activities for Dallhold. I didn't want to have everything tied up in just Bond Corporation, so I had the gold business coming on line and then Queensland Nickel. The only thing for certain about the deal was that if we couldn't make a go of it then at least we'd be able to get our $3 million back through liquidation.

I met with the management team after I took control and listened to all the problems they faced. This team was basically going along on compliance really, certain that the company would run for only another 18 months when it would be closed down. All the workers would have been sacked and the whole plant simply sold off for scrap. That meant the banks would have got back very little of the $1 billion they were owed — perhaps $50 million, if they were very lucky. Apart from that $1 billion debt, which the company couldn't even pay the interest on, the mine faced the problem of having only 18 months of ore reserves left, and as a consequence all sales contracts would expire about the same time. On the plus side though, here was a company with a huge plant on the outskirts of Townsville, in North Queensland, that would cost $2 billion to replace yet was losing money even with the price of nickel on the increase. The facility covered something like 1000 acres and employed 1100 people. It was an inefficient, high-energy consumption plant, and that made it expensive to operate. I looked at it all and thought: 'There's an interesting challenge here. How can we turn this around?'

First up I had to address the problems of dwindling reserves and a lack of long-term contracts. I had the benefit of my experiences with Lang Hancock and our Robe River days of large mining operations. Queensland Nickel's facility was a lateric nickel processing plant that needed a long-term source of high grade ore, so I started looking all over Australia, only to realise that even if a deposit was found it was going to be too expensive to get the ore to our processing plant. So, rather than be parochial in my approach, I went global in my bid to save the company.

I was told that there were large lateric nickel deposits in Indonesia and New Caledonia, so I proposed to my experts that we look at developing mining operations in those countries and import the ore to Townsville. It was a thought that was somewhat beyond the mind-set of the people at Queensland Nickel, so I quietly took myself off to Indonesia and met with all the hierarchy there, including some of the Suharto family, and struck a deal with the government. 'We'll let you have this lateric nickel,' they said, 'but we want an undertaking from you that you'll look at building a new lateric nickel processing plant up here at some stage.' I agreed. I then decided that it was a bit risky sourcing our ore from just one place, so I went and did a similar deal in New Caledonia. That way, if one source failed I could rely on the other. Among the many things we had to investigate were the quality of the ore bodies, the reliability of supply and the economics of shipping the ore to Townsville. And before we could go into major feasibility studies we had to arrange for sample shipments to be delivered from both Indonesia and New Caledonia to ensure that this ore could be properly processed in our existing plant. We soon realised that by importing an ore of higher grade than had previously been processed, and expanding the plant, there could be a $200 million surplus cash flow coming from the business.

Next came the need to deal with the federal and state governments to formulate our plans. I met with them thinking that they would welcome the news that I had made my first big step towards saving the company and the jobs of more than 1000 employees by finding fresh ore reserves: 'We want to import this ore from Indonesia and New Caledonia through the port in Townsville. How do we go about it?'

'Oh, you can't do that,' was the reply. 'It's never been done before. You just can't do it. There are no laws covering it. You might bring anything into the country, and it's lateric nickel coming in ... it'll pollute the oceans if there's an accident.' They added as an aside that the port in Townsville was not capable of handling the shipping. It was impossible to make this work.

I was undaunted, knowing that I only needed to turn a 'no' into a 'yes' to get where I wanted to be, so I went back to them: 'That's not logical to me. If we can take iron ore from Australia to Japan, then why, in theory, can't you reverse the process?'

It was a question they struggled to answer, so we thought we should make things easier for them by getting a stack of independent reports and feasibility studies done on the entire project, including one on expanding the port in Townsville so the large ships needed to carry the ore could be accommodated.

We eventually won the battle with the Queensland government and the environmental authorities. The Imported Ore Scheme was introduced as a consequence of us proving to them that it was more economical and safer to import the ore than it was to transport low-grade ore from a mine just 260 kilometres away from the plant. This in itself was an enormous gain for the state of Queensland, which was a joint venture partner in the processing plant.

The problem that then confronted us was the cost associated with the expansion of the harbour, and a requirement from the government that we pay a premium price to transport the imported ore from the port to the plant on the outskirts of the city. I found this to be quite staggering because Queensland Nickel had already paid $50 million for the rolling stock and train engines that would be used. It was as if I'd been attacked by a bunch of bushrangers while I was trying to save a company and 1100 jobs. But the government won on that one and after seemingly endless negotiations everything fell into place.

Securing the supply of ore was only part of the problem. I still had the $1 billion debt to deal with. I had my people research the situation and they discovered that the bulk of the debt was with banks in Japan and Germany and, to a lesser extent, America. The Queensland Nickel investment had turned out to be a bitter experience for them from day one because they had never received the total amount of interest they were owed, and for years they'd been forced to renegotiate, time and time again. These banks were sick and tired of hearing about Queensland Nickel.

With the help of some international tax advisers I realised that if those banks, particularly the ones under Japanese and German law, could sell the debt to another financial institution they would get immediate tax relief against their revenues. And it was an enormous tax benefit — between 60% to 70% in Japan and 60% to 80% in Germany. It was an interesting alternative, especially when it was apparent that if the company went under and these banks had to wait for the liquidation to be finalised, they could be out of pocket for many years.

Obviously I needed to find somebody overseas, an international person, to organise the purchase of the debt, and that's when I went to Jurg Bollag. We sat down and considered our options. 'It's in everyone's interest to find a solution to this,' I said. 'We need a financial institution to buy the debt because the company can't buy the debt back. It has to be a recognised financial group for the lenders to the project to be able to get the tax write-off benefit.'

We had negotiated with the banks to buy the debt for 10 cents in the dollar, or more specifically $100 million, which we had to find. Jurg and I went to Standard Chartered Bank in the UK with a proposal and they decided to take up the offer. They had already financed the development of the Super Pit in Kalgoorlie for me with a big loan of $500 million, so we had a track record. The plan was that they would buy the debt from the banks, and Queensland Nickel would then owe the $1 billion to Standard Chartered. Jurg then established a structure in Switzerland that held the option to buy back that debt for $4 million after Standard Chartered had received the $100 million and the interest on it. Jurg would then exercise the option and hold the contract to the joint benefit of Dallhold and his company. This was a totally legal offshore deal that would result in us eventually getting control of the Queensland Nickel debt. In setting up the deal with Standard Chartered we showed on paper how the imported ore scheme would work, how it would generate more nickel and cobalt, and make profits for the company.

As all the arrangements with the government and the banks were conditional upon a new long-term sales contract, I arranged for Jurg, who spoke German, to represent Queensland Nickel in Germany, which was where we hoped to find these contracts. Without sales contracts none of the deals could happen; you couldn't spend another $150 million on the development of the mine and the upgrading of the plant if you didn't have a buyer for the nickel. We arranged a consultancy agreement with Jurg's company and began payments. So Jurg went after a sales deal and before long he opened the door at Metallge-sellschaft, where I worked with him to negotiate a 20-year forward sales contract worth $6 billion — still one of the biggest contracts ever secured for an Australian company. But few people cared — especially in the media where all they seemed interested in was seeing me fail. It didn't matter that this deal meant that Queensland Nickel wouldn't fail, simply because on the back of it I was able to put all the pieces together to finance the entire project.

While the project progressed the actual agreement between Jurg and me was never formally documented because we didn't feel it was necessary at the time. One of the interesting things about this nickel asset was that Dallhold owned the shares, but the control of the asset was with the debt, because that was already in place. The shares were worth nothing unless you paid the $1 billion back to the bank. It could be argued that our agreement meant Jurg controlled that debt, so in effect he controlled the company. One of the reasons we had left the agreement in abeyance was because we weren't quite sure of the legal position as far as tax was concerned within Australia, so we decided to leave the formal side of things until such time as the deal started to generate some money. We hadn't determined what we were going to do then, it hadn't been sorted out because in reality it wasn't a priority. I was comfortable with the fact that it was a verbal understanding, as this had been a practice in my business dealings with people I could trust 100 per cent. I certainly didn't mind the thought that he stood to make a lot of money out of it. He had his document to buy the option from Standard Chartered, but I didn't have any documents to support it from my side. Jurg would also have been paid a considerable sum for putting in place the Metallge-sellschaft sales contract in place for Queensland Nickel.

What this all meant was that Jurg and I had the greatest financial deal ever because when the interest on $80 million, that's 8 per cent interest, was paid, it was tax deductible in Australia. It was then to be sent offshore where it paid the interest bill on the original $1 billion loan — so we got $80 million a year tax deduction here, then the $80 million paid for the interest went offshore. That money was then going to sit in a place where it was non-taxable, so the gain was not only the principle of $1 billion, but the $80 million per year. It was perfectly legal and a brilliant deal. We already had an international valuation saying that based on the imported ore scheme the value of the project was $US1.4 billion, or more than $2.5 billion Australian dollars.

And while this was the ultimate deal of all deals for me, our salvage of Queensland Nickel represented a win for everybody concerned. All the employees retained their jobs long term; export revenue was generated for the company and Australia; the project encouraged others to establish and operate lateric nickel mines in Australia; and thousands more jobs were created through the imported ore scheme, such as the contractors who provided plants and machinery, and in the support industries, especially in Townsville. The plant represented one of the biggest industries in the city.

What Queensland Nickel also did was show Australia was not necessarily just a mine, that we weren't just into mining resources, and that we had the potential to be a secondary producer, that is, the materials came from somewhere else and Australians did the processing work.

When Bond Corporation shares collapsed in value and the company began to founder, a series of events surrounding Dallhold investments started a domino effect across the board.

I had borrowings from a syndicate of banks, including the Hong Kong and Shanghai Banking Corporation, against some of my Bond Corporation shares, and those banks knew we had the Queensland Nickel asset on the Dallhold side that, if you could disregard the debt, was starting to generate really serious money. Here was a business for which we had paid $3 million, and which had made more than $100 million in one year and was heading for far greater things.

The Hong Kong and Shanghai Banking Corporation, as my bankers, knew about the deal that I'd done with Jurg Bollag, and while he might have been seen to have control of Queensland Nickel through the debt, they remained confident that I could control the situation because of the understanding we shared. It certainly wasn't a situation that worried me because, as a family friend, we had great trust in each other. Jurg would often look after Susanne when she was in London. Like her, he had an affinity with horses; like her, Jurg was an equestrian dressage rider and they enjoyed sharing that experience. He had also quite often acted like a private banker, paying bills for the family from time to time. He had no hesitation in doing that simply because of the income he expected to receive through his association with the Queensland Nickel deal. All I would need to say was: 'Jurg, we've got to pay such and such. Would you mind paying that for me?' and it would be done. There was a notional agreement that at the end of the day we'd add it all up and settle it through our Queensland Nickel arrangement. So a few million dollars here or there were nothing when you considered the big picture. Jurg even paid some jewellery accounts at Aspreys in London for us. It was all part of the informal arrangement.

Once the Bond Corporation shares collapsed the Hong Kong and Shanghai Banking Corporation left me in no doubt that they wanted better security:

'Look, we know you've got that asset, Queensland Nickel, and we've got guarantees over Dallhold as part of that security, but they're not worth anything because the debt exists,' was the word from their representative in Australia, James Yonge.

'Quite right,' I said, 'but it will make enough money to pay the $1 billion debt over 15 years, and it'll still pay off my debt to you.'

'Oh no, no, no. You owe $300 million to syndicated banks, so what we'd like you to do, if you can ... and we'll help you sort this out ... is get Mr Bollag to lift his agreement over Queensland Nickel, and let us put the first charge on Queensland Nickel. As part of this we will pay the $50 million balance outstanding to Standard Chartered Bank. If you can achieve this then the loans on the shares will be extinguished and we'll write you a new 15-year loan.'

That meant that their new deal was to be $350 million over 15 years and Bollag would sit behind them for the $1 billion. For me it meant that the bank would not call my personal guarantees through Dallhold and this would save me from being bankrupted.

I said: 'Oh, I don't know if Jurg will agree to do that because he is the beneficiary, whichever way you look at it, because he is to share in the profit from whatever we make out of it, and he will hold all of the securities.'

The truth of the matter was that as the deal stood, Jurg had an enormously strong negotiating position, and the bank knew that he had to give his consent, otherwise the deal couldn't be done. So I went to Jurg, and told him about the bank's proposal — that they'd give us a long-term loan and that we could pay it back.

Jurg didn't take long to consider the offer: 'Alan, I don't think I should agree to that, nor should you, because if everything falls over with Bond Corporation then at least you'll have Queensland Nickel going for you. I will go in and take possession of Queensland Nickel because I'm the lender, and I will control it. You and your family will be right for the next 100 years; they will have nothing to worry about. Why would you take this risk from the bank at this stage? You're under pressure and your share price is going down, but as a banker, adviser and as your family friend, I advise you not to do this.'

Back to the bank I went and said: 'Mr Bollag doesn't want to do this deal. His rationale is that he has had nothing to do with loans on Bond Corporation shares and therefore can see no reason why your bank's arrangement with Queensland Nickel assets, which he controls the debt on, should change.'

The bank then started arguing over who actually owned the debt: 'It's really you,' to which I replied, 'Maybe you could argue that point, however the reality and legal position is that I have no standing unless Jurg agrees. He just isn't going to buy your proposal.'

'Right,' they said, 'we'll call our loans with you and that will be that. We'll call in everything.' I wavered, and the banker said, somewhat condescendingly, 'Alan, I'll tell you what — the chairman would like to see you in Hong Kong, so why don't you go up and see him for a chat. I assure you that whatever he says will be okay.'

So I went off to Hong Kong to see the chairman, Willie Purves, who said: 'Look Alan, we know you've got a good thing in Queensland Nickel so we're going to do this 15-year deal with you, a long-term loan. Considering the situation that Bond Corporation is facing, having this loan in place may well save all the other pieces. And beyond that, if you sell the Chile Telephone Company as well and pay that money down, we can also help support Bond

Corporation directly. But you've got to do this Queensland Nickel deal for us first. If you do that we'll take over the responsibility and underwrite those other banks included in the $300 million Dallhold loan, then they will come into line. We'll make it a six-month loan initially and then get everything into place.'

Then he added the words that still ring in my ears: 'You know us well, Alan. You've done all these deals with us over the years. We've been your backstop for 20 years, so you know you can trust us to do this for you.' Then he put his arm around my shoulders and said: 'You can trust me.'

What I was being told sounded logical. After all, the bank had done plenty of deals with me on trust. But despite this and our long relationship, I remained wary: 'You're asking me to put a lot of trust in you and the bank. Shouldn't we put the loan agreement in place now?'

Purves replied: 'When the bank gives its word to you we give our word. You've been banking with us for a long time. You've relied on us giving you a $1 billion facility on my word. If we're going to do business in the future, you have to accept my word. Once we've agreed to this one we'll do the documentation.'

Purves and the bank had a gun to my head because the Bond Corporation problems needed to be solved quickly. The promise of a 15-year loan meant that I would probably be able to keep Bond Corporation, Dallhold and everything else together.

I kept convincing myself I had no reason to disbelieve Purves. We'd operated on trust so many times before. In 1987, when the stock market was in total disarray, I had a $500 million personal facility with the bank that they did not withdraw. This facility was used to purchase the El Indio mine. I'd always relied on banks through my entire business career. If a bank told me it was going to do something I knew that they would not let me down. So I told myself there was no reason to doubt them this time, especially considering my relationship with them had been so strong that the previous chairman and chief executive of the Hong Kong and Shanghai Banking Corporation, Sir Michael Sandberg, was on the board of Bond International Gold.

Convinced that things would be okay, I then went to see Jurg again. After much persuasion from me he reluctantly agreed to do the deal with the bank, but not before he said: 'I don't like it. It means that if anything goes wrong then we're second charge instead of first charge, and it would be a very difficult but probably not impossible task for me at that stage to go out and refinance the entire $350 million in Europe. However, given sufficient time, 12 months or so, I believe I could replace the loan to the Hong Kong Bank, should it become necessary. So Alan, if this is what you want to do, then I'm prepared to help.'

I told the bank that the deal was on, but within a very short time I realised that I had made a disastrous commercial decision. The bank had set me up. I should have listened to Jurg, and then maybe, just maybe, the force of the decision not to go with the deal would have seen the bank back away. If Queensland Nickel had continued to do well, as it is today, then we could have gone back later and paid it off. Instead we let the banking syndicate take first charge over the Queensland Nickel debt.

This verbal agreement with the bank turned into a documentation nightmare. The initial stage of the loan was only for six months, and the document they presented had a clause in it that required me to pre-sign the retirement of all company directors, me included. That meant that at any stage they could just put the date on the form and say, 'Thank you, you're retiring now. You're no longer a director of the company.'

Mallesons prepared the six-month loan documentation, and as we moved into the period of the loan James Yonge and his team were documenting the long-term loan ready for syndication to the market, documents that confirmed that details of Willie Purves' promise to me over such a loan being established had been passed on to Sydney. When the six months was up they gave us just three hours to repay the loan — which we obviously couldn't do. And it turned out that they never did syndicate the loan, one of the reasons for that possibly being that the world economy was slowing down following the share market crash.

Not surprisingly, after I told the judge what had happened about the promise of a long-term loan, my case was further weakened because I was suffering from memory loss as a result of my heart operation, all the stress I was under, and the associated bouts of depression, so I forgot other vital evidence, like meetings I had with James Yonge at the bank in Sydney where the term sheet of the 15-year loan was discussed. It wasn't until I started writing this book and reflecting on those times, that I was able to recall these details.

And as far as the judge on this case was concerned, well, all I can say is that he showed his true colours. I was told that the reason for him bringing the judgment down early was because he had to catch a flight to Hong Kong to attend the races. And yes, the judgment went against us.

Once the bank was in possession they said: 'Right, we're going to put the entire plant up for sale.' And who got the job as chairman? None other than Wynn Davies, an executive of the Hong Kong and Shanghai Banking Corporation who had participated in the whole loan affair. And he was ultimately rewarded with shares in the listed company.

Queensland Nickel was soon sold and the group that bought it floated it and the market valued it at about $1 billion ... and we owed only $300 million! Everything about this deal smells. Think about it commercially. Why, with all the shrapnel that was flying around my ears, would I ever have entered into a six-month deal on a loan if I hadn't been convinced that I was destined to get a 15-year loan as part of the salvage plan for Bond Corporation and Dallhold? There was no commercial logic in a six-month deal for me. You'd have to be the most naïve business person in the world. And why would I give away a prime asset? The bank just looked after their own position, and not me, a client who had dealt with them in huge amounts for 20 years. I relied on the bank's assurances and was badly burnt.

What makes this whole catastrophe even more frustrating is the knowledge that Queensland Nickel was performing extremely well and in a position to pay the bank out in a relatively short time. That also meant that Jurg was going to be paid back his $1 billion, and was destined to share that amount with me. But it never came off.

The Queensland Nickel deal answers the often asked question: 'How could Bollag be so generous towards Bond and his family?' But why didn't he want to appear in court here to defend me and our business dealings? I believe that the answer is that he would have damaged his own commercial situation. While Bond Corporation and Dallhold were falling stars Jurg was dealing with a lot of other companies around the world. The last thing he would have wanted was to have his clients see him go into the witness box and talk about what were private affairs between himself and a client, affairs that were perfectly legal but structured for minimising taxation. That would have been detrimental to any other business he wanted to do in Switzerland, or Europe for that matter. He wasn't silly, he was a clever man, and he knew that the Australian legal system was going to try to pull him down in its desperate bid to destroy me.

It must also be said that despite beliefs to the contrary, on the advice of my lawyers I did not meet with or contact Jurg to discuss the charges I was facing relative to the collapse of Bond Corporation and Dallhold. My lawyers had a couple of meetings with him, but I didn't because if I had, and he did appear to give evidence, it could be claimed that the evidence was contrived. It is hard for the non-believers to accept that there was nothing really mysterious about my relationship with Jurg Bollag, or that everything we did was legal. All I can say is that these are the facts.

While everything was stacked against us I wasn't going to lie down. I decided to take the fight to the Hong Kong and Shanghai Banking Corporation on the Queensland Nickel deal because I had a $300 million personal loan with them. So what did they do? They really put the boot in — at the end of 1991 they decided to bankrupt me over the same deal so there could be no fight. But after a lengthy legal battle, there was a settlement with the creditors and much to their displeasure the bankruptcy was annulled in 1995.

My intention was to continue the fight because while the Hong Kong and Shanghai Banking Corporation saga was unfolding I'd been to the UK and had all but refinanced the Queensland Nickel deal. Ironically it was Sir Michael Sandberg, who as I mentioned was previously the chief of the Hong Kong and Shanghai Banking Corporation and had been chairman of Bond International Gold, who introduced me to the Sultan of Brunei's representative, and I was working in London on getting the Sultan to be part of a deal where $360 million would be put up to take out the Hong Kong and Shanghai Banking Corporation loan. Then, when it was completed the Sultan would become my partner in Queensland Nickel. That all came to a dead-end rather rapidly because when I returned to Australia, the authorities, on the insistence of the banks and the bankruptcy trustee, grabbed my passport and wouldn't let me leave the country. This was part of another sinister plot to get me, which I will detail later. What it meant though was that I couldn't get back to the UK to complete the deal. I told the banks and the trustee that I was on the verge of doing the deal, a deal that would satisfy everyone involved, but their only response was: 'Well, maybe you are and maybe you aren't, who knows. And besides, if we give you your passport back you might do a runner.' After that I knew I had no hope. Dallhold was then in Bond Corporation's wake and was as good as gone.

Still, the ASC pursued Jurg relentlessly because they thought he was going to produce evidence that I had money hidden here, there and everywhere. But the bottom line was there was no money, so there was no evidence for him to produce. Yes, there were transactions that had gone on over a period of time through all the Queensland Nickel financing and other deals that I'd done, but there was no treasure chest buried in a bank vault. I explained this in court, along with the fact that Jurg was a principal in business dealings I'd done, but no one wanted to believe me simply because they were fixed in their belief. I can tell you that once the tide turns against you in this league, even when you are being wronged, it's very hard to turn it back.

CHAPTER TEN
SHATTERED DREAMS

To put the collapse of Bond Corporation into perspective we have to look at the growth of the company, particularly in the five years following our win in the America's Cup in 1983. Over that period the company literally exploded in size while our family company, Dallhold, was also expanding nationally and internationally at a rapid rate. By 1988 Dallhold was the world's largest privately owned goldminer and in 1988 Bond Corporation was Australia's ninth largest enterprise.

Much of this growth came from the realisation within Bond Corporation group prior to 1986 that we had to think globally if we were to see maximum returns for our efforts, and as a result of that approach we were, by 1988, starting to reach a size where we could make an impact on global markets. Our turnover was quite staggering, more than $1 billion a month, and we recorded an operating profit after income tax of $403 million. Our activities in buying and selling assets contributed to these profits, and were designed to gradually provide us with better quality assets. This particular part of our business was to some extent misunderstood by the market.

Our strategy was for us to be of such a size that we were dominant in international markets with our core businesses, something no better reflected than in the expansion of our brewing assets. And again, applying that wonderful thing called hindsight, it was here, and in some other areas of the business, where we were probably victims of over-expansion on our part. It could be said that in 1987 we bit off too much. But it must also be said that we were still financially solid after the stock market crash that year — we had around $423 million in cash reserves.

A big part of the reason for us being in such a healthy position was that we actually saw the crash coming at least 12 months before it arrived. That's why we were selling a lot of assets, and why our profits had been boosted that year. We could see there was going to be a big downturn, so we wanted to sell as much real estate and other assets as we possibly could.

When dealing with the Stock Exchange we would disclose only the minimum amount of information, mainly because we were doing international business and because we wanted to remain competitive. We didn't think it was smart to be running to the market every time we were negotiating a significant deal and therefore signal our activities to the world. I now think that this relationship with the Stock Exchange was something that we should have handled differently. We didn't treat the relationship with the importance it deserved, and while I didn't deal directly with the Exchange I should have been more in tune with what was happening. We didn't disclose as much to the stock market as we probably should have. Our approach at the time was designed purely on commercial grounds, and we didn't consider that there might be other consequences.

By the mid-1980s Bond Corporation had diversified on a number of fronts. Our decision then was to tighten things down, concentrate on our core businesses, and that was what we were doing. As a consequence of that move Bond Corporation had made the decision to get out of all mining involvement and at the same time increase our exposure to petroleum exploration and development. Our core businesses were brewing, media and communications, property and petroleum, and our master plan was to see each of the Bond Corporation entities separately floated to the public at some stage.

Dallhold, and all other Bond Corporation shareholders, were to receive a slice of each of these companies, and each entity would be designed to expand with its own management structure, including its own board. This way we could bring in substantial capital without diluting control — and we were a long way towards achieving that. It was a move that meant Dallhold, and all other Bond Corporation shareholders, would have a share in four different divisions of Bond Corporation instead of just one.

As far as Dallhold was concerned, it was changing its direction towards becoming more of an investment company than anything else. The company was continuing to expand globally with its goldmining activities, Bond International Gold was destined to become one of the top ten in the world. But Bond Corporation was the real focus, and because it was expanding so rapidly, some important decisions needed to be made, decisions that would let us continue on this growth path while retaining control of both our Australian and international interests.

The principal decision that we made in 1985 was for me to be based out of Australia, primarily in Hong Kong, for the ensuing three years so I could concentrate on Bond Corporation International (BCI). BCI would control the bulk of our international interests, like the Chile Telephone Company, property developments in London and Rome and Hong Kong TVB. This move meant that for the three years prior to the collapse of Bond Corporation I spent 10 months each year outside Australia — not an excuse, just a fact.

Our headquarters in Australia was to look after all the brewing interests, including Heileman in America, property, media and our petroleum business. In effect the company was split up geographically and the management restructured. I became chairman and anything international, other than those entities with roots in Australia, came under my direction. Peter Beckwith became chief executive in Australia.

Peter had made an impressive climb through company ranks to his new position. He had a background in accounting and joined the company as a real estate salesman in 1969, aged 28. It was an interesting introduction — he came across from South Australia to apply for a job, and when I said: 'You're hired. Will you move across to Perth?' he replied: 'Yes, I'll move across here, but I'm a bit short of money to bring the furniture across.' Even though I'd only met him that once I had no hesitation in saying, 'Don't worry, I'll pay for it', and with that I pulled out my chequebook and wrote him a personal cheque. Peter impressed me from the start; he was very dedicated and his talent saw him moved up to a managerial position, and then up again to a director and later managing director.

Tragically, Peter passed away in July 1990 from a massive brain tumour at a time when Bond Corporation's fight for survival was becoming increasingly intense. He had been complaining of headaches for about a year and died within about six weeks of the tumour being diagnosed. Notwithstanding the difficulties Peter always remained a true friend, a friend I miss to this day.

While I desperately do not want to be seen to be laying any blame on Peter for some of the decisions he made over a considerable period, surgeons and oncologists told me that his judgment would have been impaired for quite some time prior to his passing, and they confirmed that he would have acted in ways that one would not expect of him.

When we changed the structure of the company it was a toss up between Peter Beckwith, Tony Oates and Peter Mitchell as to who would become the chief executive. This was the period when I applied the much-publicised 'golden handcuffs' to keep the key executives of Bond Corporation on board. With the company growing as fast as it was I realised that I needed to know that the team was going to stick together. The 'golden handcuffs' involved them signing a non-compete contract of exclusivity; they entered into a restrictive covenant agreement where for a significant capital sum they agreed to stay with the company for five years. The terms of the contract depended on their position within the organisation, but everybody included in the arrangement got a share of what was a tax-effective bonus.

I was certain that Peter Beckwith was the right man for the top job, even though Mitchell and Oates were equally talented. Tony Oates, a lawyer with an exceptional ability on the financial side of the business, became financial director while Peter Mitchell, a very talented corporate strategist, would concentrate on the expansion of the business. David Aspinall headed media and communications and Dr John Jackson, petroleum. I was certainly very comfortable leaving the Australian side of the business under the direct control of Beckwith, Mitchell and Oates because they worked well together. There was good rivalry between the three because both Oates and Mitchell believed they held claim to the position of chief executive. It was a healthy situation for the company because it meant there was always a strong person behind Beckwith through the rivalry that existed. However, my decision to go hands-off in the day-to-day operation of Bond Corporation in Australia would prove to be a costly mistake.

While this restructure was happening, our international treasury division, which was under the direction of Oates, became so large that we decided to move it from Perth to Sydney where we could establish a huge trading room for around-the-clock currency transactions. The decision to move was reinforced by our need to be closer to the action, particularly the international bankers we were dealing with.

I left the eventual control of this new treasury operation to Oates and Beckwith, but the move would prove to be one of the biggest internal mistakes the company made — we essentially lost control of our treasury functions. Our daily turnover on the international money market was massive, and the minute this operation was moved to Sydney we were relying on reporting rather than any of us being able to go into the office at any time and get the feeling for what was happening with our money. This reporting system made the chain of command far too long, and as a consequence the Bond Corporation board struggled to stay abreast of what was occurring in the division. Regardless, one of the most ridiculous allegations to emerge when Bond Corporation collapsed was that this division was losing money. It's a fact that we did have to write-down some values, but it then became an accounting argument as to whether or not we made as much profit as we publicised. The debate was based around the fact that some one-off profits were in there; it all revolved around the management of the cash and loans. There were hundreds of millions of dollars in those movements and it could always be argued as to what represented profit and what didn't.

I accept responsibility for losing control of the treasury function even though my involvement in international matters led to me being treated in Australia as if I was an external director. I must say though that all the divisions I was controlling out of Hong Kong were reporting directly to me, and they didn't have any problems. It should have been the same when treasury was moved to Sydney, but obviously the right procedures were not in place for us to identify problems when they arose.

The immediate aftermath of the stock market crash in 1987 didn't impact on us too much. The company continued to power ahead on many fronts, including the acquisition of shares in the UK hotel and investment company, Lonrho. At that time we also had 10 per cent in a UK brewer, Allied Lyons, and it's around these two deals that I made a significantly incorrect decision on company direction. As time would show, what we should have done was just go for Allied Lyons as part of our brewing portfolio and forget about Lonrho. Our association with Lonrho developed into a very unsavoury and expensive experience. I believe Bond Corporation would still be alive today and going from strength to strength if we had stayed away from Lonrho, but there was certainly no sign of what was to follow when we made our move into the company via the shareholding.

We found ourselves in this mess as a result of our efforts to help the Western Australian government save its political neck by trying to rescue the merchant bank, Rothwells, from financial disaster. That led to much of the cash reserve we held after the stock market crash quickly being squandered on a petrochemical plant deal that the government promised us but never delivered. Then came the final straw, our investment in Bell Group, which could have been so good yet turned into a disaster. It was a very sticky web, so sticky that Bond Corporation underestimated the impact of all these events, in particular the aggressive reaction from Lonrho's Tiny Rowland in 1988 towards our purchase of shares in his company.

After encouraging us to buy into Lonrho, Rowland then did a complete about face and decided he didn't want us in there — we had served our purpose. And to get rid of us he masterminded a very deliberate assault on Bond Corporation aimed solely at wrecking our company. He was ably supported by the former owner of Bell Group and Bell Resources, Robert Holmes à Court. I would say that if Rowland was the orchestra conductor then Holmes à Court was the piper playing his tune. Holmes à Court was involved to such an extent that he personally passed onto the banks, particularly ones we were dealing with, copies of the malicious Lonrho report on the supposed poor financial health of Bond Corporation. Rowland's ploy was to crush us by deliberately undermining Bond Corporation in the eyes of the banks by telling them we were insolvent. They went to all our banks with two documents they had prepared, one detailing Bell Group assets and liabilities, and the other the Bond Corporation position as they saw it. They put one over the other, and not surprisingly, it showed a very negative position for Bond Corporation. That was all they needed to do to ring alarm bells.

Certainly the efforts of this pair influenced the Hong Kong and Shanghai Banking Corporation's attitude towards us over the Queensland Nickel deal where they refused to extend the loan beyond six months, the loan that could have saved the company. The Hong Kong and Shanghai Banking Corporation was on their list when they set out to do as much collateral damage as they could to the group of companies and me. And I'm told by various banking personnel that as well as using scare tactics with their falsified documents they actually made threats to the banks: 'If you don't take note of your exposure to Bond Corporation and do something about it then the issue will be raised at your next shareholder's meeting, Mr Banker.'

But while Rowland's actions played a significant factor in the downfall of the company, our problems really came with the National Companies and Securities Commission (NCSC) investigation into Bond Corporation a few months earlier in 1988, and the subsequent Sulan Inquiry.

The sequence of events around this entire saga started with James Yonge, from Wardley's, coming to us and saying that Holmes à Court was in financial trouble and needed cash. There were two 19.9 per cent shareholdings in Bell Group for sale, and he recommended we should look at them because it was an asset-rich business. What he didn't tell us was that the Western Australian government through the State Government Insurance Commission was looking at buying the other parcel of shares.

Our first reaction when we discovered that the government was wanting to get into the deal, was that it was a very unusual move, but once we did have discussions with them their reasons became apparent: they saw an opportunity to gain significant cash from a sale of Bell assets, and this cash could be tipped into the gaping financial hole that was facing Rothwells following the unsuccessful rescue attempts that started in 1987. In short, it was the state government trying to help out their mate Holmes à Court while at the same time digging itself out of trouble. And if there was another reason it was probably that they were eager to get some level of control over the newspapers Bell owned. I guess that's why, when we started talking, the government felt comfortable about us buying the other 19.9 per cent; they hoped Bond Corporation would be a friendly shareholder that would work with them for their desired results.

We looked at the deal and in April 1988 the Bond Corporation board approved the purchase of a 19.9 per cent share of Bell. We didn't want any more than that because we didn't need to be in a position where we might have to make a takeover bid for the company. But when it became apparent to the outside world that both the government and Bond Corporation were buying into Bell it was suggested that we had been acting in concert from the outset. We were accused of scheming to take joint control over the company, even though this was a long way from being fact; it wasn't until we had commenced negotiations that we knew of the government's moves. The truth is that there had never been any collusion between the two sides, but once we did know that the government was also involved we did have discussions with them on what our respective intentions might be for the future of the company. But there was no way we worked together on the deal.

Holmes à Court had become extremely depressed by his looming corporate demise. He was struggling to stay on top of things, so much so that he had moved out of his office and gone to work from his home, which was where I met with him to negotiate the share deal. Even then, despite all the problems he was facing, he impressed me as being a very clever man, although his motives behind some of his deals were not always very clear. He was certainly very sharp in his dealings with us, which was probably a reflection of his desperation. Still, I did become concerned about what was really going on behind the scenes when we started talking with him about Bell Group assets. There were some unusual elements to our discussions, like when I told him that the Stoll Moss Theatres in London, which were on the books as an asset, were properties well worth owning and consequently made the deal more appealing. He then told me he'd forgotten something. The theatres weren't included because there was a purchase option on them, and that option would be exercised before settlement. He wouldn't say who the buyer was, and we soon discovered why. The Stoll Moss deal was with his mate Christopher Skase. Holmes à Court had done a back-door deal and sold the theatres notionally to Skase for well under their true market value, then *bingo*, about four weeks after we had secured a share of Bell, the Stoll Moss Theatres found their way back into Holmes à Court's hands. By doing the deal with Skase he got the theatres out of the company without having to account fully to the shareholders. In fact, we discovered that during the period he owned Bell Resources he had taken out tens of millions of dollars, money that we had to put back into the coffers following the revelations at the National Companies and Securities Commission inquiry into the entire affair. Their question was: 'Where has that money gone?' We later found out that it had been used for the purchase of preference shares in the Bell Group.

The NCSC inquiry came about as a result of the Commission's chief, Henry 'Big Ears' Bosch, making huge noises about us and the Western Australian government purchasing the shares in Bell. While it is true that we did have discussions, the legal advice we had was that providing we conducted our own negotiations for the 19.9 per cent shareholding and did not discuss the final terms of the arrangement with the government, and the government acted quite separately and did the same, we were not acting in concert. As we now know, the government's agreement was quite different from ours, in that not only did they purchase the shares from Holmes à Court, they also purchased a substantial amount of convertible bonds — well in excess of $100 million. The government was also advised by the Attorney-General that it was not subject to the laws relating to takeover provisions.

Looking back on the image this transaction conveyed, I can see that there was a sound basis for the assertions made by Bosch, regardless of the merits of the argument. It must also be said that evidence was given at the inquiry by the state government's Minister for Energy, David Parker, and the head of the State Government Insurance Commission that we didn't act in concert.

While our legal advice left us in no doubt that there were no problems associated with buying into Bell, Bosch made enough noise for the inquiry to be established, an inquiry that did us no favours simply because it was getting us considerable negative mileage in the media at a time when we certainly didn't need it.

Incredibly, the threat from the inquiry was that we would be de-listed from the Stock Exchange, a threat that put Bond Corporation under enormous pressure. Just by the NCSC announcing the inquiry we were made to look guilty by association, even though we had not been able to plead our case. We also knew our backs were to the wall even before the inquiry started because of Bosch's reputation. He had no time for entrepreneurs — if you weren't a large company with an establishment board based out of Melbourne then you were in for a torrid time.

Not long after proceedings started we realised that there were only two options open to us. One was to let them reach a finding, and if that finding went against us then fight it in the courts. It was a fight I was sure we would win because even if we were found to have acted in concert with the government, the fact was that the government was not bound by the rules of the takeover provisions, rules that state that if you own 20 per cent or more of a company the obligation was there for a takeover bid to be made. The only other option for us to consider was whether or not we wanted to keep our shareholding in Bell.

And as I've mentioned, hanging over all this was the threat that Bond Corporation might be de-listed. It was a sufficiently serious scenario for me to call a meeting of the Bond Corporation board in Hong Kong so we could consider our position. We decided that the consequences of being de-listed were so serious that we should immediately despatch Peter Beckwith to Australia with the imprimatur of the board to meet with Henry Bosch and find a commercial solution, whatever that might be. Nothing was heard for around 48 hours, then, without coming back to me to discuss it, Beckwith announced through the media that we were going to take over Bell. The full takeover of Bell (a decision which admittedly was not Beckwith's own), caused Bond Corporation to lose hundreds of millions of dollars.

To the best of my knowledge no other members of the board knew anything of the deal prior to Beckwith's announcement. I tried to keep my cool, something that was very difficult as I continually reminded myself: 'Jesus, the commercial solution wasn't to put us in the net for another $400 or $500 million payout — in 30 days!' What Beckwith had done was speak to a couple of banks and they'd said 'yeah, we'll fund it'. The only plus side I could see at that time, if there was one, was that our bid did not include us taking over the government's shareholding in Bell Resources.

Beckwith's plan sounded okay when it came to preventing us from being de-listed, but when we got back to Australia and started doing the numbers, Pete Mitchell announced to us: 'Shit, this deal doesn't look too good at all. Holmes à Court's numbers just don't add up. I'm struggling to justify the price we will have to pay.' Fortunately though, he saw a solution: 'We can justify doing the deal if we can turn Bell Resources into a single purpose company, and we can do that by putting all the brewing assets in there.' It made sense to all of us so that became our plan, right from the start. And to be fair to Peter Beckwith, that was also the concept he had in his own mind — it was why he decided to go with the bid after being pressured by Bosch. It was the only way the deal made sense. However, I wish we'd had the chance to do the numbers before he announced the deal. It could have been negotiated better than it was.

Even so, while Beckwith's unilateral decision was to buy Bell, there was another course that we could have taken, a course which, when you consider that this deal was what really brought our biggest headache, would have resulted in Bond Corporation remaining afloat. Given time we would have realised that our worst position on the 19.9 per cent deal was that the shareholding could have been confiscated from us. There was no precedent for this happening in Australia, and it was our worst-case scenario, but had the NCSC inquiry decided that we did act in concert with the government on Bell, and remembering that with 19.9 per cent of the shareholding we weren't in a position where we could be forced to make a bid for the company, we could have walked away. In fact Southcorp and Allied Lyons were already negotiating to buy our brewing assets, even while we were looking at our own option for selling that division of the Bond group into Bell Resources.

The more we dug into Bell Resources the more it turned out to be a financial disaster. We discovered that Holmes à Court had a pile of debts in a group of subsidiary companies, debts that were very difficult to pick up because they were offset in consolidation. The long and the short of it was that we paid $600 million for Bell and 90 days later that $600 million was worth nothing. In effect, because of all the hidden debt, we got nothing. There's no doubt that with proper due diligence we would have picked up the true debt position in Bell, but because of the pressure coming from the NCSC inquiry and Bosch, everything had to happen in a hurry. We were by then desperately trying to save our company. We were on a financial conveyor belt that we didn't need to be on, and it was one that we couldn't get off.

There was another consequence of our forced takeover of Bell. The original Bell deal was to be Premier Dowding's life-raft in the Rothwells salvage debacle, but then when we were forced to take control of Bell his life-raft began deflating. Things immediately went from bad to worse as his plans to save the government from financial disaster began to submerge. Frustration set in to a huge degree — at one meeting I had with Dowding where we discussed developments he picked his chair up and smashed it against the wall. I couldn't believe what I was seeing. He just exploded. He was desperately trying to extract himself and the government from a huge mess, the WA Inc. mess that Premier Brian Burke had left him, but it wasn't working out. And the harder he tried to get the government away from the problems, the deeper his troubles became. I have always found it interesting that he denied smashing the chair that day, but I was there and I can tell you he just blew up.

Yet another interesting aspect of all this was that Holmes à Court seemed to have found a saviour in David Parker. Theirs was a quite unbelievable relationship that was accentuated by the fact that desperate men were doing desperate things. Over one weekend just a couple of weeks before the government encouraged Bond Corporation to get involved in helping Holmes à Court, Parker and others had negotiated for the government to purchase from Bell some city buildings in Perth plus a swag of BHP shares — at a cost that was apparently somewhere between $400 million and $500 million. It was a deal done to help Holmes à Court out of his mess, but it still wasn't enough. This intriguing situation became even more interesting. Before our purchase of the shares in Bell Group from Holmes à Court was completed, Bond Corporation was asked by the Western Australian government to get Holmes à Court to put $50 million from Bell Resources into Rothwells. This was because the government believed that he should assist them because they had helped him by acquiring the property and shares. Holmes à Court agreed and the funds were transferred, not that the amount was enough to help Rothwells. The next step for the government after this was to call on Bond Corporation to help with the Rothwells rescue because they knew that we were, at the time, still cashed up.

The inquiry turned out to be a bit of a shambles, but Bosch would eventually get his satisfaction by convincing the federal government to establish the Sulan Inquiry into Bond Corporation in March 1990, an inquiry that turned out to be, in many ways, a futile exercise and a waste of taxpayers' money. But it would prove to be very expensive for Bond Corporation.

I have no doubt the federal government wanted to look inside Bond Corporation because we were seen to be too powerful. They essentially panicked when we bought all of Bell, because it meant that we claimed Bell's media interests and held a media portfolio so strong that we could influence the outcome of an election. At that stage Bond Corporation had more than $9 billion in assets worldwide, while in Australia we controlled the Channel Nine television network, nine capital city and regional radio stations, the *Daily News* and *West Australian* newspapers in Perth, British Satellite Broadcasting and the Hong Kong TVB television network that broadcast into China. And among our many divisions we were very prominent in the oil and mining industries, Bond Motor Corporation imported Hyundai motor vehicles from Korea, and Bond Corporation International was also doing big things. Along with this, our physical profile in Sydney could not have been higher than it was with our Chifley Square development set to dominate the city skyline.

I know that there was pure jealousy behind the federal and Western Australian governments' moves against us — they saw our wealth and power essentially making us another Australian state in our own right. We were way ahead of their thinking commercially, spending as much as $30 million annually on legal advice, so they decided that as their public service mentality couldn't keep up with us they should curb our activities. They had to stir something up, create enough mud so that it would stick, and the Sulan Inquiry was the way to do it.

But while the Sulan Inquiry looked to all intents and purposes to be purely politically motivated, some unanswered questions still weigh heavily at the forefront of my mind to this day. Why did the federal government press for this inquiry when they knew that such an inquest would almost certainly destroy the company? Was there an ulterior motive? Was it a guise for something else? Who really propelled it and why? Did someone from the corporate world who believed they had a score to settle with Alan Bond push the government's buttons? Why am I asking these questions? Because I am reliably informed by my contacts in the right places that the federal government's interest in us was influenced by powerful commercial interests who wanted to get us, and hopefully get their hands on some of Bond Corporation's prime assets, if we were forced into a position of collapse.

The prelude to the Sulan Inquiry was that there had been great speculation on the stock exchange and in the media about what Bond Corporation had done with the funds belonging to Bell Group subsequent to our purchase of that company and the following investigation by the NCSC.

While all this was going on Bond Corporation was suspended from the Stock Exchange for periods of time, something that caused irreparable damage. Simultaneously there were a number of shareholders' meetings called to approve the purchase by Bell Resources of all Bond Brewing assets for some $3.5 to $4 billion.

Bond Corporation was able to derive some benefit from the cash that was in Bell Resources via the movement of funds directly and indirectly through merchant banks both domestically and internationally. It was simply a question of approving a loan or business transaction between one group of public companies and another group of public companies. No one went off with a barrow full of money — there was an inter-movement of money that was permissible. At all times they paid a proper interest rate for the money, and those funds were returned in their entirety to Bell Resources to enable that company to pay the $1.2 billion deposit for the worldwide brewing assets of Bond Brewing, including Heileman Brewing in the United States.

The Sulan Inquiry was established while this brewing deal was being structured. It was initiated in most unusual circumstances by the federal Attorney-General who worked behind closed doors when seeking the support of each of the states to have a formal inquiry in Adelaide into Bond Corporation, even though Bond Corporation was not based in Adelaide. Nor indeed were any Bond Corporation companies. Sufficient states agreed, so the inquiry was enacted with South Australian QC John Sulan conducting proceedings. It went for almost 12 months until one day somebody woke up to the fact that all the information they were gathering — tainted or otherwise — could never be used for any other challenge against the company. It was just like someone coming over your back fence to have a look around because they felt like it, and then making assumptions about what they think they saw, and what the neighbours told them.

We knew from the outset that this inquiry would do massive commercial harm to Bond Corporation, because the government wanted to be seen by the public to be a powerful watchdog acting on their behalf — and they made sure they got every ounce of publicity to show just that. It was to be yet another one of the fatal blows we were destined to receive, and the more we tried to protect ourselves and prove that everything we had done was within the law — as anyone in our position would — the worse it was made to look for us. As a result we were unable to recover from the commercial bombardment that came about through what people said at this inquiry, even though they didn't have to justify their statements or have them tested under law. It was untested evidence that we could not cross-examine. Not only that, but people were given immunity if they gave evidence against us.

It was as a consequence of this inquiry that seven years later the charges were laid against Tony Oates, Peter Mitchell and me alleging that we stripped money from Bell Resources. These charges were beyond comprehension. The purchase of Bond Brewing by Bell Resources was an incredibly complex affair where we had gone to every conceivable length to confirm the legality of the transaction. The legal documentation was so complicated, especially relating to the protection of Bell Resources, that we had senior partners from two prominent legal firms, one representing each side of the deal, attend board meetings to ensure that all directors understood the values and consequences of the sale before deciding how they wanted to vote. It was critical for both sides to know that there were no legal breaches in this transaction. If you want evidence of just how legal this transaction was, it's this — even after five solid years of investigation, investigators could find no breaches whatsoever. But then, with the Statute of Limitations about to expire, meaning that no charges could be laid thereafter, they sought an extension of time with the federal Attorney-General and were granted it — without any consultation with us! This shows how desperate they were to get us.

We went to extremes to confirm that everything was legal within Bond Corporation. In 1987 we paid millions of dollars to law firms to set in place the proposals for the Bell Resources transaction and to make sure that every aspect of the deal was clear and binding. Wherever possible, on 99.9 per cent of occasions, all documentation was done by external lawyers who were supported by our own internal law management team comprising more than 10 lawyers.

And in the case of the breweries going into Bell Resources, the documentation also had to be accompanied by an independent valuation by Whitlam Turnbull, a process that was completed for a fee of $1.2 million. With so much at stake, the company always ensured that everything was done to the letter of the law.

The timing of the Sulan Inquiry was also perfect for our opponents because it came when interest rates were extremely high, and that made the company very vulnerable financially; we were under threat because of the large debts we were carrying, debt that became even more pronounced once we were forced into buying the Bell companies as a consequence of the NCSC investigation. If achieving nothing else, the Sulan Inquiry sent the price of Bond Corporation shares through the floor and accelerated our dive into oblivion.

In addition to this, our position was further damaged when the Western Australian government reneged on its agreement with us regarding the petrochemical plant, an act that left us holding a worthless investment after paying $400 million for it. Peter Beckwith went on record publicly saying: 'You are not honouring the commitment you made to us and you are lying to the public and us. We spent money trying to help you with Rothwells and we went into the petrochemical plant because you promised all the necessary support — you gave a letter of commitment to us then withdrew it after we'd spent our money preparing for the project.'

There was a lot of political embarrassment brewing for the Western Australian government and to avoid it they too contributed to the commercial damage that began with the Sulan Inquiry.

Holmes à Court was out to get square with us because we were then the holders of the trophy companies he once owned. He couldn't cope with the thought that he'd failed and was facing a buy-out from an arch-rival — Bond Corporation. He turned into an adult version of a spiteful child who was fuelled by jealousy, deciding that the only way to save face and get some level of satisfaction would be to try to drag Bond Corporation under with him, and that's why he turned against us. It was total vindictiveness, to put it mildly.

He knew that Tiny Rowland didn't want us as part of Lonrho. So once the forced sale of Bell to us was complete he went off to London and met with him, and between them they worked out a scheme for ridding Lonrho of the Bond Corporation shareholding using a method that would more than likely bring the company down. It was Holmes à Court who supplied Lonrho with all the information on Bond Corporation and the true financial position of the Bell Group, a terrible financial position that we only discovered after the deal was complete.

One consolation for us in the Bell deal was that there was considerable cash in Bell Resources, and by putting this money together with our plan to become a single purpose company for our brewing interests, there would be sufficient money for us to rectify Bond Corporation's struggling financial position. But there was more trouble brewing. After we had completed the purchase of Bell Group shares, Adelaide Steamship, under John Spalvins, set in motion a purchase of shares that he would attempt to use as a greenmail against Bond Corporation. Several meetings took place and finally Spalvins said to me words to the effect of, 'if you want to put the brewing deal into Bell, buddy, then you have to deal with me. The only way you'll get me out and get your way is to buy me out at a higher price.' But we couldn't buy him out because we would have had to make the same offer to all the other shareholders in Bell Resources, so in effect Spalvins was attempting to hold us to ransom, preventing us from turning Bell Resources into a single purpose brewing company.

Then, thanks to Tiny Rowland and his mate Holmes à Court, other external pressures continued to undermine us. When we did the deal Holmes à Court had confirmed with us that all the loans in his group of companies were five- to seven-year money, something we could cope with. But once the circumstances changed around the ownership of Bell so did the attitude of the banks, because Rowland and Holmes à Court had been very successful in taking their manufactured documents to the banks. The banks Holmes à Court had in place for Bell decided to call in their loans and as a result Tony Oates was flat out selling Bell assets to pay them. I will admit that better due diligence on our part would have exposed the true nature of these loans, but with time rapidly going against us we took Holmes à Court's word on them being for up to seven years.

What Holmes à Court was doing in effect was alerting the market that he'd sold us a pup. I believe his long-term plan was to show the world that he could also save himself. He was hoping his deal with Rowland would lead to Bond Corporation collapsing, thus putting him in a position to buy back some of the Bell assets at fire sale prices. It was a nice plan, but he died before he could carry it out.

The other thing we realised in all this, after it was too late, was that the deal with Lonrho was an absolutely premeditated trap for Bond Corporation into which we walked wide-eyed. I had met Tiny Rowland on a number of occasions, socially and professionally, and I thought I got to know him quite well. One day Diana and I were invited to his home and during the visit he said: 'Alan, there's an aggressive shareholder in America who has bought around 14 per cent of my company. I've been watching how you've been operating around the world and I think we've got a lot in common. I'm thinking of retiring shortly, so why don't you buy into the company? It gets the Americans out of my hair and lets Bond Corporation get a solid foothold in Lonrho. This would let you come onto the Lonrho board and put you into a position where you can gradually take over Lonrho.'

It made sense ... until we bought the shares from the American institution. From that moment on Rowland did not want to know us. I went to see him in his office in London to develop the arrangement, only to be told by his assistant that he did not want to see me. Suddenly, we realised that the only reason Rowland wanted us to buy the shares was because he was scared of the American group and the power they might wield within Lonrho through the enormous financial resources they held. He wanted us to buy the shareholding to eliminate any threat of a takeover from the Americans and, as we had served that purpose, his next plan was to eliminate us. The only other thing I'll add about Rowland is that he set out to stuff us from the outset, and he did a good job. He is the only really evil man that I have ever met.

So there we were under attack from all sides. While Tony Oates was still trying to sort out the Bell Resources mess, I was faced with the Lonrho problem, and it had only one solution. I told the board that we had better bid to buy Lonrho. It was by then our only option if we were to save Bond Corporation — Lonrho had a lot more assets that we could sell off.

Incredibly I found the £1 billion needed to make the bid for Lonrho through Ed Roberts at the American Express bank group. He gave me a letter of commitment for the amount — one bank for the lot! However, the Bond Corporation board decided that the timing was wrong and we didn't make a bid. The whole affair with Lonrho, I must admit, was a big mistake.

While interest rates had rocketed to an unbelievable 20 per cent-plus we were managing to hang in and service our debt at the time, even at that level, because we had some really wonderful cash flow businesses. In another six to nine months, when rates came down, we would have been home and hosed. But for Bond Corporation all the dominoes were falling at a rapid rate and there was nothing we could do to stop them from tumbling. The market knew the banks were calling in the Bell loans and that we had to sell our assets in a bid to save the company, so they naturally played hardball on price. It was a Catch-22 situation for us because the last thing we wanted to do was sell assets under pressure — interest rates were up and asset values down. Even so, we stuck by our obligations to the best of our ability, so much so that we got rid of almost all the debt in Bell Group, other than to the bondholders.

It was suggested during this period that we were over-valuing our assets to provide a healthier financial picture of Bond Corporation, but that wasn't the case at all. Yes, we did revalue the brewing assets up by $1 billion to offset some of the losses that we'd incurred. The increased value was based on independent valuations. We were entitled to revalue these because the brewing assets were being held at historical values — they were in the books at the original cost. There were some differing opinions on values. We believed that the brewing assets should be valued at $4 billion while the independent valuation from Whitlam Turnbull came in at around $3.5 billion. But Whitlam Turnbull said that under the circumstances it was fair and reasonable to ask $4 billion because it was a monopoly business. The fact was that the assets in question were really prime assets, and quite frankly they justified a premium price. So, yes, we were asking Bell Resources to pay us more for the brewing asset than some of the market thought it was worth. Even so, if the market and the shareholders had come back and said, 'Look, notwithstanding it's a fair and reasonable price at $4 billion, you must sell it for $3.6 billion,' then we would have done just that. The deal would still have been okay for us. If we had managed to get the brewing assets into Bell, our companies would have all been saved and Bell would have made its money. There is no question about that.

The figure of $1.2 billion has continually popped up in stories about the Bell deal, namely that we had stripped Bell Resources of this amount. The $1.2 billion referred to was in fact the deposit that Bell Resources paid legally to Bond Corporation for the brewing assets. Independent directors on both the Bell and Bond Corporation boards considered this deal separately and voted in favour of the sale of the brewing assets to Bell. I agree that not every shareholder supported the plan, John Spalvins being one. But he had his own agenda. I always thought that he would support it at the last minute because it made commercial sense but what I didn't know was that the company he headed was in a desperate financial state. It was difficult for him go along with the Bell proposal even if he wanted to because he was struggling to stay afloat in his own pond.

The simple explanation of the Bell transaction, where Bell Resources would purchase the worldwide brewing assets for approximately $4 billion, is that from the deposit of $1.2 billion Bond Corporation would retire any inter-company loans. The balance of the purchase was to be satisfied by taking over the existing long-term debt within the worldwide brewing operations. Along the way there was to be a little bit of fine-tuning relevant to the deal that was to be based on the company's net asset position from time to time. Security was put in place to cover the $1.2 billion until such time as the transaction was completed. This was in the form of a promissory note secured by various assets, including the equity that we had in the brewing companies. While Bond Corporation was confident that the transaction would be completed there were clauses written into the agreement by the independent lawyers, stating that in the event that the shareholders did not approve of the transaction then the $1.2 billion was required to be repaid some three to six months later. It was felt that as there were other interested buyers for the worldwide brewing assets, this was a realistic approach. I stress again that the best legal advice confirmed for us that this deal was not fraudulent — it was all very legal. Sure no one knows how good any contract is until it is challenged legally, but as far as we were concerned the Bell deal could not have been structured any better legally.

Even so, while we were struggling to keep the wolves from the door the dogs were barking, grabbing every opportunity they could to make the headlines and state that we were stripping Bell Resources. If these individuals and the media had not tried to destroy us in the name of personal profile and sensational headlines then everyone would be very happy today. It was a case of 'let's create more panic by kicking Bond again'. Even so, while things were looking bad from the outside, Bond Corporation was still operating. We had no small creditors and held substantial cash in the bank — enough money to operate with cash. And we were selling off assets while not incurring any more liabilities.

While all these problems were unfolding in Australia the international companies I was developing and expanding were going very well. None had any problems. I had good audit committees in place and monitored each company's progress very carefully. But I now realise that I should have been doing the same thing in Australia. The problem was that once things started going wrong in Australia it all blew apart like a spring in an over-wound clock. It was something like six months from boom to gloom.

Even though a lot of people believed otherwise, the Bell moneys never went to Alan Bond — there was no treasure-trove of cash from Bell out there waiting to be claimed by me. Yes, some of the money associated with this transaction was lost, but it need not have been lost if the purchase of the brewing assets had been completed; if those assets were still in there today they would be making healthy profits. Yes, I did have some private investments that were owned outside Australia, like the *Irises* painting, and assets like an estate in England that is owned substantially by Eileen and my children in a trust. Even so, the family had to sell off many assets, including my son Craig's house in Queensland, to pay substantial settlements to the liquidators of Dallhold and Bond Corporation.

It was the National Australia Bank (NAB) that provided much of the ammunition for others to fire at us when it put a receiver into Bond Brewing by stealth in December 1989 over what it claimed was a $500 million debt. If you put a receiver into any public company then its credibility is destroyed. Our only recourse was to get the receiver out, and we did. The court threw him out, but the damage was done. We had faced tough times in the previous six months, but this action really put us on the back foot because all of a sudden everyone wanted their money.

The NAB was running scared at the time because of the tough financial conditions, yet Bond Corporation was one client they shouldn't really have been concerned about because they had plenty of security over our assets and they could call it. The problem they had with us was that our accounts were very complicated — for perfectly legitimate reasons. They were worldwide consolidated accounts which were a bit too much for the NAB to comprehend, and as a result panic set in because they saw us lending moneys backwards and forwards between companies, even though this was a normal part of our operation.

I had just launched a new maxi ocean racing yacht, *Drumbeat*, only a short time before the receiver arrived on the scene and I was looking forward to contesting the race for line honours in the Sydney to Hobart. It was to be a brief but pleasant respite from all the pressures that were surrounding the company and me. Certainly, had I sensed what was coming I wouldn't have done the race; so obviously, when we set sail on Boxing Day in 1989, I had no idea that problems were in the making for Bond Brewing.

It must be understood that Bond Corporation was not behind in any interest payments to the National Australia Bank, or anyone else for that matter. The basis of their argument when they went for a receiver to be appointed was that we were re-investing money outside the brewery business, putting cash from Swan Brewing into other assets, which is true. That made it a technical issue, the bank claiming that we were acting in conflict to the loan agreement. The fact that the court ruled in our favour when we appealed against the receiver being appointed and threw him out proved otherwise. The judge said: 'No, it is not a conflict. It's what they are entitled to do.' Tony Oates was a smart lawyer and he had devised a system for the movement of money, an action that we already knew through the best legal advice was not in conflict with the loan agreement. It involved deposits and investments and was perfectly legal.

I can only guess that the NAB went to the court as late as possible, just after Christmas and while I was on the high seas, to catch us unawares and make sure that we weren't there to fight. If that was their plan then it was very clever; they succeeded because there was no one from our side in court to say that we weren't doing anything illegal and that there were no grounds for the appointment of a receiver. It was as though the bank was a bully going through the back door of the court, having the judge listen to their story, who in turn said, 'Well if you want a receiver then here, it's granted.'

The first thing I knew about it was when we reached Hobart

aboard *Drumbeat*. We sailed home first and I was absolutely elated, but the moment I stepped ashore my friend Tracy Tyler took me to one side and told me that the receiver had been appointed to our brewing interests and that everything was falling down around our ears. My elation went from hero to zero in a flash as I desperately tried to gather my senses and comprehend the consequences of the move.

In fairness, I must say that part of the problem for the NAB might have been due to the fact that we had changed auditors, from Price Waterhouse to Arthur Andersen & Co. Price Waterhouse were our auditors up until about two years prior to the collapse of Bond Corporation. There had been an argument between Price Waterhouse and Tony Oates and Peter Beckwith relating to the sale of the TV stations into a new entity, a sale that recorded a profit. Price Waterhouse would not allow that profit to be recorded, despite having earlier agreed to it. They reversed their views at the very end of the audit period, so suddenly we lost a big swag of profit. I think it was about $90 million. Needless to say Tony Oates was not very happy, having relied on the assurances given earlier that the deal was acceptable. Tony subsequently decided to put the audit business out to tender and Arthur Andersen & Co got the job. I'd used Price Waterhouse for many years and continued to retain them for Dallhold because I liked the way they operated. I'm sure Arthur Andersen & Co was not as tight on the Bond accounts — they let things go that they should not have, and that had an impact on our credibility in some areas. These are all points based on reflection. It's easy to talk about it now, but that wasn't the case at the time.

Regardless of this though, nothing justified the NAB's actions in having a receiver appointed.

One thing Australia needs, unequivocally, is a Chapter 11 provision in company law as is the case in America. If such a system was in place we would have been able to save Bond Corporation, even after the NAB receiver was appointed to Bond Brewing. Chapter 11 is a protection mechanism that stops everyone for up to 12 months from grabbing assets or demanding loans be re-paid, something that gives the company much needed breathing space to get their house in order. More often than not receivers are appointed in Australia on a Friday evening and as a result the company has only the weekend to sort things out, and you can't continue to trade if you're insolvent on Monday morning.

Chapter 11 recognises that you may be insolvent, but it doesn't stop you reconstructing and having an orderly sell-off of assets. You are allowed to trade on and work towards getting your company out of trouble. This would have been particularly important for Bond Corporation when you consider the worldwide assets we held, including our major investment in Heileman Brewing in America.

With a Chapter 11 provision, secured creditors are prevented from claiming the asset until all of the stakeholders' considerations are put forward. Stakeholders include employees, lenders of various secured and unsecured classes, bondholders, shareholders, customers, and the communities that the company operates in. Chapter 11 stops a greedy bank coming in, taking the asset and saying, 'we're going to flog this off to the market to get our money back, and damn the rest of you.' That's effectively what they do. It allows everything to remain status quo so you can re-group and stave off bankruptcy. It doesn't stop the bank from getting their money back. However, the independent judge will take into account all of the stakeholders in considering any proposed reconstruction. This puts a company in a position where it can go and reconstruct the business with the existing shareholders, and can bring in new shareholders. Most importantly, you are not fighting fires all over the place at the same time. Interest payments also stop and you're not forced into a fire sale of assets; you are in a position to negotiate the best price. Nothing has to be liquidated tomorrow. Also under Chapter 11, if you need new working capital money so that you can continue operating in an orderly manner then the new money ranks first, above all the securities you already hold. For example, if the Hong Kong and Shanghai Banking Corporation held a $1 billion security over your major asset and you needed $300 million to keep going while your problems were addressed, the new money ranks before any other and is not at risk — so the opportunity is established for everyone to get a fair distribution. It is a very important issue because it puts the banks into a comfort zone. Chapter 11 means there is encouragement for the same banks to refinance a business, and that's what is needed in Australia.

In America, by having the Chapter 11 provision available, many banks step in to assist clients who are heading for financial difficulties before disaster arrives because they know that the safety net of Chapter 11 exists. And very importantly, there is no stigma in the financial community in America associated with this process, yet in Australia the appointment of a receiver conveys every possible dark image.

There is no question about the effectiveness of a Chapter 11 provision. Many important American companies faced with financial ruin have gone on to prosper and become great once again.

If there were only one more thing I could do for Australia it would be to see the government introduce a Chapter 11 process built on the American model.

At its peak Bond Corporation employed around 17 000 people and was worth about $2.7 billion in net shareholders' funds while Dallhold had 8000 employees and was worth $1.4 billion. To see both organisations sink so ingloriously, knowing that they could have been saved, was an emotionally crushing experience. I was also absolutely mortified by the fact that I was being accused of not caring about the shareholders and the losses they faced. It was because of the shareholders and not the losses confronting me that we fought so hard to fix the problems and protect the shareholders' investment. But the odds and time were stacked against us. Corporate snipers, whose sole intent was to wreck the company, ambushed us. So much of it came through surprise attacks that we just could not counter, especially when a massive tide of media sentiment was going against us. I accept that the media has a vital role to play in our community — and it must be remembered that media ownership was a significant part of our company — but it's extremely difficult to counter biased and totally negative reports.

Even though I was the biggest loser as a shareholder in Bond Corporation, it was distressing for me to know so many shareholders had lost so much. One doesn't like to see anyone lose in any deal where shares have been purchased in good faith. In reality though the stock market is not dissimilar to gambling, it's like going to the racetrack and putting your money on the horse you believe will win. Investing in companies is speculative and investors have to accept the fact that they can lose their money. There are many, many losers in the stock market every day — one could argue that for every buyer and seller someone is losing. We have seen around $3 trillion wiped off the American NASDAQ market over a three-month period with huge write-downs in stocks; investors took hard hits on their investments. As far as Bond Corporation shareholders were concerned, we did everything possible to protect them, but our attackers just would not give us the time to do the job. When you are a shareholder you are behind all the lenders, and all the liabilities of the company have to get satisfied before the shareholders get anything. If the company assets are large assets then a temporary downturn in values could be critical. But given time they will come back, usually in less than 12–18 months, as we have seen with so many of the former assets of Bond Corporation and Dallhold.

Take for example the Chile Telephone Company and what happened to us there. Today it's worth billions of dollars, and at the time of our demise it was an asset we definitely didn't want to sell. We sold that, not because we had a debt we couldn't pay — it only had a small debt of $25 million that we could have paid any time — but because the Hong Kong and Shanghai Banking Corporation said: 'If you sell that asset and send that money ... $500 million, or what ever you can get for it ... back to Bond Corporation by the end of the month we will extend all your other loan facilities for you.'

So in a period of three weeks we did as they demanded and turned the money back into Bond Corporation. Now I believe that part of the reason, if not the entire reason, for the bank wanting us to do that was because their image was being damaged in the media and through their exposure to us. This was one of the banks that following our America's Cup victory in 1983 was clamouring to deal with us, and then suddenly we were out of favour, particularly because of the Sulan Inquiry.

The fact is that no one needed to lose and Bond Corporation should not have collapsed. I'm not talking years to sort it out — I'm talking about taking between six and nine months. That's all it was going to take. Bond Corporation and Dallhold had fantastic assets — we had simply financed the wrong way when interest rates went out of control and reached 25 per cent.

It must be said that what followed the final collapse of the company was the most shameful sell-off of assets that has ever taken place in Western Australia. Look at West Australian Newspapers, a monopoly business, and a premium business with a brand-new plant that cost about $500 million to build. It was worth every bit of $1 billion, yet the bankers forced a fire sale and sold it for $290 million. Within six months it was refloated and the market valued it at approximately $1 billion.

CHAPTER ELEVEN
TRIAL BY MEDIA

The repercussions from the collapse of Bond Corporation and Dallhold reverberated around the world, but the impact was no greater than on the Bond Corporation and Bell shareholders.

But while we continually hear about their losses, which were awful, there is one thing that is very much forgotten. Bond Corporation shareholders made very good money for many years. There were a lot of people who bought in at 10 cents a share, but we never heard about them and how much they made when they sold out at anywhere between $2 and $5. The fact is that many Bond Corporation shareholders made more money over the years than they lost. It must also be remembered that we paid dividends for many years.

And it shouldn't be forgotten that the biggest loser of all when these companies went down was Alan Bond, who held 51 per cent of Bond Corporation. Dallhold, through its subsidiaries, had also loaned Bond Corporation $250 million in convertible loan notes and lost all of that. And that was only the start.

Bond Corporation could have survived a very substantial write-down, and a significant loss, but wasn't given the chance. Compared with other corporations around the world, like AOL Time Warner, Marconi and even AMP in Australia — to name a few — ours just didn't compare. But the fact is that these things do happen to companies, and it must be remembered that it's not something that the executives want to see happen. These situations can come about if the growth of the company is too quick and one hasn't analysed the consequences if something goes wrong, like interest rates that become exorbitant. And once things do start exploding all around you your brain explodes with them. It doesn't stop — you just keep tossing things over and over in your mind. I continually asked myself: 'What could I have done. Why did I let it happen?' The anguish of failure is not a pleasant experience.

Above all, the one aspect of the disaster that hurt me most was the realisation that I had let people down. I let my family down, my friends, people who had worked for me all their lives, and the shareholders. It was emotionally devastating. I had the weight of the world on my shoulders and it's extremely difficult to cope because there you are one minute a high achiever, a billionaire, who had done so much in life, and the next minute there's a catastrophic failure to face. It is very difficult to live with. It wasn't the money that I lost that mattered, it was the emotional trauma that came with realising the impact of the disaster on others. I kept relating back to the old adage that you come into the world with nothing and leave with the same. I asked myself if this catastrophe was meant to happen for some God-given reason. Was my piece of enjoyment on earth coming to an end? Was I being prepared for a better life ahead? I do believe an after-life exists. I am a fatalist. Events don't 'just happen' — they happen for a reason.

Also hanging heavily over me was the realisation that Bond Corporation and Dallhold had sunk when salvation was so close. There were so many opportunities to stop the loss and turn things around. A classic example came with Geoff Hill, a merchant banker who went into Bell Resources as the chairman, appointed by John

Spalvins after I lost control of that company in 1990. If Hill had completed the Bond Brewing purchase as we planned it for Bell then everybody's assets in Bell Resources would have remained intact. It would have become a beautiful business. Hill originally came in as a supporter and adviser to Bond Corporation while at the same time supporting and advising John Spalvins from his side of the Bell deal, as a Bell shareholder. That meant that when all the problems came for Bell Resources, Hill had to play for both teams. He caused assets to be sold off way too cheaply, instead of keeping them and building them.

Compare what happened with Bell and what was done with Adelaide Steamship Company when it struck trouble. The banks didn't push Adelaide Steamship and that allowed the company to build the asset over a number of years so it could be sold for the right price. The banks got almost all their money back, all because there was a good custodian in there to manage the business. The Bell Resources shareholders would not have lost the money they did if the brewing deal had been completed after I got out of Bond Corporation. And I must stress that the Bell loss wasn't $1.2 billion as we keep hearing. They got hundreds of millions back through the sale of assets, but they could have got a lot more. Better still, if they had kept the brewing assets, taken up the debt and then raised additional capital to reduce that debt, they would have owned 45 per cent of the brewing industry in Australia and a big slice of the industry in America. I have no doubt that if the deal had run then the company would not only have survived but become an enormous brewing business, like Allied Lyons today. That was where we had it headed. It could have returned a fortune to Bell Resources shareholders, just as we had planned.

My corporate relationship with Tiny Rowland came to an end in September 1989 when we were forced to sell out of Lonrho at a loss of $120 million — a fire sale triggered by the dire financial straits Bond Corporation was facing, but a sale I was very pleased to see behind me because it ended the relationship. By then the financial floodgates were open and there was no way we could shut them. One month after quitting Lonrho we were confronted with having to announce Australia's then largest-ever corporate loss — $980 million. Then in December 1989 came the NAB's deceitful move on Bond Brewing. The end was nigh for Bond Corporation and Dallhold.

The following year, 1990, was the worst. In August, after reaching an agreement with the NCSC I resigned from the Bond group. It was stated that for there to be any hope for a reconstruction of the company there had to be a change of chairman. My resignation came at a shareholders' meeting and the moment I announced it the majority of the shareholders present were calling for me not to go. At this meeting I passed the role of chairman over to Peter Lucas, from Sydney. It was not long after this that Tony Oates and Peter Mitchell followed me out of the company.

By this time it seemed we were keeping the Australian judicial system in business as we battled our opponents on many fronts. They were coming at us from every direction and we had no intention of surrendering. We knew what had happened and why we had been brought down, so we were going to fight for our rights wherever possible. Dallhold succumbed to liquidation in July 1991 and the following month Bond Corporation went into a Scheme of Arrangement.

But the worst situation for me came in December 1990. The debacle around the failed rescue of Rothwells had resurfaced and I was the centre of attention. I was charged with dishonestly inducing Brian Coppin to support the rescue.

This whole sorry saga started just days after the stock market crash in 1987 and ended with me in jail, simply because I answered a call for help from leading federal politicians and the then Premier of Western Australia, Brian Burke.

I believe that it is here, the rescue attempt of Rothwells, that the roots for all the problems associated with the collapse of my empire are found.

It all started just after I arrived in Rome on our company jet for important meetings. I received a telephone call from Peter Beckwith who told me that Rothwells, the merchant bank privately owned by Laurie Connell and his family, was on the verge of collapse. There had been a run on its cash reserves the day after the stock market crash on 20 October, Black Tuesday. Everyone wanted their deposits back and the bank didn't appear to have the money. The government said that if Rothwells went down there would be carnage in companies and institutions throughout Western Australia, and the whole of Australia for that matter; it could well have lead to a panic situation in the entire Australian banking system. Burke and the federal politicians wanted me to return to Perth immediately to coordinate a rescue mission.

The important point to consider here is that there was nothing in the rescue mission for me or Bond Corporation. I was just asked to help, and considering who was doing the asking I had no hesitation in turning the plane around straight away and heading home. Later, it did eventuate that our breweries had some deposits in Rothwells, but they weren't significant amounts, certainly not enough to worry us or make me want to rush to the rescue.

One thing for certain is that I didn't go into the rescue mission for Laurie Connell's sake — my relationship with him wasn't what many people would have you believe. He was no great mate of mine, but he and Peter Beckwith were good friends; that's how my apparent alignment with him appeared to be maintained. Laurie and Peter shared interests in racehorses and gambling. When it came to business deals between Connell and Bond Corporation, they were negotiated between Beckwith and Connell. I wasn't involved. I had to agree to them, but I was what you might call once removed. I was not removed, however, when it came to this rescue attempt and the public exposure to Rothwells. I looked upon the effort as being good for Western Australia and Australia. Bond Corporation supported it publicly on that basis.

I was exhausted when I arrived back in Perth so I grabbed a few hours sleep before going to the Rothwells office to help get a plan of action in place. It was a weekend and all the key players were there, including Laurie Connell, a big team from Bond Corporation, the managing director of Wardley Australia (the Hong Kong and Shanghai Banking Corporation's Australian merchant banking group) James Yonge, and senior Wardley's men Kerry Roxborough and John Dickinson. The state government, which had about $50 million with Rothwells, was represented by the Deputy Premier and Treasurer, David Parker, along with Kevin Edwards, Premier Burke's most powerful adviser and deputy chairman of the State Government Insurance Commission. Brian Burke participated by telephone and in private meetings with Connell over the weekend.

The first sign of trouble for Rothwells came only 24 hours before I got the call in Rome. The state government had then asked Peter Beckwith and Tony Oates to take a look at the situation and see if there was anything Rothwells could do to save itself. That meant we had the benefit of Peter and Tony's brief investigation to guide us, but it still wasn't much. Peter had asked Wardley to give an independent financial evaluation and see if they could assist in a rescue operation and they agreed, so Bond Corporation sent a plane to Sydney to pick up the Wardley team and fly them to Perth.

When we sat down and started pooling all the information that was available I realised the extent of the problem we were facing. It was huge. What I saw on paper was confirmation of something I'd sensed for some time — that Rothwells might be travelling badly. But it wouldn't be until Wardley's had completed their investigation of the figures that we would get a real idea of what funding would be required to save Rothwells. The only figure being offered was Connell's estimate of $100 million. All we knew was that we were faced with a total disaster, and we only had the weekend to sort it out because if the run on the bank continued on the Monday morning then it would go under.

Rothwells was a little unusual in its structure in that it was a second-tier lender holding a lot of deposits from mums and dads around town as well as a large number of institutions, like the Catholic Church, which had $50 million in there belonging to its Schools' Fund. These two points concerned me greatly and influenced my decision to help. Additionally, the Western Australian government was exposed for about $50 million, and there were deposits from trade unions, deposits that had been encouraged by Connell's political connections within the government on the premise that Connell was someone on the way up, a major political supporter and a close associate of Premier Burke. Connell had become one of the government's favourite sons because he was lending money back into businesses in Western Australia, something the bigger banks weren't doing. As far as the government was concerned, whatever he did with Rothwells would help the community.

As there was no certainty as to exactly how much money was needed to salvage the bank — our best calculations at the time put it at somewhere between $100 million and $160 million — I saw only one solution. I said to everyone: 'Look, we're only going to get one shot at raising the money, so let's get twice the amount of money we think we need. That way we make sure we have every chance of saving the bank and making it strong for the future.' So the decision was that we would seek $160 million equity if the National Australia Bank would provide a matching amount. The bank agreed, but only after the state government gave a quasi-guarantee to cover the NAB's involvement. Also, the reason Peter Beckwith and Tony Oates had organised for Wardley's to come in and help was because we needed an organisation to underwrite a $160 million share issue, which they did on the proviso that there was a certain level of sub-underwriting. It was proposed to be a rights issue, where existing shareholders were to be given the opportunity to subscribe, although this was not expected to bring a great response.

Using a whiteboard a plan was developed that had input from David Parker, James Yonge, Kevin Edwards, Peter Beckwith, Laurie Connell and myself, where we would contact people around the country who we thought might be able to help by putting some money in. To make that happen we split into small groups and took to the phones. I called the likes of Brian Coppin, Dick Pratt and other prominent corporate people and arranged commitments of $5 million or more to the cause while Bond Corporation sub-underwrote about $17 million of the preference issue that was established. We all worked around the clock and by the end of the weekend we had a satisfactory list for Wardley's to commit to the underwriting of the $160 million.

With the job complete, or at least with us believing the job was complete, there were smiles all round from the state government, which announced with great relief at a press conference on the Monday, that the rescue mission for Rothwells had been successful. We had $160 million promised from the share issue and a further $160 million from the National Australia Bank conditional on the Western Australian government's guarantee for that amount. We saw that this $320 million would make Rothwells an even stronger second financing institution for Western Australian business than it previously was. At the same time any depositor who wished their money to be returned could be accommodated.

For me it was time to get back on the jet and head for Rome, where I had a meeting scheduled with the city's newly elected Mayor. But before I left Perth Peter Beckwith suggested that with so much effort having gone into this 48-hour salvage job on the part of Bond Corporation, we should follow up on a discussion that we had had with Connell the previous evening where it was suggested that a success fee might be considered appropriate. I said that it should be discussed with Connell, and that's where I left it. Subsequently Connell agreed with Beckwith that the fee was appropriate, as did the government representatives, including David Parker. But nothing was set in concrete in those discussions and nothing was put in writing. It was a case of 'if, if, if, if and if ...' all very wishy-washy. It wasn't until about 11 days later that Beckwith and Connell discussed the fee once more, and it was decided then that a letter should be formulated outlining an arrangement for Bond Corporation to receive $16 million, subject to certain success parameters within the Rothwells organisation.

Another thing I did before leaving for Rome was visit Brian Coppin at his home, which was close to mine, early on the Monday morning.

When I returned to Perth from that Rome trip I had a barbecue lunch with Brian Coppin at his home. He asked how things were going with the Rothwells rescue. I told him I believed everything was okay, and knowing that Beckwith and Connell had by then negotiated a fee and outlined it in a letter, I told Brian that it had been decided that Bond Corporation was going to get a fee for its part in putting the rescue together. It was something that I didn't have to tell Brian, but I chose to do so because the offer of a fee was an afterthought and was only going to happen if the rescue bid was successful. As it turned out Bond Corporation never did receive any fee.

It was the fact that I didn't mention the fee to Brian when I saw him on the Monday morning after the rescue mission was completed — which I couldn't do anyway because nothing was confirmed and it was possible that it might not even happen — that led to Malcolm McCusker QC, the state government's special investigator into the eventual collapse of Rothwells, deciding he had the ammunition to go after me. He interpreted this to be a secret commission that should have been disclosed to those who put money into the rescue bid.

Subsequently, I was charged with not disclosing a commission to be gained not by me, but Bond Corporation — there was no personal gain. The entire scenario was beyond comprehension. Here I was on the wrong side of the law, even though the thought of the commission, and the letter detailing it, didn't exist at the time of the money-raising effort and was never paid.

The run continued on Rothwells and within a matter of weeks the whole $320 million we had raised was gone. Fortunately though, a lot of people and institutions we initially set out to help were able to get their money out, including the Catholic Church.

Panic was starting to set in for the state government because they were exposed through organisations like the State Government Insurance Office, and there were question marks over the approval of these investments.

With the situation looking much worse for Rothwells, Laurie Connell really had his back to the wall. He said to me: 'We've had that rescue mission and it's still left me in the shit. The government's now up for another $160 million because of its guarantee to the National Australia Bank, $160 million they won't get back if we go arse up.' Connell said the government faced another dilemma — its guarantees were provided without proper cabinet approvals. These guarantees came via associated entities, the State Superannuation Board and the State Government Insurance Commission. The government had organised, through Edwards, to have these moneys put in but few people knew about it; it was all done under the table. In short, the government was in cahoots with Connell and destined for a lot of strife if ever details of what they had done surfaced. Their backsides were completely exposed.

Soon we were confronted with the fact that Bond Corporation and everyone else might lose the money put into the rescue bid because the Rothwells financial hole was enormous. The government was becoming desperate because it then knew that it might see Rothwells go under and as a consequence also lose the Kwinana petrochemical plant it had planned to build with Connell and his partner, Dallas Dempster. If those two deals fell over then the government's failure of due diligence on Rothwells and its deposit of money there without the right approvals would become public knowledge. As a consequence, the government would inevitably fall. Their only option was to put the pressure on Connell and Dempster by telling them that they needed to find another $400 million for Rothwells.

In the ensuing weeks there were extensive discussions between David Parker and Peter Beckwith with regard to developments around Rothwells. Things were still looking bad, so in a desperate bid to stop Rothwells from going 'arse up' Connell came to me and said that he had an idea based around the petrochemical deal. He told me how he and Dempster, the developer of Burswood Casino in Perth, had a company, Petrochemical Industries, which held a mandate from the state government for the establishment of the petrochemical plant at Kwinana. The site had been allocated and all the engineering drawings had been done. Connell said: 'Why don't you buy this from us for $400 million? If you do then the government will do other things for you so you can get your money back.' His plan was to use the $400 million to again try to buy Rothwells out of trouble. The fact was that the petrochemical project as it stood was probably worth only $100 million, and it was going to cost in excess of $1 billion to develop. Our company, Bond Petroleum, had originally applied for the contract to create the plant, but somehow it went to Connell and Dempster, despite their lack of experience in such a project. We were one of the very few groups in town capable of doing the job, something that we showed in developing the Harriet Oilfield. Our ability to build the plant was further reinforced by the fact that we had Zoltan Merszei, the former president, CEO and chairman of Dow Chemicals in America as a director of Bond Corporation. His vast experience in the industry was an exceptional asset for us in projects such as this.

Connell's Kwinana deal was put to the Bond Corporation board where it was knocked back. It was one of the few times that there had been a split vote on the board. Peter Beckwith, Tony Oates and Peter Mitchell were insisting that we should proceed while the independent directors sided with me because we were not satisfied that the government would meet its commitments. Again our board policy that a majority vote didn't necessarily rule had surfaced, the understanding being that no project would go ahead if there were a number of negatives associated with it. Basically you had to have unanimous support for proposals. For me, paying $400 million for the initial deal, and then being faced with investing an additional $1 billion to get it up and running didn't make commercial sense. There were too many uncertainties, the biggest one being that the government offered to supply the gas but would not guarantee a price.

The decision by the Bond Corporation board to reject Connell's proposal meant only one thing — Rothwells would fail. The pressure immediately returned to the government, and Premier Burke and his deputy David Parker literally began harassing Beckwith, Mitchell and Oates, asking that they try to get me on side and have the board reconsider the proposal. The question from

Burke and Parker was: 'What does the government need to do to get Bond Corporation to step in again and help save the day?' We were the only people with cash in the bank after the stock market crash; we were still running pretty well, so as far as the government was concerned, we were the only game in town that could help. They knew they weren't going to get any more money for Rothwells from anywhere else. The decision from the top was that the government would guarantee the $1 billion needed to develop the plant by in turn guaranteeing not to charge us for the supply of gas to the plant. Suddenly Kwinana was a very appealing project for us because the gas component of the plant's operational costs was around $100 million annually, and we weren't going to have to pay for it — it was going to be a highly profitable venture.

While all this was going on I was in London on business. Beckwith, Mitchell and Oates liked what they were hearing, so Beckwith and Mitchell rang me and asked if they could come to London to put a further proposal to Alan Birchmore and me. Alan, a fellow director, was with me in London. This time the proposal contained a letter from David Parker guaranteeing that the government would provide not only the gas but also a financial guarantee. It should also be noted that by this time the government and Connell had renegotiated Dallas Dempster's position — he was to receive only $50 million from the sale while Rothwells received the remaining $350 million.

On what was being offered, our projections showed that for an outlay of $400 million the plant would be up and running and providing us with a couple of hundred million profit each year. Better still, the numbers said the value of the plant would probably be $3 billion. It was almost too good to be true, a no-lose deal for Bond Corporation, and on that basis I then supported the proposal. I telephoned the other Bond Corporation directors, discussed it with them, and they also agreed.

When I approved the deal it was subject to the government signing a document guaranteeing their end of it, otherwise it was not going to go ahead. The government then advised that an act of parliament needed to be passed to do this; however, in the meantime the relevant minister, David Parker, who was the Minister for Mines, would sign it on behalf of the government. He did just that and we held that signed document in our safe. That was good enough for us to proceed, and with so much pressure on the government to keep Rothwells afloat, we put our money into the deal so that Rothwells could continue trading. In the process the government grabbed the opportunity to withdraw much of the money it had deposited with the bank.

Our trust in the government was totally unjustified. My original fears that they wouldn't stand by their promises were right. They reneged on the deal. Incredibly though, while we had played a fair game on this deal, when this entire debacle finally unravelled and was investigated, we were classified as being the bad boys, regardless of the fact that we put up our money and stood by our end of the deal. We proposed suing the government because we had the guarantee document in our possession signed by the minister, but as it turned out other circumstances overtook the situation, namely me being charged over the supposed secret commission followed by the financial slide of Bond Corporation.

It was when Rothwells foundered, about a year after the first rescue attempt, that Malcolm McCusker entered the scene to investigate. David Parker and Premier Brian Burke went to prison as a result of this inquiry, although the only thing they could get Burke on was a deal over stamps.

I was dragged in and charged with dishonestly concealing a commission. It was beyond comprehension for me — McCusker was claiming that I hadn't disclosed the commission to Brian Coppin, but I had done just that after I learnt that there was to be a commission to be paid to Bond Corporation. It must be said that Brian didn't initiate the action that resulted in me going to prison — it was McCusker. He went hunting and found me. I was in his firing line. My relationship with Brian Coppin is still good today.

Time would tell that we weren't even remotely close with our original estimates on the amount needed to salvage Rothwells. It would eventually be revealed, years later, that around $600 million was missing. Connell had been using depositors' money to finance personal share purchases, transactions that were cleverly hidden in the accounts, yet they tallied hundreds of millions of dollars.

The shock of appearing in court on a criminal charge when you know you are innocent is almost beyond description. It brought considerable humiliation for me, and even more grief when I saw greater humiliation being heaped upon my family.

The first realisation of what I faced and what my family and friends were going through came as I entered the court the first time as the charged party. It's one of the most humbling, emotionally crushing experiences anyone can have. You come up to this particular court in Perth from the cellblock underneath by climbing a winding staircase to the dock where, when you arrive, you find a police officer waiting to sit alongside you. My immediate reaction was to avoid looking out into the gallery because you know everyone is looking at you — it's humiliation beyond anything else you've ever endured. At the same time you try to put on a brave face for the family and friends who you know are out there in the courtroom. I'm sure it's the same experience for everyone who appears in court, but I think the level of devastation is proportionate to the walk of life you come from. I'd been dragged down from the top to the lowest possible level by the system itself.

After a four-day trial in May 1992 I was convicted on evidence, particularly from Laurie Connell, that would eventually prove to be false. Needless to say it was a high-profile case — one of Australia's richest men was being vilified — so the headlines were horrible. In court I kept asking myself why this was happening, and before long, as the case progressed, one thing became very apparent — Western Australia's Director of Public Prosecutions, John McKechnie, was on a very definite vendetta to get me. And he was not the only one. There's no doubt in my mind that McKechnie's eloquent theatrics before the jury contributed in a big way to me being sent to jail. He should have been on Broadway. He would stand there looking like a vampire in a black cape, waving his arms around while saying something like, 'we're talking $16 million dollars here. They were going to get $16 million out of this and not tell anyone.' The jury got caught up in this emotion. To the average person who makes $40 000 a year, $16 million is a lot of money. The fact that in the end there was no money didn't seem to matter. On the other hand my lawyers just dealt with the facts, not the emotions.

If the court experience wasn't enough then hearing the jury declare that I was guilty absolutely gutted me. I was shattered — the victim of a political and corporate assassination. And to cap it off, Laurie Connell, the man who was so pleased that I had been able to do so much to help save Rothwells, had lied to put me in jail.

I was sentenced to two and a half years, the judge saying that a jail term was the only appropriate sentence because of the amount of money involved. The minimum term I would be required to serve was nine months. Small consolation. The emotion in the court at the time the sentence was announced was overwhelming. Eileen was distraught, and friends just sat there looking at me in stunned disbelief.

I was escorted out of the court to be shipped off to Wooroloo Prison, which is in the hills just to the north of Perth. The police either inadvertently or deliberately put me in a small prison panel van for the trip, a move that created the perfect photo opportunity for the press photographers. I was put into the cage-like back of the vehicle where there were no seats. You could only squat or sit on the floor. It turned into a feeding frenzy for photographers as the van left the court. Their cameras were pressed up against the windows of the van as they desperately tried to get shots of me in this most desperate state. I was again paying a price for profile.

The feeling of emptiness I endured for the 40 minutes it took to transport me to the prison was indescribable. I was mortified. I had done nothing wrong, yet here I was on my way to prison. The time the journey took was also enough for word to go around among the prisoners at Wooroloo that I was on my way there. When I arrived and was taken from the van I could hear them cheering. They were welcoming me in a very positive sense. And it was interesting to listen to the comments from the officers when I did get there. Some could not believe that I'd been found guilty and were quick to say: 'You'll win on appeal straight away. Things like this just don't stand up.'

After I was processed I was assigned to a bed in a dormitory with 11 other prisoners, including a number of Aboriginal men. It was a horrid baptism by fire into prison culture. I immediately learnt that my new world involved the law of the jungle, survival of the fittest, because as soon as I would fall asleep others, usually the Aborigines, would come and pinch my blankets. There was nothing I could do about it, especially if it was the Aborigines doing the taking because there were four of them prepared to take me on if I tried to get the blankets back. What made matters worse was that it was winter and the small windows up high in the dormitory had been broken, so the cold air whistled through the place. It was like living in an icebox. I sat there night after night and froze. I'd put on every bit of clothing I had and climb under two big blankets on a wire bed that had a mattress about one-inch thick. All the time I'd be sleeping with one eye open, ready to fight for my blankets if anyone came near me. One day I asked about getting the windows fixed and was told by the wardens that it would only be done when the inmates stopped breaking them.

The bleak conditions, and the stress I was under, had to take its toll and not long after I entered Wooroloo I suffered a minor heart attack and finished up in hospital. This heart condition worsened with time and not long after I was released from prison I had to have open-heart surgery to replace my aortic valve. That was in February 1993. During the heart operation I unfortunately suffered five embolisms — minor strokes. These, together with the trauma of the six-hour operation, caused me some level of memory loss, something that is not unusual in major open-heart surgery. In addition I began to experience bouts of depression that would last for some time.

Hygiene in the prison was one of my biggest concerns, a concern I would carry with me in the prison experiences I would endure in the ensuing years. There is a very, very high percentage of the prison population who have herpes in one form or another. Some had it before they were jailed and others contracted it through their drug habits, but it is true to say that every prisoner is potentially exposed to the disease. You have to be very careful when it comes to what food you eat, where you take your food from and what utensils you use. I used to sterilise my eating utensils in hot water before I used them. I was fortunate, but other prisoners I met did contract the disease while in jail.

As soon as I went to Wooroloo my lawyers started preparing an appeal, and 90 days after I arrived at the jail the appeal was successful. The judges in the Appellate Court said that I must be released immediately, quashing the conviction on the grounds that a jury could well believe fresh evidence alleging that Laurie Connell lied at the trial — and had the original jury heard the same evidence it is highly likely that I would have been acquitted. The new evidence came from a builder, Max Healy, who told the appeal court that Laurie Connell had told him that as he did not want to be seen to be standing alone in the aftermath of the Rothwells disaster it was his intention to bring down as many leading businessmen as possible by associating them with the collapse. Healy also said that Connell had asked him to lie in another court case where Connell was charged with criminal offences. The judges also said that even if I was guilty the maximum penalty should be no more than a $4000 fine.

It seemed that as soon as I was out of Wooroloo the Crown decided I should go on trial again on the same charge, notwithstanding the fact that they could only secure a $4000 fine if they were successful. As I expected, I was found not guilty, but the experience started me wondering how many people out there wanted to get me. And why? I was also wondering what the jury in the original trial must have been thinking when I was subsequently acquitted; they'd listened to all the emotion, watched the theatrics, struggled to understand it all and still found me guilty, only to learn later that their verdict had been overturned.

There was one big winner in all this — the prosecutor, McKechnie. He had a rapid rise up the ranks following his theatrics in this trial. I was his ticket to success.

All this time, leading up to and during the period when I was charged then sent to jail over the Rothwells deal, the dogs had been let loose via the Sulan Inquiry, which had a mandate to investigate our companies and determine if there had been any breaches of law in our dealings while we fought to keep the group afloat.

This and two other investigations would go on for more than six years, but even after that period there was nothing the investigators could lay their hands on as an offence. They came up with a number of recommendations for charges, but if there had been an offence it would have been obvious from the outset and I would have been charged then. But no, it was just an ongoing search and destroy mission.

Eventually there were two lots of charges purported to be emerging from the inquiries. One related to the purchase of the painting *La Promenade* in 1983 for around $4.6 million, and the other was about our acquisition and operation of Bell Resources.

La Promenade was first on the agenda in June 1993. This charge was seen by members of the judicial system across the world as more of a joke than anything else. It was a trumped-up charge that alleged I took away the opportunity for Bond Corporation to buy a painting at the end of a lease arrangement. I went to jail for three years as a result of it. Remember, I owned 51 per cent of the company, and the company owed me a lot — I'd already loaned it $250 million. And, if it had been right for Bond Corporation to buy the painting, if they wanted it, then they could have had it. Again, there was no illegal action on my part, but unfortunately for me circumstances prevented Tony Oates and Peter Mitchell giving evidence to support me, and Peter Beckwith had passed away in 1990. They were the only people who knew exactly what the arrangements were.

It's quite a complicated story. *La Promenade* is a painting by 19th century French impressionist Edouard Manet, which was leased by Bond Corporation from an American bank soon after the America's Cup win in 1983. Bond Corporation and Dallhold had separate offices in the same building in Perth, and because I held a desire to have the Bond Corporation executives develop their own managerial talents without me being continually there looking over their shoulders and applying the strong will that I have, I deliberately had my Bond Corporation chairman's suite in the Dallhold offices. It was a planned move on my part to get some individuality into Bond Corporation as it expanded. I had all my Bond Corporation personal assistants and general staff working around me in the Dallhold headquarters.

It was because so much Bond Corporation business was done in Dallhold offices that Bond Corporation agreed to pay me a reimbursement of costs, and that included the decoration of the offices, boardroom and dining room. Many paintings from my private art collection were on display in the Dallhold office as part of this decoration, which as I have said was as much a headquarters for Bond Corporation as it was for Dallhold. In fact, when overseas financiers and bankers came to do business with Bond Corporation they would meet with me in my office at Dallhold.

La Promenade was hung in the main dining room at Dallhold after it was leased. The lease led to an arrangement whereby Bond Corporation could make the lease payments on the painting and obtain a benefit by writing off to tax the lease costs of the painting. At the same time this arrangement was recognised as part of the payment to Dallhold for office facilities and decorations. The point here is that a company cannot, by law, say it owns a leased painting because the convention is that when you lease something, it actually belongs to the leasing company. Ownership comes when you pay the residual at the end of the lease. The *La Promenade* lease was for five years and I made an arrangement with Peter Beckwith where, when the lease was up, I or Dallhold would pay the residual amount and have the painting valued, and I would then account to Bond

Corporation for the money it had paid and half of any increased value. Bond Corporation never actually had possession of the painting as it was always on display in Dallhold's premises. Dallhold was also responsible for the insurance of the painting and its maintenance.

This arrangement around *La Promenade* was outlined in a three-line notice at a Bond Corporation board meeting in 1983. The lease cost was $100 000 a month, not a significant transaction when you consider that at the same meeting we were dealing with the $276 million acquisition of the Grace Brothers department stores. It meant that with so much happening at the meeting the *La Promenade* deal was far from a major event. So *La Promenade* got little attention at the meeting. I do know that we purposely left the arrangement somewhat open ended so Bond Corporation could manoeuvre it to a point where it could claim the maximum taxation advantage at a later date. There was nothing illegal about what we were doing, but when I was faced with the charges in court I was left to explain a peculiar three-line paragraph in the notes from the board meeting all those years ago. The note said in effect that Bond Corporation was the owner of the painting, but it could never be the owner of the painting because the leasing company always owned it. In hindsight, the arrangement was not detailed well enough in the minutes at the time.

This Dallhold/Bond Corporation agreement on *La Promenade* surfaced with the company auditors, Arthur Andersen, in the mid-1980s before the expiry of the lease. It was nothing extraordinary, but the auditor quite rightly asked: 'What's this payment that's been made for the lease of this painting? What's the situation? Bond Corporation has been making the payment. Where is the asset?' Peter Beckwith explained the arrangement, including the fact that Bond Corporation had been getting the tax benefit from it. There were some differing views on the tax benefit at that time, but the fact was that Bond Corporation had no right to actually acquire the painting at the end of the lease.

The auditor then said that the arrangement had to be formalised: 'You've had an informal relationship going with a director and you can't do that. It must be a formal agreement. You have to have a proper contract done, the board must approve it, and it has to be disclosed to the shareholders.' That's exactly what happened. The contract, which was quite complicated, was drawn up under the instructions of Peter Beckwith, the bottom line being that any profit on the painting would be shared at the end of the lease. The long and the short of it was that the contract went to the board and the board retrospectively approved it — 11 directors approved it, and I didn't vote. The contract went through and was disclosed in the annual accounts. There was no problem with the shareholders, however the government investigators picked it up later on, and they decided that the deal hadn't been done in accordance with the law.

Bond Corporation's financial woes were continuing to accelerate so the decision was made to contact the lease company and finalise the $1.2 million residual payment that was verbally agreed to at the time of the lease. However, there was nothing in the lease arrangement with the Australian subsidiary of the American-based bank detailing the actual arrangement over the payment of a residual. But such an arrangement was the convention and adhered to by Australian finance companies and banks on the lease contracts they held. Our approach obviously rang a bell for the bank because the next thing we knew the American headquarters of Chemical All-States had decided that it wasn't going to accept a residual payment — it was going to keep the painting. The bank's attitude was influenced by the fact that it was quitting Australia so didn't give a damn about convention. Obviously they wanted to auction off the painting, which had increased in value substantially, and pick up a tidy profit. However, I didn't care how much it had gone up in value because I didn't want to see it sold.

Bond Corporation was the face of the deal as it was making the lease payments, so the decision was that the bank should be sued. Their response to that suggestion was simply: 'Okay, take us to court if you like. Sue us wherever you want to sue us. The contract doesn't say anything about a residual.' An American representative of the company who came to Australia to discuss the contract with us confirmed the latter point. He said: 'It's not your painting. The bank is going to sell it for as much as it can get. They're not interested in the $1.2 million you want to pay for it.'

I asked Tony Oates what he thought we should do, to which he replied: 'We have enough difficulties here. We are not going to go into a court case in New York against an American bank and to try to defend what is the convention in Australia. We don't have a lot of strength other than it is the practice here. Besides that, I'm not going to use the company's money; we're short of money and could blow a couple of million on this very easily.'

He was absolutely right about the cash flow situation. The erosion of the capital base of Bond Corporation had by then reached a stage where we were paying cash for everything. But my thought on *La Promenade* was that we couldn't just let it go. Oates quite logically concluded: 'You've got the benefit coming to you. Dallhold is going to get half the gain. You've got the obligation to pay the money out so you go and do it.' He was very strong on that point, and beyond it he could see that if Dallhold took it on then Bond Corporation still stood to get half the gain. That way he didn't have to use Bond Corporation money and be put in a position of suing one of its bankers, a move that may have had an adverse reaction with other major banking institutions we were dealing with in America.

So Dallhold instructed lawyers in New York to begin proceedings against Chemical All-State Bank, which by then had taken the painting because the lease had expired. Then the issue became more clouded because Macquarie Bank had taken over some of the Australian operations of Chemical, including the lease portfolio, which in turn included *La Promenade*. That meant that Macquarie Bank then actually owned the painting. In the meantime Bond Corporation gave a letter, signed by the company secretary, Noel Reed, saying Bond Corporation was not interested in pursuing the painting and handed the right to negotiate on it over to Dallhold. This action alone confirmed that Bond Corporation was never in the business of buying art, something that is very relevant when you come to the *La Promenade* case. How do you take away a corporate opportunity when the company never wanted that opportunity? Bond Corporation wasn't in the art business — it was into brewing, media, property, oil and gas. Where did a painting fit in? It didn't. But the jury in this case couldn't see that.

So, off we went to Macquarie Bank where we said: 'You bought the lease business but we are entitled to that painting, and we're going to pay you $1.2 million as the residual under Australian convention.' They said that they didn't know about that — that they'd bought the business in good faith and that the painting was part of it. We left them in no doubt that we would challenge them in the courts if they didn't do the right thing, and Macquarie knew that what we were saying was the convention. They also knew that it wouldn't look good for writing new lease business in Australia if they were taken to court for reneging on a deal.

After much ado, and with both sides deciding there was no real desire to involve legal challenges, we struck a deal. They said: 'You give us an additional million dollars as a fee and you can have it.' So it became $2.2 million, which Dallhold paid, and I still had to account to Bond Corporation if it was sold because that company was due half of any profit made on the painting. Coincidentally the Bond Corporation liquidator later claimed and received that extra $1 million from Macquarie Bank.

Unbeknown to me, Macquarie Bank decided to send a letter to Bond Corporation before it would finalise the deal, saying in essence that they were going to dispose of the painting and asking whether Bond Corporation wanted it. Macquarie wanted to cover their position so Bond Corporation replied with two letters, both of which were produced in court, saying: 'No we don't want it. Dallhold can have it.' I didn't sign the letters, I had nothing to do with them and I certainly did not influence them or know what wording they contained. Lo and behold, I was subsequently charged with taking away the opportunity from Bond Corporation to buy the painting.

Consider all this information and you can only conclude that it was an absolutely ridiculous charge.

Then the agreement with Macquarie Bank became a lot worse. While the deal we struck with them was obviously the best way to wrap up the lease agreement and give Dallhold ownership, there was one more big surprise. The American bank had somehow got the painting to America where they planned to auction it. By rights though, Macquarie Bank became the owner before settling with us because they had taken over the American bank's Australian leasing operations; and once Dallhold had paid the $2.2 million over to Macquarie then *La Promenade* became Dallhold's asset.

By that time the painting's value had increased significantly. I didn't want to sell it, but the dramatic financial pressures both Dallhold and Bond Corporation were then experiencing left me no option. In a very complex transaction, Bond Corporation received back $7 million. Peter Lucas, the new chairman of Bond Corporation who came in after my resignation, confirmed that it was a legal and satisfactory conclusion for Bond Corporation.

The saga continued. Enter the Bank of Nova Scotia, which somehow knew that the painting was in America. They went along, seized it to cover another Dallhold debt and subsequently sold the painting. Dallhold, the family company, had paid out the $2.2 million to Macquarie and $7 million to Bond Corporation, and never got the painting.

CHAPTER TWELVE
BAD TIMES

For years the emotional pressure had been building and building for me as my corporate empire came crashing down around me in highly questionable circumstances. All the time I was trying to work out who was really behind these moves and why. I was trying to work out their motives so I could consider what tactics I should adopt to defend myself.

As the pressures went up my health went down. Rapidly. I was at the stage where I just couldn't cope with the stress; the human mind and body will only take so much. By the time the committal proceedings on the *La Promenade* charge were due to be faced in 1993 I had deteriorated so badly, both physically and mentally, that my lawyers went to court in Perth, first in October then December, and argued that I was in no fit condition to face court. Tim Watson-Munro, a forensic psychologist from Melbourne who had assessed me, confirmed this to the court. He found that, among other things, I was anxious, depressed, suicidal and suffering from memory impairment. The inevitable emotional landslide had arrived. My brain was not functioning properly and I couldn't think straight. It was as though I'd been running on adrenaline for all those years, fighting for my life, and then suddenly it had evaporated. I'd known plenty of stress on previous occasions, but what I had encountered and been trying to fight was beyond belief. And making things worse was the fact that I believed that nothing I had done was illegal. As a consequence the call to defend myself had never been greater, but I wasn't in a fit condition to face court there and then.

My lawyers were successful in getting the trial postponed six months, but the fact that I was obviously very ill didn't stop the media bombardment, and other doubters, from harassing me. It was like a feeding frenzy for the media — they were like blood fish coming at you, biting at you again and again. Outside the court immediately after the hearing in December a female television reporter walked up to me and asked something like: 'Is it true you have tried to commit suicide?' She was being an absolute smart-arse, desperately looking for an angle for her story. For me it was like being asked: 'Did you beat your wife today?' My spontaneous reaction was what I'm sure a lot of people have wanted to do when the media is harassing them — I grabbed the microphone from her and hurled it across the car park. I didn't need such a horrid invasion into my space.

The fact was that in the true sense of the word I wasn't suicidal. I was clinically depressed and not well enough to attend court and defend myself. Still, there is no denying that I'd had dark thoughts, but they were thoughts that I'd rationalised and I knew I wasn't going to go there. I remember thinking: 'Oh yes, wouldn't it be easier just to end it all — go down to Cottesloe Beach and go for a swim, and keep swimming out so far that you can't get back.' It was no more than a fleeting thought, but it had been there when I was experiencing my lowest moments. That was when I was really depressed. I was shaking so much that I was considered to be on the point of a nervous breakdown. My mind was so scrambled that at times I just didn't know where I was.

In March 1995 I was finally committed for trial over the *La Promenade* painting, and I went back to court in Perth for the trial in July the following year to answer four charges — two of failing to act honestly in my duties as an officer of Bond Corporation with intent to deceive and defraud, a charge of furnishing information to Bond Corporation directors that I knew to be false, and finally a charge of allowing false information to go to the Bond Corporation auditor. It was all just so ridiculous, and in fact the story doing the rounds in legal circles across Australia was that these were just holding charges while those in pursuit of Bond Corporation and me could work up the charges over the Bell Resources deal. I was reliably told more than once that the Crown never believed that they were going to succeed with the charges over *La Promenade*. It was a sham.

The charges of stripping Bell Resources of $1.2 billion were made against me, Tony Oates and Peter Mitchell in January 1995 and at a hearing 12 months later I was committed for trial. That was to make 1996 a horrendous year as the trial over the *La Promenade* charges was also on the agenda.

Why did it take so long for the Bell charges to emerge? Because the investigators couldn't find evidence definitive enough to lay a charge. Talk about a witch-hunt! It was more than six years after my empire collapsed that the Bell charges came. The investigators had been looking into extremely complex transactions where the best lawyers had prepared all the documents, the relevant decisions had come from independent boards, and independent valuations had been obtained. Everything had been done in accordance with the law, but these sleuths were desperate to find a charge — they wanted to get me and make an example of me, so they hung in, and hung in.

Their desperation saw them go to a lot of the key people in Bond Corporation, entice them with an offer of immunity under the possible threat of charges, then say: 'Now you tell us everything you know. What was the real expectation behind this deal?' My belief is that these people became convinced that when they appeared at the committal hearing they had to give a distorted view of situations just to get themselves off the hook. They knew that our lawyers had done everything correctly, that everything was legal. But of course it didn't take much for them to twist things around and make me look bad. I was told the prosecutors pressured them to the degree where they were left in no doubt that they might be charged, so they reacted. It was a case of: 'Here are the charges that we are going to make against you. If you want to get off these charges then you must tell us what we want to hear, give us some evidence so that we can get Bond, Oates and the others. Give us the evidence so we can have a go at these guys. But don't forget, if you don't give us the information we want, in the way we want it, you may be charged.'

I'm not sure if any of them had done anything wrong or not; that wasn't the issue. The issue was that they bargained untrue information on me for freedom from prosecution for themselves. So there was a Judas in our camp. It is a despicable man who would actually do such a thing — give a version of events that was so concocted as to support charges against Tony Oates, Peter Mitchell and me, just to get themselves off the hook.

The investigators did everything they could to throw the book at us at the committal hearing, coming up with all sorts of charges from events perceived to have taken place. They went after us for conspiracy and breaches of the law involving the duties of company directors. They were desperate to find something that would stick. They were like vigilantes, trying to ride high on investigations costing tens of millions of dollars. And who was there trying to ride as high as any of them? John McKechnie, the Western Australian Director of Public Prosecutions — the same man who played a starring role in sending me to jail over the Rothwells deal on evidence that was later shown to be false. I was high profile and, having succeeded in getting me once, he obviously thought he could get me again. But this time he knew he would have to be more careful in pursuing Bond Corporation and me because he'd finished up with egg all over his face after I was acquitted on the Rothwells deal — a trial result that had eventually gone against the government's desire to nail me. That explains why it took so long for the investigations to be completed and for charges to be laid — they had to work even harder in their desperate bid to get me. Really though, if somebody has done something wrong it doesn't take nearly seven years to bring a charge. Maybe though, if you're trying to manufacture a charge, it could take seven years. And realising all this, I wasn't surprised when I was committed for trial.

Unfortunately, the fact that I had such a high profile brought added weight to my situation by again making me a target in the media. Never before had the old adage 'bad news sells newspapers, good news doesn't' been so true. What amazed me was that some people, especially in the media, believed that I should just roll over, do nothing and cop the rap. How incredible! They only knew one side of a lop-sided story. Why wouldn't I do everything within my means to defend myself against charges that I knew had no foundation? All the time I wondered who was out there cheering that day I was committed for trial. Who in what high place — government, corporate or judicial — was celebrating the fact that the posse had finally gone out and got their man? And what were the real reasons behind their celebrations? What was in it for them? The tall poppy syndrome was alive and well.

Soon after the *La Promenade* trial opened, my legal team fought to have the case thrown out. That was when there was a claim in the newspapers that a cache of paintings belonging to me had been discovered overseas, the inference being that I'd stolen them and had them in hiding. The newspaper posters at the newsagent's just metres from the court in Perth screamed: 'Bond Art Found'. The jury had to see those posters when entering the court, so my QC, Julian Burnside, took a poster into court, saying: 'Look, you can't let this case go on. It's unfair to my client. He can't get a fair trial with this going on.' The legal argument went on and on, but then Justice Antoinette Kennedy ruled: 'I will direct the jury to take it out of their minds.' What a joke. There was no way they could take it out of their minds. There had been so much adverse publicity already, and this just added to it.

Justice Kennedy also struck at the start of the trial when she would not allow me the time to get supporting evidence from fellow directors. Peter Beckwith had died and only Mitchell and Oates were left, but both were overseas. Neither wanted to return to Australia but had agreed to give evidence in America and Poland respectively. In refusing to allow me the time to get the evidence, Justice Kennedy commented that the trial had been delayed long enough and that it was in the public interest to proceed.

I was still far from being a well man. I collapsed on the very first day of what would be a six-week trial that ended in August 1996. Apart from my heart problems, I had a terribly painful kidney infection, so bad that I was actually peeing blood and vomiting almost every day during the trial. I had to be taken to hospital at one stage for an ultrasound. Even the prosecutor knew I was sick because he came out and saw me barking into a bucket. I was so weak from the infection that my legal team, especially my lawyer, Andrew Fraser, considered stopping the trial so I could go to hospital. But going against that thought was his belief that we were going very, very well with the case; we had such a cast-iron defence that he believed I couldn't possibly be convicted. On those grounds it was decided that I would have been foolish to stop, especially considering that to do so might bring an entire change to the balance of proceedings next time around. For a start we wouldn't have been able to keep the jury on hold if I had a lengthy stay in hospital. The process would have had to start again. Still, it was a very fine line between deciding to continue or to stop, and when I look back on it now I question Fraser's advice to continue. I now know it was bad advice for more reasons than my health. I really was too ill to proceed. I started to think I might die due to the stress I was under. I couldn't think straight and I went through periods where I could not remember anything.

Even more detrimental to my position was something I didn't realise at the time — my lawyer had problems of his own. It was only later that this became obvious. I was always wondering why, when I went to conferences in his offices in Melbourne, he would not write everything down. And he hardly gave me any briefing when it was time for me to go into the witness box. As we now know, Fraser was living the high life in Melbourne and was addicted to cocaine. Had I even had a hint of this at the time I would have done what I was entitled to do — absolutely refuse to attend the court and gone to hospital to be treated properly. Then, when I was well, I would have been in a much better position to fight the charges. But no, on the advice of Fraser, who said we were looking good in the case, I pushed on, something I very much regret now. One wonders whether his drug-taking affected his thinking and advice on the way the case should have been run. Although Andrew Fraser has now been convicted and jailed on drug offences, this gives me no comfort.

As hard as we fought to prove my medical condition was serious, especially when it came to my recollection of events, the prosecutor and court doctors fought equally as hard to try to prove that I was feigning ill health. Some sections of the media lapped up that side of the story and really put the boot in, not stopping at any time to consider the fact that I genuinely was a sick man. These vultures saw this as an opportunity to drive more nails into Alan Bond's coffin. All I can say is that I'd like to see them go through the wringer as I had, subjected to such relentless persecution, and see how they came out of it.

One point I later realised was not presented to the court by my legal team related to our threat to challenge the bank over ownership of *La Promenade* in a court in America. There is no way that we would have made that challenge if there had been any doubt in our mind about the legality of the arrangement between Dallhold and Bond Corporation. A court case in America would have required extensive disclosures and depositions from Dallhold to support its case, so we would certainly have not accommodated the thought of litigation there if we knew the agreement between the companies was illegal.

With neither Oates nor Mitchell to support me, one of the few things that I had left for my defence was the legal document signed in 1985 detailing the transaction that was approved by the full board of Bond Corporation. The fact was that Tony Oates had prepared the minutes of that board meeting and I had signed them for that meeting in 1983, but at that time I didn't give the paragraph relating to the painting a second thought.

One person with whom I was very unimpressed during this trial was Noel Reed, the Bond Corporation company secretary, who delivered some extremely damaging evidence against me. He was part of the group that signed off on the *La Promenade* deal at the board meeting, yet he came up with an opposing view at the trial. His attitude at the trial appeared to be: 'I've retired from the company so now I can say I didn't like the deal.'

I think one of the biggest problems the jury faced was that the case was extremely complicated. It was even complicated for legal experts, so how could you expect these jurors to understand the technicalities surrounding company structure and the lease arrangement on the painting? They'd be asking themselves: 'Well it's a lease so how could somebody not own it and at the same time own it? That's confusing.' At the end of the trial the jury went out for 36 hours to deliberate — 36 hours to consider a deal relating to a painting! The time they took to consider their verdict left Burnside and Fraser in no doubt that we'd won. And all the time the jury was out I waited at Perth Central in a holding cell, a small, stark and bitterly cold concrete room with no windows and only a concrete bench. The officers refused to give me more than one blanket so I had to wrap it around me while I shivered all night in the corner of the cell.

It just smashed me when the jury came back and delivered the verdict of guilty. Either they didn't understand the case or the jurors holding out in my favour for so many hours were finally convinced to change their opinion. The whole thing seemed like a joke, and what made it more ridiculous was the fact that during the entire trial

I was confronted by one juror winking at me the whole time, obviously saying everything was going to be okay. I did my best to ignore him.

Diana, my family and supporters in the court were devastated as the guilty verdict was announced. Di had been in court for every day of the hearing, something that gave me strength, although it was a harrowing experience for her.

Following the verdict came the crunch. Having first expressed concerns about my health, the stress I had already faced, and the humiliation heaped upon me by some sections of the media, Justice Kennedy handed down a sentence of three years' jail. It was as if my world ended there and then — three years in jail for what had been a perfectly legal transaction over a painting. I went into shock. My first thought was: 'I'm going to die. I can't take much more of this. I'm going to die in prison.' Then, before I knew it, I was whisked away in a prison van to the diabolic Casuarina maximum-security prison to be processed. I could only think that just one group would be more surprised by this conviction than me — the prosecution.

After a couple of weeks in Casuarina I was transferred to Karnet Prison where the first thing that struck me was the cold. All the memories of Wooroloo Prison came flooding back, and I could see the pattern repeating itself. I started out living in dormitory-style accommodation in a communal block where each prisoner was accommodated in his own cell overnight. The officers would put you in there and turn the key at 7pm and open up again after 7am the next day. It was a crushing experience each night. I was longing to see a sunset or a sunrise, the moon and the stars, but there were no windows. Sleep was a fitful experience because the mattresses were hard and uncomfortable. It was a very difficult situation to come to terms with and from the outset the words kept echoing in my mind: 'You're not going to survive this. You're going to die in prison.'

My one salvation came in the never-ending support I had from Di and the rest of my family throughout my entire ordeal. They came to see me every possible time they could, but in reality a one-hour visit over a weekend is not enough to give you the total support you need when you are so mentally crushed. Overwhelming humiliation re-entered my life. In my eyes I'd been tainted as a criminal, and my family and friends could only look upon me as a prisoner. Incredibly though they didn't see me that way. I was still their loved one, or their great friend, but even so it was always a hard drive back home for everyone after a visit.

Di and the family always tried to get to Karnet early each time they visited so they could get a table under a tree in the grounds for our gathering. To make the most of each visit we always tried to block from our minds the knowledge of where we actually were. I did everything possible to make everyone feel comfortable. Di used to laugh, telling me that the way I was treating them, by bringing out the biscuits and afternoon tea, was as if we were having it at the Ritz. In my mind such a fantasy made everything bearable, but only just.

This emotional support I was receiving reinforced my determined bid to stay on top of things, an effort that sometimes waned because of the pressure I was under. Still it was always a wonderful feeling knowing they were there, family and friends, especially friends from the yachting community. Eileen, quite understandably, hated coming to the prison, but she did as often as she could. And my incarceration led to her and Diana establishing a strong bond. They had many telephone conversations and Di was included in Christmas celebrations at Eileen's home as part of the extended family.

I had many other friends who just could not come and visit me in prison, and I accepted that. I knew I had their support and realised that they just could not handle entering a prison environment. They, like 99 per cent of the population, had never seen inside a prison, and they didn't want that experience. But there were others who didn't step forward to be counted at this time, simply because they were too embarrassed to be associated with me. These fair-weather friends certainly reminded me of the true value of friendship, and how shallow it can be for some.

The one thing I had to be careful of during all the visits from family and friends was that no one outside our group took photographs. I learnt there was a photographic bounty on me from the media — they were offering money for any photograph of me inside jail supposedly having a good time with friends so they could make out that I was getting it easy. The media were obviously hoping they could entice a guard or a prisoner to smuggle a photograph out to them.

Emotionally, my lot certainly improved when I got my own self-care hut six months after I entered the prison. It was a little wooden structure that provided me with some very valuable independence, but it was bitterly cold to live in during winter. Living in a hut meant you could have anything you could scrounge from around the prison, so I finished up with a little bit of well-worn carpet and a swivel chair — they were the main features of the room. I even planted some flowers outside the hut, only to have them removed by the officers soon after because they were considered a benefit to one prisoner and not others. I was determined to win on that one, so I put the flowers back in again. They didn't come around a second time and take them out.

Although I had my own accommodation I had to accept the fact that I was in jail, and even though everything possible was being done to get an appeal in place and get me out of there I had to help myself as much as I could while I was waiting. It wasn't easy for me, and often depression was my closest ally. Keeping my mind active was the challenge. I decided there were opportunities to help the prison officers and some of the inmates to get a better understanding of the world of business, finance and wealth creation. I also helped the officers with the structure of their superannuation funds. One officer owned six houses but had the entire package of rental income and mortgage repayments badly structured, so I helped him to make the most of his assets. Some officers made money on share investments I suggested for them. Generally speaking they wanted to talk to me more than they did the other inmates because they didn't hold common interests with them. There were a few nasty officers there who I had no time for, ones who went out of their way to be very difficult, but the Superintendent and the people with intellect, the senior officers, were very fair towards me. Many couldn't understand what had happened and why I was there. They read the charge sheets and they couldn't believe them. I actually got to know the Superintendent fairly well. He was a good sort of a fellow, and very approachable and I'd wander into his office quite frequently for a chat. He also respected my efforts to improve things for prisoners. I became chairman of what was called the Prison Committee and we did things like have a playground built for the kiddies so they could entertain themselves while the prisoners had family and friends visiting.

While in Karnet I made a successful application to have my own doctors continue to treat me. Apparently it was agreed to on the grounds that I was a high-risk medical inmate; the state had a duty of care so could be held responsible if anything happened to me. I got the feeling that the Prisons Department was quite happy not to have the responsibility. Still, the attitude of the officers varied greatly, some wanting to sit right there in front of me while I was having a check-up while others were quite happy to wait outside. The good officers would try to make an outing as interesting as possible for me when I went to these medical appointments in the city, while others went out of their way to ensure I received no favours whatsoever. The good guys would see to it that we travelled to and from Karnet different ways, just so I could have a look around town. In fact the Superintendent, on a number of occasions, provided his own car for me to go from Karnet Prison to these appointments.

As Karnet was a minimum-security prison I never expected to travel to my doctor as a high-risk prisoner, in handcuffs and the like. But that's exactly what happened one day during the early stages of my incarceration when I was taken to Charles Gairdner Hospital for a check-up. At the time I was having trouble with a blood clot that created a condition where the blood is cut off to the bowel and the bowel effectively becomes ulcerated. When we arrived at the hospital the officer insisted that he put me in handcuffs to take me inside, the only obvious reason for this being that he wanted to cause me as much embarrassment as possible. So there I was walking through the hospital in handcuffs with people everywhere pointing at me and whispering, 'that's Alan Bond. Look, he's in handcuffs.' As soon as I got back to the prison I put in a letter of complaint to the Superintendent saying: 'I'm not going to go to any other hospital in handcuffs. I'd rather die here in prison than subject myself to the embarrassment of walking through a hospital in handcuffs.' The Superintendent, who I always found to be a very fair man, immediately came back to me saying: 'You should never have been placed in handcuffs. It's only a requirement from the unions when they are transporting prisoners who are considered to be a risk. You were never classified as a risk and it should not have occurred.' It did not happen again.

One of the more memorable days with a kind officer came when a visit to a heart specialist I had scheduled was delayed at the last minute because of an emergency the doctor had to deal with. It was around lunchtime and we had time to kill so the officer took me on a drive along the beachfront at Cottesloe. We stopped along the way and he offered to buy me a cup of coffee. I said: 'Wonderful, that's great'. He was a nice fellow and we had a good chat over a cup of coffee and a cake. I was dressed up in my drab prison garb — my greens, a baseball cap and joggers — and the officer was easily recognised because he was wearing his brown uniform and badges. Four young guys in a sports car drove past, recognised me sitting there and saw I was with a prison officer. One called out: 'Hey, let him go. He's done nothing wrong. Let him go,' and threw a couple of obscenities at the officer. It was all in good humour. Next thing these guys had driven around the block and pulled up out the front of the cafe, so we only had one option — get up and go.

On another occasion, in similar circumstances, I was out with a prison officer having a cup of coffee and some sandwiches for lunch at a little corner cafe in West Perth. While we were in there somebody who spotted us called the newspaper saying we were there having lunch and picked up $50 for a news tip. By the time the newspaper had finished with the story we had been having a three-course lunch, and they wanted to know who paid for it. The story caused great embarrassment for the officer and he was severely reprimanded when we got back to Karnet. Two internal investigation officers from the Prisons Department came to Karnet the next day and decided they would have one of their kangaroo courts in the Superintendent's office. It was a wet and miserable day and I was summoned to the office. I wasn't aware that there was an investigation going on, so when I walked in and looked at these fellows sitting there looking as official as they could behind a table I asked who they were. They said nothing, so I then asked what they were doing:

> *Officer:* 'We want to talk to you.'
> *AB:* 'Talk to me about what?'
> *Officer:* 'We want to talk to you about your outing for lunch.'
> *AB:* 'Who do you work for?'
> *Officer:* 'We work for the prison.'
> *AB:* 'I have no obligation to talk to you whatsoever,' and with that I turned around and walked out.

The one thing many people don't learn in life is that there's no obligation to talk to these people. The only people you have to talk to are liquidators because it's required under the legislation. But as for the rest, you are not required to give any evidence or have any discussions. Until you know what it's all about you're better off keeping your own counsel. And the good thing about this incident was that the other officers almost immediately found out what I had done. It went around the prison very quickly that Bond had said nothing. I had new respect because it was very unusual for a prisoner to protect an officer.

There was another similar incident for me at Karnet in 1999. The Bond Corporation liquidator, Richard England, convinced a South Australian judge to come over to Western Australia and interview me in the prison to inquire into millions of dollars allegedly missing from Bond Corporation. It was little more than a junket for the judge and his entourage, and the inquiry wasn't anything like it was supposed to be — impartial.

The judge arrived and duly set up his 'court' in the Superintendent's office. Unbeknown to them I'd developed a good rapport with many of the prison officers so had been tipped off that the judge and his team were coming. As a result of that tip, my lawyers and QC were there waiting for them when they arrived. The one thing I knew was that the prison authorities didn't have the right to hand me over to an inquiry, even though I was inside the prison, unless a court order was in place. The judge and his cronies simply expected me to come into the office, sit down, and tell them everything. And they also thought that their element of surprise would help their cause.

The Superintendent wandered out to my hut and asked if I'd come up to the office.

I simply stated: 'No, my lawyer has advised me I have no obligation.'

He then said: 'There's a judge here to see you and you're required to appear.'

'No, the advice I have is that unless there is a court order the prison has no jurisdiction when it comes to asking me to attend. I'm not coming. I don't have to so I won't.'

I was only standing up for my rights. Eventually, when my QC put his case, he told the judge that he needed a court order to start with, and secondly he had no jurisdiction in Perth. Soon the judge realised that he had no option but to go and get a court order to force me to appear, so he headed into Perth to do just that. But the Western Australian judge refused to issue the order, saying that he needed to hear both sides of the story, so the South Australian judge and his team headed back to Adelaide empty handed.

Apart from visitors, my mail kept me going while I was in prison. In Karnet I used to get up to 40 letters a week. Some were even fan mail. The majority of letters were from people who didn't know me but wanted to register their support for me. One couple from

Melbourne, Bob and Joan Garnett, wrote to me religiously every month, encouraging me with great words and items of general interest. They even flew to Perth to visit me once when I was in prison. These were people I had not known before. They proved there is still a lot of goodness in Australian people and they were special. Many officers hated me getting so much mail because they had to write down the name and address of every sender. I suspect that a lot of my mail was just thrown out because the officers were too lazy when it came to registering these details. The average prisoner usually gets one or two letters a week, so it was a bit embarrassing for me each time I went to collect my mail because the letters were put out in piles and it was obvious that I was getting more mail than everyone else combined. At times some prisoners, just to be spiteful, would pinch some of my letters before I got there to collect them, but you accept that such a thing comes with the prison environment. I answered as many letters as I could and eventually started writing a regular newsletter that I could send out. I would tell those interested what was happening in my life and give my views on certain news items from the outside world.

Of all the mail I received in Karnet, one letter really upset me, and I made sure the writer knew it because it was yet another unjustified kick in the guts for me. This official letter stated that seeing I was in prison I was required to show cause why the Order of Australia award I had received after winning the America's Cup in 1983 should not be rescinded. I couldn't believe it. Then again I could, because I was a high-profile target. I wrote back to these people, the ones who originally handed out the award, and said that the Order was given to me for the America's Cup victory. Whatever happened to me later in life shouldn't have any impact on the contribution I made to Australia through the America's Cup. I also stressed that my sentence was to be appealed. The other point about this move was that there is never a contract issued when you receive the medal that states: 'We'll give this award to you under these specific circumstances.' They just give it to you, and I don't think they have a right to take it away. Surprise, surprise, I didn't even get the courtesy of a reply, even though I'd taken them up on their original request to explain why I should keep the medal. The next thing I knew was that I was no longer Alan Bond AO, an act that as far as I am concerned denigrated the award. Whether, in fact, they can take an award away has not been settled legally at this time. At least they could have waited to see what happened with my appeal, but no, they were just another group wanting to get some prominence by having a swipe at me while I was inside. At least no one could take away the fact that in 1978 I was named Australian of the Year.

Many of the letters I did receive in Karnet were full of admiration for me. I had impressed a lot of these people by not 'doing a Skase' and fleeing the country. The thing was that I had plenty of opportunities before everything collapsed to leave Australia and not come back. I had a number of approaches from people wanting to fly me out. But I took the view that I'd messed things up by virtue of decisions that I'd participated in, and those decisions, along with significant outside influences that I could not control, had brought about the collapse of Bond Corporation. I wanted to see the entire process through because my children and my grandchildren meant everything to me. I wanted to have the matter resolved and not left on the books as a problem for them to inherit. To 'do a Skase' was the coward's way out.

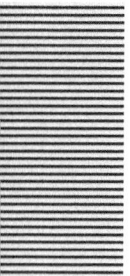

CHAPTER THIRTEEN
INDIFFERENT JUSTICE

Ian Callinan QC began preparing an appeal on the *La Promenade* conviction virtually from the moment I was imprisoned. By the time he had finished he had a 1000-page document to back the application and was certain that we had an exceptionally good chance of being successful, particularly considering that Justice Antoinette Kennedy refused to allow evidence from Peter Mitchell and Tony Oates to be taken from their respective domiciles overseas. Also, Callinan believed that I didn't get a fair trial because the charges were too complex for the jury to properly understand. He was also certain that the media bias that was shown in the period leading up to the trial was very detrimental for me publicly and that this had carried through to the jury. He reminded me that Perth is a small city where everything is so easily coloured by the media. But I knew all along that I was paying a high price for my profile, a profile that was influenced by a widely held belief, even before the trial, that I was guilty. It was an attitude built on the fact that a large company had collapsed and shareholders had been affected, so somebody had to be held responsible. I was the only one there and as captain of the ship I had to go down with it. Regardless of being innocent or guilty, I had to pay a price because justice had to be seen to be done.

It was while Callinan was preparing the appeal, during my early days at Karnet, that pressure started coming from the authorities over the Bell issue. Now that I was in prison they had me where they wanted me, and they wanted to make sure that I stayed there. Suddenly they saw their job of getting a conviction becoming a lot easier.

My lawyers soon advised me of something that I sensed but didn't want to hear — that the Bell case could well take a year to defend. I didn't really want to think about that after what I'd already experienced. I was still very ill, and defending the charges would mean that every day during the trial I would be transported between Karnet and the Perth court in the back of what they called the 'meat wagon', a claustrophobic little van with a metal floor, no seats and little slits for windows. I'd have to leave very early each morning, be placed in a holding cell under the court until proceedings started, spend the day in court and then be shipped back to Karnet when the court closed. However, my day wouldn't end there because each evening I would have to go through the transcripts so I could continually brief my lawyers. My mind became totally preoccupied by what the consequences of all this might be and what I would have to endure to defend myself. Considering I was so ill, the big question for me was: 'Could I go the distance?' The answer was 'probably not'. I didn't think that my body could take it, that I would die before the year was up. I thought about Laurie Connell, Robert Holmes à Court and Peter Beckwith — they all died at a time of high stress in their lives. I was already on medical watch in prison and was still seeing heart specialists in Perth.

With this case coming so soon after the *La Promenade* trial another question I had to consider involved whether or not I would get a fair trial. What bias would there be against me? I was a prisoner and would be appearing in the dock in prison clothing. What influence would that have on the jury? And how would the jury feel after being locked into this incredibly complicated case for a year? How would they react? They were ordinary people trying for a year to understand something that it took investigators seven years to get their heads around in their search for charges. The average juror would not come across something like this in a lifetime — these people were being unfairly asked to determine elaborate accounting procedures and legal arguments. This case involved loans from one public company to another — we were not talking about something going in Alan Bond's pocket, even though I was the one being charged. This case against me was based on nothing more than circumstantial evidence, but that wouldn't matter. I weighed it all up with my *La Promenade* experience and rated myself almost no chance.

There was also the question of cost — around $1 million a month to defend myself. The best legal brains in the country would be needed to understand the details of the case and then present my defence. A year-long case meant $12 million would be required, and I didn't have anything like that sort of money available to me. Mind you, if I did have that pot of gold stashed away like so many people suggested, then I assure you that I would have spent it on my defence. So, as there was no heap of money available, financial support could only come if my family sold their homes and other assets, assets they had created themselves from a financial base that I had established for them decades earlier. Denuding the family of a financially secure future and a life that they had worked so hard to establish was out of the question.

To reinforce their case the prosecutors were trying desperately to get people associated with Bond Corporation and Bell on side because they could get no hard evidence against me; that's why it took them so long to lay charges. I acted as a chairman of Bond Corporation, but I wasn't on the board of Bell Group. Yes, I approved a loan, there's no question at all about that, and that's all legally documented, but there was nothing wrong with that transaction. Their only hope in pinning me was to say that I had a mind-set to defraud the company, nothing more. Still, my belief was that considering my predicament at the time there was no way I could get a fair result in court.

I met with my legal advisers to discuss all the options, and at that meeting the most important consideration for them was that my health was just not good enough to face a 12-month trial. I was still depressed, clinically depressed, from the impact of the *La Promenade* trial, a trial I believed would find me innocent, and yet I was found guilty. I also remembered all too well how the judge did not allow the evidence of Tony Oates and Peter Mitchell. That attitude meant I would have no suitable witnesses in the Bell case, especially seeing that so many of the former Bond Corporation hierarchy had grabbed immunity from the prosecutor to protect themselves, even though nothing illegal had happened in the Bell transaction.

Callinan told me that he had met with another QC and discussed the case, and that discussion had confirmed everything he already believed. He basically said to me: 'Alan, I don't think that we are going to get a fair trial in Western Australia or anywhere else for that matter, primarily because of the amount of adverse publicity you have received, and the heat that is still around from the previous trial. I also think that it's unreasonable to assume that any jury will understand this case. It's far more complicated than the *La Promenade* case, and you know what happened there.'

He also reminded me that the Crown had virtually unlimited resources at their disposal for this case while we didn't. So after much discussion we concluded that while we all knew the charges weren't sustainable, our best and really only option was to go to the Crown's solicitors and discuss a plea bargain.

The Crown was very receptive to the idea of a plea bargain because they would get their man without a fight. My legal team went into discussions and after a period of negotiation it was agreed that I would plead guilty to two charges of breaching directors' duties based around failing to act honestly as a director in allowing the company to pay a deposit on the brewing assets. There was no suggestion in any of the charges that I took any money. The Crown solicitors were more than happy with that — on the proviso that they added the line 'with the intent to commit fraud'. But while it might have appeared otherwise to the outside world, I had no intention of committing fraud. To agree to the inclusion of that line was as good as committing commercial suicide. I was not guilty of fraud. The other aspect of this plea bargain was a suggestion from Andrew Fraser that we would not proceed with the *La Promenade* appeal, an appeal which Ian Callinan was confident we had every chance of winning. However, Callinan agreed with Fraser, saying that our cause would be helped if we dropped that appeal. He assured me that the Crown solicitors would then be satisfied and subsequently not challenge whatever additional sentence the judge handed down as a result of the plea bargain. And there was some consolation towards me from their side — a 'conspiracy to defraud' charge was dropped by the Crown, as were four Company Code charges.

We knew the Crown would not budge on their wish to have the line 'intention to commit fraud' included, but while I didn't agree with it I did discuss my position with my solicitor, who advised: 'Four years will be the maximum that you get. They've never given more than two and a half years on directors' duties charges. And because these events occurred at the same time as the *La Promenade* charges, they must run concurrently as a sentence.' This meant that with the two sentences combined I would have to serve only an extra four to eight months to put everything behind me. That's what they told me — but it would turn out to be total bullshit, as was the Crown's promise that they would not appeal the court decision on the extension of my sentence, as was told to me by Andrew Fraser!

I thought about the offer and decided that I had no alternative but to agree to the Crown's offer. Above all, the most important influence on my decision was that in taking the plea bargain and not fighting in court for another year my health might not deteriorate further — I was still worried that I would die in jail. I also considered the fact that I was already disgraced by being in jail, and I had lost everything that I had worked for over so many years. The plea bargain meant that this terrible chapter in my life would soon be behind me. I'd get my life back.

So I agreed to the inclusion of the additional line that the Crown's solicitors insisted on, and from that moment on they had me exactly where they wanted me. It was time to stick the knife in once more: 'We will prepare the statement, and you will not change one word of it.'

The frame of mind I was in by then said *'just sign it'*.

The document that was read out in court was full of flamboyant adjectives and did not represent the charges to which I had pleaded to. It contained interpretations without the facts being married to them. But there it was for the world to see. After almost seven years of investigation the Crown had got their man — and they didn't have to prove a thing: Alan Bond was pleading guilty to failing to act honestly as a company director, with intent to commit fraud.

For the first time in a long time I was starting to feel relief — but it was for the briefest of moments. The judge, as expected, gave me a four-year sentence on the plea bargain, but *added* it on to the three years I was currently serving on the *La Promenade* deal, so I was confronted with seven years in prison with parole after serving two years and six months. I'd been had!

This plea-bargain hearing came about four months after I entered Karnet, and while the four-year extension to my sentence was difficult for me to accept, at least I was going to be able to stay at Karnet, or that was what I thought, until the Crown reneged on the promise not to appeal the additional sentence that I had received — the Commonwealth Director of Public Prosecutions appealed what he thought was the leniency of the sentence on the last possible day.

As soon as the appeal was lodged I was called into the Superintendent's office and told that because of the appeal I'd be going to Casuarina. I asked why I was being sent to maximum security and was told that because of the appeal I was considered to be a flight risk. 'They want you to go down there to do an assessment. I'm sure you'll only be there a couple of days.'

Shocked as I was I said to the Superintendent: 'Okay, I'll go and get my gear.'

His response threw me: 'Don't worry about your gear. The vehicle is out the front so just go and get in it.'

I didn't realise then that what was happening to me was what prisoners referred to as being *'shanghaied'*. I was on my way to Casuarina, Western Australia's worst prison and while I was told that I would be there for only a 'few days' it would be 18 months before I'd see Karnet again. To this day I can only wonder why I was ever sent to Casuarina, an overcrowded hell-hole that was lacking all basic considerations of humanity. There were provisions in the rules of the prison system stating that anybody jailed for a white-collar crime, and specifically a company director, did not have to spend time in maximum security. But I was destined to call Casuarina home, all because a case officer determined it that way. It was further evidence of the system having a go at me under the influence of powers at the top.

The appeal proceeded and my QC, Ian Callinan, was totally frustrated by what happened when he went into court to oppose the Crown's application. He came back to me after making his address and said: 'Alan, I didn't get the message through to them at all. It was as though they had made up their minds before I made my address.' I wasn't surprised to hear it because I'd already sensed that just by listening to the questions of the female judge during the appeal. She'd only recently been appointed to the bench and all along I was aware of the aggravation in her voice. That, coupled with her body language, told me that things were not looking good. I ended up with another three years on top of the seven I had already received — 10 years in total. It felt like a death sentence!

Our only option was to appeal.

There was an interesting reaction from a lot of people right across Australia when I agreed to the plea bargain, a reaction that became evident to me through much of the mail I received, and via word-of-mouth from friends. People couldn't understand why I didn't tough it out and fight the charges. They said things like: 'We thought you were innocent until such time as you were proven guilty; that's why we've believed in you.' These people would have understood it better if I'd remained defiant to the end, doing everything possible to prove that there was no offence committed. Only then would they have accepted it if I'd been found guilty. That is what they would have preferred. In not knowing the reasons for me taking the plea bargain they thought that I'd just given up, decided to surrender with a guilty plea, and taken the easy way out.

I didn't realise until some time after I was released from prison the true impact my taking the plea bargain had on a lot of people I knew, especially people who had worked for me. All along they had stood by me, saying: 'Of course he's not guilty. He's just caught up in the system. It's all part of the tall poppy syndrome. That's the only reason he's in jail.' They thought along the same lines as my government friends in Chile who told me I was in effect a political prisoner, something that I agree with to a large extent, even though it would be impossible to prove. As I've said all along and will say until the day I die, there were forces behind my crash from glory, pushing and pushing the government to bring charges, and the government got on the bandwagon. I'm convinced of this by the mere fact that the federal and Western Australian governments were involved either directly or indirectly in so many of the deals that brought about my downfall. They knew that the only way to prevent the government from being exposed, and subsequently being brought down, was to bring me down first. That's why they pressed for seven years to get me — looking for any opportunity, even just three words in a 1000-page document that might hint that I was guilty of an offence. That's the reality of the game when you get into the league that I was in.

I can say from experience that the emotional trauma associated with being sent to a maximum-security prison is far worse than anyone can ever imagine. You are living with the worst of the worst, men who have been jailed for brutal crimes that are beyond comprehension; Casuarina was home to every murderer in Western Australia. I could not go any lower in life. But there I was, and there was nothing I could do about it. But as difficult as it was, I had to convince myself that I should make the best possible use of my time, and that led to me deciding two things — I wanted to add to my life the amount of time I spent in prison, and I'd do that by adopting a new attitude to my health. I also wanted to wake up every morning that I was in there — I did not want to go into the history books as having died in prison.

To achieve my goals I had to apply my mind to things that would keep it active and stretch me mentally in new directions. Helping me to retain my sanity were the all-important visits from family and friends, but they were far more difficult and impersonal in Casuarina. They were awful experiences for both sides, and being limited to exactly one hour every Saturday and Sunday meant that every minute together mattered. It was easy to become frustrated by the time it took to get your visitors to the visiting room and seated. Quite often your one-hour visit was reduced to just 50 minutes. These were extremely difficult times for me, but while I was never in good mental shape during visits I did my best not to let the others know how I was really feeling. I always did my best to put on a brave face so they could go away from the prison feeling as comfortable as possible.

My mental state at the meetings was also influenced by the fact that I had been strip-searched before seeing my visitors. It is a harrowing experience. The officers take you into the holding section where you are required to take off all your clothes and face a search, which includes opening your mouth to ensure you've got nothing hidden, then bending over and touching your toes to prove there's nothing concealed anywhere else. They even have you lift your feet to check underneath. When the search is complete you're given a dull grey T-shirt, a pair of grey leggings, and a pair of thongs. You have to endure this strip-search procedure on the way through to the visit and also when you come back from it.

But there was an even worse side to this procedure — any one of your visitors could be strip-searched before coming to see you, a thought that weighed heavily on my mind, especially when it came to Diana, who visited me as often as possible. Visits to Karnet were just bearable emotionally for her, but the experiences at Casuarina were quite horrible. Fortunately she was never selected for a random strip-search, but I know that had she been chosen then she would have gone through with it just to see me. She would not have turned back, and this is something that makes me love her even more. Still, a lot of women were searched, and sometimes while waiting outside the prison before a visit, Di was confronted with taunts from other women who were checked. 'I bet they won't search Bondy's wife.'

The visiting room was small, too small in fact for the number of prisoners and visitors using it, and it was stark and devoid of any warmth in every sense. There were plastic chairs and tables positioned across the room and when your visitors got there they were sent to a particular table to await your arrival. There was always tension in the room because, apart from a brief kiss or handshake as a greeting, there was a ban on physical contact. Loved ones could hold hands across the table separating you, but that was it. At times these rules were too much for some prisoners. One day while Di and I were sitting there chatting, a prisoner went totally berserk and hurled chairs in every direction across the room. He was eventually subdued by the officers and taken away.

I'm sure Di's religious upbringing helped her cope with this terrible time in our life together. I get very emotional when I think about what she subjected herself to just to support me. It's only at times like this that you appreciate the deepest meaning of love, family and friendship. I'm a better person from having experienced it.

As the visits were so limited, the telephone became my lifeline to the outside world, but prisoners were limited to one 10-minute call a day, and those calls were monitored and recorded to ensure that you were not abusing your privileges. The phone room was open for only one hour each evening, which meant there were always too many prisoners wanting to get on, so the only way you stood a chance of making a call was to write your name on a board and wait in a queue. The calls weren't cheap either, the prisoners' rate being four times the normal telephone rate, and that came out of the $20 you earned each week for working in the prison. Inevitably, most of your money was spent on calls.

This phone room, which was adjacent to the dining room, was always a dangerous place because many prisoners who did not want to follow the accepted call procedures started to throw their weight around. Some refused to put their name on the board — they wanted to call at a certain time because that was when their wife or girlfriend was available to take the call. Inevitably there were fights, often vicious and ugly fights that were fuelled by prisoners who were on drugs. And while the officers could see what was happening when a fight started it took them quite some time to get in and break it up because they had to come through two doors to get there.

I knew I was in danger from the moment I entered Casuarina because, as a high profile white-collar crime prisoner, I was seen to be a soft target by the worst of the inmates — getting to Alan Bond would be seen by some as a form of entertainment. I was always expecting problems in the phone room, and it was only two weeks after I'd arrived at Casuarina that my worst fears were realised. As I went to use the phone one day an Aboriginal inmate, who was obviously high on drugs, rushed up from behind and wrapped the metal cord attached to the phone around my neck. He was out of his mind and determined to kill me. I struggled for breath and tried to fight him off, but he was behind me and pulling the cord tighter and tighter. I was beginning to black out — there was nothing I could do, and incredibly the officers who could see what was happening weren't rushing to my aid. I was convinced I was going to die, but then another of the inmates grabbed this bloke and hauled him off. While this wasn't the most frightening incident to confront me in Casuarina it is the one that still haunts me today. I get emotional every time I think about it. I was certain I was going to die.

Casuarina was always recognised as a very violent prison, and I was right in the middle of it. It was inevitable that there would be more attacks on me, so I had to consider what I might be able to do to lessen my exposure to the threats. With 40 per cent of the prison population on drugs, just like the guy who'd tried to kill me, I had to find a safer existence.

I went to the officers and they told me one option was to be put into the prison's Protection Unit, but they warned that one only went in there as a last resort because it was a horrible place, where you are locked up 24 hours a day. I was told that going into this unit was the only way the officers could guarantee that they could protect me. Having drawn their attention to my concerns about my safety it then became compulsory for me to sign a waiver if I wanted to stay in the general prison population, a waiver that gave away any rights I might have had which would allow me to make a claim against them should I be attacked. It stated that I acknowledged I was facing a threat in the prison, and that the prison officers were not responsible for any attack, fatal or otherwise. In thinking about my alternatives and the associated consequences, I reminded myself that my ultimate desire was just to get out of prison alive, but I wasn't prepared to go into what was, in effect, solitary confinement. I took the other option available to me and went into the Self-Care Unit even though it held 48 prisoners, 24 of whom were convicted murderers, each with their own cell. But the fact that murderers surrounded me was less disconcerting than the knowledge that there were stabbings in the prison all the time. I actually saw people stabbed right in front of me. One day while I was there they discovered 18 knives, and that was only among the few prisoners they searched. My guess is that half of the nearly 700 prisoners had knives, or access to knives. It's extremely difficult for the system to keep knives out of the place, especially when the prison is as overcrowded as Casuarina. When you have a workshop in any prison there is always the opportunity for someone to make a knife by simply taking a piece of metal or other hard material and working on it.

I knew that if I was to further minimise the potential risks I faced I needed to create a time-management plan that would limit my exposure to any danger. I discovered that there were only five prisoners attending the art school in the prison's Education

Centre, and that it was considered a very safe place even though a couple of them were multiple murderers. I quickly applied for an entry into the school and was accepted. The school operated from 8am until 5pm each day, so the only time I was in any real danger was during the two hours I was out of my cell before and after art school. Incredibly, the happiest time of the day outside school was when they turned the keys in the door of my cell at seven o'clock each night. I was then locked in and no one could attack me.

While I was at Casuarina there was a sequel to the failed attempt by the South Australian judge to gain evidence from me at Karnet. They successfully applied to the courts to have me extradited to South Australia. This little adventure turned into a one-week junket for the prison officer who flew there with me, but it was a ghastly experience for me.

When I got to Adelaide I was sent to one of the state's oldest and worst jails, Yatala, because they wanted me 'in safe security because there have been a few prison deaths lately'. That was a load of rubbish. I could have been put into a motel if they wanted because there was a prison officer there to watch over me. Where they actually held me was worse than maximum security — they put me into the punishment section of the prison which was notorious for its bad conditions. Yet again I became convinced that the system was out to break me.

There was nothing pretty about Yatala. My accommodation was a solitary confinement cell where there was no window light, just concrete walls, a concrete bed, and a couple of blankets. There were also a couple of towels and before being taken to court each day the guards insisted that I had them rolled up in a certain fashion. Then they would also inspect the stainless-steel sink and toilet before I left the cell, and if there was a mark on either one I would have to polish it out before I could leave. Then each time I was to take a shower I had to first put my hands through the cell door so the guard could fasten handcuffs on me. It was a blatant attempt to break me mentally, and when I protested they simply said: 'You have to conform with the rest of the prisoners.' I reminded them that I was only there for an inquiry. They laughed.

At my age, almost 60, and in my condition it wasn't hard to fall ill in that environment, and that's exactly what happened at Yatala. I complained about my treatment, stressing that I was a low-security risk at Casuarina, but no one cared. Part of the problem was that I was being forced to eat a no-option diet, and I hated it. By the time they got me back to Yatala after each day of the inquiry it was too late for a hot meal. All I got was a cold meal left on a concrete bench in the cell.

The one bonus for me was that Di came across from Perth to be in court when I was there. But I was only allowed to make direct contact with her during the short lunch break period.

Back at Casuarina my studies involved computers as well as art and, as I kept myself sufficiently active, I did not have any desire to leave the Education Centre during the day. Eventually I got myself to a stage where I convinced the authorities that my time would be better utilised if they would let me run a special education program for selected prisoners. My proposal was to teach business management, how to run a small business and how to motivate yourself in business. I saw it as a great opportunity for both the prisoners and me to get some self-esteem back. It turned out to be a very successful program run under the guidance of outside teachers and the prison Superintendent. Each term they had to approve the curriculum that I had established. There were only 12 students selected by the prison for the class, something that presented problems from time to time as many of the prisoners who were not considered by jail authorities to be suitable would set themselves up outside the centre and hurl abuse at the students and me. In the classes I explained to prisoners how they could go about buying a home once they were released. I told them that because they had a prison record they could not secure loans, so they would need to get family or friends to go as guarantor. We went through all sorts of exercises, including hypothetical share-trading deals, so prisoners could see what opportunities might be open to them once they were released. I was always trying to rebuild their confidence for their return to the outside world. I wanted to show them how they didn't need to do anything dishonest to exist once released.

Even though the risk of harm to me was minimised by being in the Protection Unit and the Education Centre, I knew I would still need to look after myself in those four hours each day when I had to mix with other prisoners. So I did a trade with the prisoner who came along and saved me when the beserk prisoner was trying to choke me: if he watched my back everywhere I went in the prison I would teach him to read, write and use a computer. It was a good deal all round. Still that didn't stop a couple of guys with knives from trying to get me. It was a brutal life in there, and many of the worst prisoners saw an opportunity to raise their status within their chain of command if they could knife someone with a high profile, and that meant me. In what was the most terrifying moment of my entire time in Casuarina, even scarier than when the guy attacked me with the cord, a guy got to within a few metres of me with a knife. He was coming straight at me with a frenzied look on his face and I was left in no doubt that he was determined to kill me. But my man and others leapt on him and pummelled him in what was a massive fight. Eventually my would-be attacker was subdued and taken off to the containment cells.

As I became accustomed to being in Casuarina another thing that became apparent was that the greatest risk to me would probably come from the Aboriginal community in the prison, as they were the only real gang in confinement. To further protect myself I went to the oldest among them, the one you might call the tribal elder, and made a peace offer before it was needed: 'If any of your guys need any help in preparing applications for parole or anything else, then call on me and I'll help.' It worked because I had shown that I cared and I gained their respect. I genuinely felt sorry for the Aborigines because no one suffers more from imprisonment than they do. It's a cultural thing. Many of them are used to being in open space; many are nomadic people who are very different from the rest of us. It's no wonder there are so many deaths in custody among them. Even while I was in the self-care wing there were two suicides, one right opposite my cell and the other just around the corner. The poor chap in the cell opposite had serious emotional problems and was trying desperately to see the prison psychiatrist. He was told very bluntly by the wardens that he'd have to make an appointment and come back next week. But this guy needed help there and then. He'd committed a horrific murder — he'd killed his wife in a fit of rage even though he desperately loved her. His children wanted nothing to do with him; all he wanted was to be with his wife. He even had a shrine to her in his cell. He took his life because in his mind that was the only way he could get to be with her. There was no hope for him — he had nothing to live for. It was disgusting to see the system let him down. If the prison psychiatrist had realised the urgency of this man's need he'd probably still be alive today.

There was a prisoner in a similar predicament who another inmate and I tried to counsel in the days prior to his suicide. We tried to convince him that life would get better with time. I encouraged him to go with me to the prison church where a priest conducted a service each Sunday. We sang songs and prayed. It was a fantastic experience for him because suddenly he was in touch with humanity. He really enjoyed it so I tried to get him further into the church environment for support. I had no hesitation in doing this, despite his crime, because in my mind while you can't change what a person has done you can find some forgiveness, even for the worst of human beings. There's nothing else you can do but try to show them the right road in life — they can't move forward within themselves unless they start to accept what they've done and then seek some forgiveness. They must get their emotional self together before they can go anywhere. But try as we did we could not get him on the path to redemption. He was on a one-way street.

There was one more suicide in Casuarina that really depressed me. For two years one of the inmates had been establishing a beautiful little garden in front of the cellblock where he had planted flowers and shrubs and built a little waterway. When the shrubs had grown a little, one bloody horrible, vindictive officer decided: 'Hey, someone could hide in there and we mightn't see them.' So, with that decision made, he sent a tractor along and smashed the entire garden. The poor guy came back from his prison work one day to find his garden gone — the one thing he was living for. Next thing, only hours later, he committed suicide. That's how fragile someone's existence can be in prison.

With time, I started to feel safer, primarily because most of the prisoners realised I was actually prepared to help them. I was moulding into the scene. Quite often a prisoner would come up to me and offer a couple of oranges they'd been allocated from the canteen if I'd help them fill in their release application papers. That had also happened at Karnet. The officers would often say: 'Listen, go and get Alan to help you. He knows how to get it done.' I had set up standard forms on the computer in the Education Centre that would help them with their applications for parole, early release and for getting support for their families. While some prisoners somehow managed occasionally to get money and drugs into the prison from the outside, the hard currency in the system were cigarettes or cans of cola, and it seemed that everybody had to have their own way of getting their hands on them. The barter system was quite amazing. Some people would do washing for another prisoner, some would wash floors, others would do some cooking for people — there were all sorts of things going. In my case I chose to write letters for prisoners to the parole board, and letters for prisoners who had problems with the Family Law Court. In return I'd get a couple of oranges or apples, soft drinks or even an ice-cream. But the payment didn't really matter for me — I worked on the principle that if I could help one soul get out of such a dastardly place then I would feel better for having helped. Every day that you are in a place like Casuarina is a day of unmitigated suffering.

Apart from playing tennis on a small court with a wooden bat as often as I could to keep fit, I spent every spare moment I had available to me painting. It was really helping to keep me occupied, fill the time and get my own self-esteem back. I was doing something positive. There is a limit to what people can take as a result of the depression that stems from prison life, and I went very close to that limit. For 18 months the only thing I could see of sunlight when I was in my cell was when it reflected off the two rolls of razor wire I could see through the slots in the window. You don't ever see any bird life, you don't see a tree and you don't see the sun come up or go down. Fortunately, painting took my mind outside the prison, beyond the impenetrable high fences and razor wire. If I was painting a French impressionist style, I was in France. It really helped to get me motivated. I enjoyed painting copies of the French masters more than anything else because it helped me learn how they mixed their colours and bring vibrancy to their work through their brush strokes. This led to me developing my own sense of colour; I really like strong colours in my paintings, even my watercolours. Of all the paintings I did while in prison my favourite was the copy of Renoir's *The Boating Party*, and yes, I did a number of copies of Van Gogh's *Irises* that I later gave away to friends.

I also negotiated for the students in the art school to do some work for the outside world, including backdrops for a theatre in Fremantle that was staging a play. But while the Superintendent approved it, the prisoners wouldn't do the job until a barter deal had been negotiated — a new CD player for the art school.

What happened to Peter Mitchell and Tony Oates during this period?

Before I elaborate I must again stress that as the chairman of the company, as the captain of the ship, one must accept responsibility for what happened. And as unfortunate as it was, I did just that.

Still, Peter Mitchell was committed for trial on the Bell charges along with me and came back to Australia from America on a plea bargain that resulted in him spending 12 months in prison. To this day I stand by him as being a wonderful human being. Anyone who knows Peter well will state most emphatically that he is a sound, hard-working and honest man. I'm pleased to see that he and his family are now resident in America and going along very nicely. As far as I am concerned, Peter did nothing wrong.

Being a lawyer, Tony Oates took a different view from Peter on the scenario relating to Bell Resources and the crash of Bond Corporation. Tony went to Poland with the backing of some Australian investors to undertake business opportunities and met a woman, whom he married. He decided to make Poland his new home.

His legal background convinced him that while we could and should have done things differently within Bond Corporation, we hadn't breached any corporate laws. He is emphatic that there is no case to answer. Having been returned to Australia to face charges he now recognises that it may be difficult to get a fair trial because of the feeling that has been whipped up by the media and the government against Bond Corporation and its hierarchy. Tony's feeling is similar to mine. Obviously different rules apply for different companies when risks are taken and they don't work out.

It should be said that I believe Tony Oates did nothing wrong and hopefully the legal system will reach the same conclusion.

I was at the mercy of a complicated and protracted legal system in my bid to have my appeal heard against the extended sentence that came as a result of my plea bargain. It would be easy to use the word 'conned' when it comes to what the Crown and the investigators did in manipulating me into their desired position. It meant that they could all walk away comfortable in the thought that their job had been seen to be done because I'd made the admissions that they sought. The fact that they'd reneged on their end of the deal probably didn't lose them any sleep. Meanwhile, I sat in prison and vegetated, waiting for an opportunity to right the wrongs that they'd forced upon me. There was nothing more that I could do but wait for the system to catch up.

The only good thing you could say that happened to me in this period was that I was eventually transferred from Casuarina back to minimum security at Karnet, a huge relief after the nightmare experiences I'd had during my 18 months at Casuarina.

It was not until March 2000 that my appeal against the three-year extension of the sentence was heard by the High Court in Canberra, and in a unanimous decision by the seven judges it was ruled that the Commonwealth Director of Public Prosecutions had no right to appeal against the original four-year sentence. While it was an enormous relief to know that I was going to be released it did not come as a surprise because we knew all along that the move by the Commonwealth was not legal, we just had to get to the High Court to prove it.

I'd served three years and eight months in prison, 14 months longer than I should have, but there was nothing I could do about that. Actually I went very close to spending an extra night in prison after it was announced that I would be released. It was 7.15am Perth time when the High Court made its decision, but it would be more than nine hours before I was actually released. Incredibly, just after the release papers were completed, Karnet was hit by a bolt of lightning that caused a power failure and crashed all the computers. The prison was thrown into turmoil and ten inmates were taken to hospital after suffering some impact from the strike. Had the lightning hit only minutes earlier then my papers would not have been processed until the following day.

Just before 5pm I was in Di's arms a free man. The media was there in force as she drove me away from the prison on what was an emotional trip back to our home at Cottesloe. Di had been a tower of strength and inspiration throughout my ordeal and all I wanted to do was spend time with her, my family and close friends. Still, the media felt that they should also be part of my new life. For days they hounded me, camping outside the house and following my every move.

It was a beautiful feeling being in familiar surroundings once more. I could take a deep breath, sink into a lounge chair, and listen to the chatter and chuckling of the family around me. I wanted to savour the moment and not think about the future. The only thing I knew for sure about my future was that I never wanted to be the head of a large corporation ever again.

CHAPTER FOURTEEN
REFLECTING FORWARD

Just four months after I was released from prison in March 2000 the heart was ripped from our family when, tragically, Susanne died. She was only 41.

It was not a suicide through a drug overdose, as some quarters of the media reported.

For some years Susanne suffered from a rare and extremely painful disease, coeliac disease, which attacks the lining of the small intestine and results in poor absorption of food and nutrients. It is caused by gluten intolerance and as a result you need to be on an extremely strict, almost intolerable, diet. Apart from the pain, coeliac can cause chronic fatigue and malnutrition and an attack brings severe swelling of the stomach, so bad at times that hospitalisation is the only option. Morphine is more often than not used to counter the pain.

It was this medical condition that forced her to give up her wonderful career as a competitive rider, and with time on her hands she went back to her studies, attending University of Notre Dame in Fremantle to study for a degree in literature.

Susanne had returned home to Perth from England on the afternoon of the day she died. She was so tired by the time she got to her house she planned to go to bed early. She had a bath with her 18-month-old son, my grandson, Charlie, dressed him in his tracksuit and put him to bed. She then called some friends around Australia to tell them she was back and to generally say hello. She told them that she was very tired and was looking forward to going to bed because she hadn't slept during the flight.

Susanne did have a dependence on morphine because of the pain she faced when she had a coeliac attack, but it wasn't an addiction — she knew the limits. She suffered a pain attack during the evening so took a morphine tablet then lay down on the couch with her head propped up on the armrest at the end. The combination of extreme fatigue and the tablet put her into a deep sleep, so deep that her head slipped down from the armrest and her chin was buried in her chest. She asphyxiated.

My Princess...

Only people who have lost a child will understand the emotion the family faced, but we have a bonus in Charlie, a curly-haired little rascal who is absolutely full of life. In her will Susanne nominated Eileen as Charlie's legal guardian, so today Eileen, along with Jody and Damien, are bringing him up. My lasting memory of Susanne and Charlie, now tinged with great sadness, was when she so proudly brought him in to see me in Karnet — a tiny little bundle of happiness only 11 days old.

Another consolation for me emotionally is that I often think of Benny Lexcen now being with Susanne, who he loved very much. He would have welcomed her with his big, broad grin, his trademark blinking and with his arms open wide. I imagine Ben getting Susanne to hop aboard a yacht with him, putting up a spinnaker and sailing away, the two of them laughing like crazy kids and talking about the good times at the America's Cup. It was sad to see them both go to a better place when so young, but I know they are in good company.

■ ■ ■

I guess if there was a 'coming out event' per se following my release from prison then it was the America's Cup Jubilee Regatta in Cowes, England, in September 2001. It was to celebrate the 150th anniversary of the inaugural match for the Cup on the very same stretch of water. When it originated in 1851 it was called the '100 Guinea Cup', the amount put up as the prize for a single race around the Isle of Wight between a fleet of England's finest racing yachts and the schooner *America*, which was built specifically for the event. The British yachts were no match for the American entry and the trophy was taken across the Atlantic to New York. And it wasn't until we came along with *Australia II* in 1983 that the Cup was to leave America and have a new home in Australia.

The Jubilee was a very personal celebration for me, a celebration of being accepted back into society and welcomed by true friends. Until then it had been a struggle since being released from prison. Diana and I had wanted to stay in Australia but there were too many obstacles. Being disqualified from acting as a company director in Australia for five years was one thing, but the real problem was that I was too high profile and that made things very difficult. Every time I moved in the public arena the media wanted to sensationalise something. While I was trying to be positive and get on with my life they'd bring back the negatives all the time, so reluctantly Di and I agreed that we had no option but to go and live in Europe.

It was a great honour for us both to be invited to the Jubilee as guests of one of the America's Cup's greatest sponsors, Louis Vuitton. As soon as we arrived in Cowes people were reminding me that the real reason for the Jubilee Regatta, and for the America's Cup contest being what it is today, was because I'd led the team to victory in 1983. It was wonderful to be the focus of so much of the celebration.

Not so pleasant though was the reception I received from certain elements of the contingent from Perth that had organised for *Australia II* to be at the regatta.

When the decision was made to organise for *Australia II* to be at the Jubilee as a centrepiece of the celebrations the yacht was in Perth awaiting the completion of its new home at the Maritime Museum in Fremantle. For a long time it looked like the money would not be found to cover the costs, until eventually a number of companies and individuals came to the party, including the Bond family. The good news was that everyone associated with the 1983 winning syndicate was invited, and they managed to get all but one of the Cup-winning crew there. Still, I wasn't to be seen to be part of it.

In Cowes, Warren Jones tried to make out to everyone that Di and I were most welcome, but that was not the case. This is not sour grapes on my part, but I say without hesitation that the way we were treated by the leaders of a contingent from my own home city was disgraceful. These people were only in Cowes lapping up the good times because of my determination to win the America's Cup. I couldn't believe that Warren, who came to see me during my incarceration, and who I considered a special friend, had let himself be bought for sponsorship pennies and dragged into this mire. I kept saying to myself, 'I've paid my debt to society; what else am I supposed to do?' I don't think there's anywhere else in the world outside Australia where a sentence is perpetuated upon somebody the way it is here. Overseas the general attitude is: 'Well, he faced up to whatever the circumstances were. Now he should be allowed to get on with his life.' What this treatment in Cowes did was teach me to again hold my head high because I had done everything that was asked of me by the Australian legal system, and helped other people during the process.

The one conciliatory gesture by the *Australia II* group was that I was invited to sail aboard the yacht in the Jubilee's major event, a re-enactment of the race around the island. It was great to be with the old team onboard the boat, but the discomfort factor still didn't go away. Sadly, Warren has passed away, but he knew my views before he died. Like Benny Lexcen his passing came way too early, due in part I believe to the fact that he would keep things bottled up inside — he didn't know how to spit the dummy every now and then to release tension.

In contrast to my reception around *Australia II* was the welcome we got from everyone else in Cowes. Every time I walked down

High Street people would stop to tell me how wonderful it was that we'd won the Cup in 1983; we had changed the course of sailing history. They knew who I was and they knew what had happened to me, but they accepted me as a person. Even the Aga Khan rushed up to welcome me and again say what a great victory *Australia II* delivered the sailing world. Sir Max Aitken's daughter, Laura, had a special dinner for 40 guests, including Di and me, at her house, as did a number of others in Cowes. There was one dinner party where a judge made a speech aimed directly at me, saying: 'Alan, what happened to you in Australia wouldn't have happened here in England. We want you to know you're among friends, all of us here. We recognise your contribution to not only sailing but to so many other avenues in life, and you're welcome in our midst.'

It was a very emotional moment for Di and me, having the hand of friendship extended so superbly after such a terrible period in my life.

That hand of friendship also extended to the actual sailing side of the week with me being invited out on a number of yachts, including the majestic *Cambria*, a 124-foot classic K Class cutter owned by John David from Sydney, and one of the stars of the event. And the Jubilee Ball, staged at what was Queen Victoria's stately summer residence located on the northern side of the island, Osborne House, capped a great week of social fun. The ball also saw one of the most amazing charity auctions ever. On offer was the Hennessy America's Cup Jubilee eaux-de-vie cognac collection — 31 bottles, one taken from the vintage each year that the America's Cup had been contested. It was presented in a custom-made cabinet and was valued at £20 000. Bidding started at £40 000 and quickly passed £100 000. The final scene was American billionaire and America's Cup winner Bill Koch standing in the middle of the dance floor permanently holding his bidding card above his head while a rival bidder, rumoured to be the Aga Khan, kept upping the ante. Koch won the day, paying a staggering £310 000 for the collection.

The trip back to Cowes from the ball was another highlight for

Di and me. Some Australian sailing friends had been loaned an incredible double-decker bus, one that was designed to convey the stars of entertainment across England in five-star comfort. It even had a double bed in a special compartment upstairs. Everyone was having a great time, laughing and watching rock videos on a large screen as we drove through the island countryside well after midnight. Then someone took control of the sound system and played the Kevin 'Bloody' Wilson CD, *Living Next Door to Alan,* a song about a family of Aborigines moving in next door to 'Alan's' luxury home in Perth. No guessing who the song was aimed at. Anyway, it was played at full volume and next thing everyone on the bus, Di and me included, was singing along to the chorus. From that moment I knew I was back in the company of real Australian 'mates', and the past was slipping away.

After the final day of racing at the Jubilee Regatta there was a presentation of trophies on the waterfront outside the Royal Yacht Squadron with hundreds of people present, including royalty. At the end of proceedings there was a special presentation to *Australia II* for being 'the yacht that had done the most to further the image of the America's Cup and contribute to the success of the Jubilee'. Warren Jones bounded onto the stage with the rest of the team, but there was no invitation for me to join them. It took the cheering crowd only a few seconds to realise that I was missing, and next thing a chant started, 'Bondy, Bondy, Bondy ...' Before I knew it, Bruno Trouble, the French America's Cup skipper who was coordinating the regatta for Louis Vuitton, grabbed me and pushed me onto the stage, and much to my delight an enormous cheer went up. A beautiful trophy was presented which I was told later was supposed to go to me, but I never got to see it. Someone from *Australia II* grabbed it and it disappeared. Obviously certain sponsors couldn't forgive and forget, even though it was a sporting event. At least the Hennessy Cognac people made sure that their special award in recognition of my contribution to the Cup got to me.

And in more recent times there has been a magnificent honour bestowed on me. I was inducted into the America's Cup Hall of

Fame at a function in New York in late 2003 alongside such great names as Sir Thomas Lipton, Dennis Conner, Ted Turner, Harold S. Vanderbilt, Sir Peter Blake and our own Sir Frank Packer, Sir James Hardy and John Bertrand. The Hall of Fame is based in the famous Herreshoff Marine Museum in Bristol, Rhode Island.

Living in Europe is giving me a real opportunity to re-establish my life, even though my heart is still very much in Australia. Di and I have very definite plans to move back to Fremantle in a couple of years when we hope people will finally give me the proper opportunity to recover.

Fortunately my health has improved considerably, due in no small way to seeing the stress and problems I faced fading into the past. And without the stress and associated depression my memory is also improving, as doctors said it would. My memory loss was so severe that it is only recently that I have remembered meetings I had with James Yonge of Wardley's in Sydney at the time when the Hong Kong and Shanghai Banking Corporation was claiming the Queensland Nickel project from me, meetings that would have provided crucial evidence in my case against the bank and, I'm sure, turned the result in my favour.

While it has been difficult to get going again, my life is now very much on the improve. It took me a year to get my head together after the ordeal of being in prison. For the first 12 months, while I was on parole, I felt as though I was shell-shocked. I can now understand how the prisoners of war felt when they came back to Australia — having been in such a foreign environment for so long I was very disorientated for quite some time. Then it took another 12 months after that for me to regain my confidence and to work out what I could do with my life. I now look on life very differently — I have new values and meanings. While many doors have been shut it is astonishing how many new ones have opened. I've had to look at my commercial future from a very different perspective.

Having had Bond Corporation and Dallhold hold interests in 27 countries I still have many contacts who are willing to help make things work for me. I am acting as a consultant in London, Europe and Africa, developing strategic projects for companies and individuals. In organisations where someone is needed to say: 'Let's look at the bigger picture and work out what we can achieve', this is where I am playing a major role. At the same time I have the opportunity to participate in the equity of new ventures.

My background has given me vast experience, experience that I can bring to the table across a lot of industries — development, goldmining, the oil industry, property, plus financial engineering in many markets. And then there's the benefit of hindsight, what the consequences might be when a business carries too much debt. Even if these clients don't use my vision in its entirety, I am in a position to stimulate their thought processes. I am in a better position than most people to contribute to their outlook and what strategy they should adopt. The big bonus for my clients is that I am a better businessman today because I am now able to temper my views of the business world with my more recent experiences — I've got the yin and the yang, the experience of success and failure. All the signs are that the projects I am working on will be successful, but this time more so for other people than Alan Bond. I am enjoying participating in the success of others; it's fun. I'm quite happy to see others take the limelight and be successful, yet when it comes to limelight I can well advise them from my own experience how a high profile is not always in their best interests. I'm still paying the price, even though I've moved to Europe.

There are some exciting opportunities out there for me, but I am being very selective as to which projects I take on, as I no longer have the desire to overwhelm myself with work.

Thankfully my family has supported me financially while I have worked towards rebuilding my business life, and a few friends have presented me with some solid commercial opportunities to consider. But I'm certainly not looking to make a fortune again. I just want a comfortable lifestyle without becoming a billionaire once more. As

I've said before, I have never been driven by money and I'm not driven by it now.

Unfortunately, while I try to move ahead, there are still people who don't believe the penalty I paid was strong enough. All I can say is that if they feel that way then they should insist that the same rules that applied to me also apply to the heads of other large public corporations in Australia where billions of dollars of shareholders' money have been lost. These losses have come because someone's commercial judgment was wrong, which is no different from what happened in Bond Corporation, yet all that happened to so many of those corporate chiefs was that they either stepped aside or were relieved of their duties. End of story.

One important point that Australia needs to remember is that we should not crucify entrepreneurs — they are the people who can inspire nations and individuals to go out and do great things. These entrepreneurs might start out in life by building a small home and on-selling it, or opening a small business and building it. They are a vital ingredient in the business world and should be encouraged. If we want development then we need people to go out continually and try new things. That is how the free enterprise system of our society works. Yes, there will be failures along the way and mistakes made, but people learn from mistakes and improve. We should encourage people to be successful because we all benefit. All too often in Australia the tall poppy syndrome emerges. It seems to be obligatory to chop down someone who has been successful. What I would like to see is for Australians to adopt the American attitude, where there is no permanent stigma associated with actually having failed at something. Our society should be able to forgive and encourage rehabilitation.

I hope that one day I experience some level of forgiveness from those people who still don't want me to be able to get on with my life. And while I remain adamant that I should not have gone to prison on any of the charges that were laid against me, it must be realised that I have paid the price asked of me, and on top of that I lost more than $1 billion of my own money.

Looking back on my achievements in life I see three significant contributions that I have made for Australia. First up there was the fantastic win in the America's Cup where we showed the world that a small nation with determination and dedication could do the impossible. We went where no one had been before. Then there was the *Endeavour* project, which came as a result of a vision I developed from Bruce Stannard's concept. I saw this ship as a gift to Australia and a wonderful way to showcase the nation. My vision was that it wasn't to be a museum piece — it would sail the world's oceans under the Australian flag, and that is what it is achieving today.

Above all, the project of which I am most proud is Bond University, Australia's first private university and one that was created without federal government support. Despite the government being completely against us and determined to drive wedges into everything we tried to achieve, we succeeded, and in doing so have set new standards in university education. In 100 years, when I am long gone, Bond University will still be there making outstanding contributions to Australian society and the world.

From a business point of view there are some notable achievements of which I am very proud. One was the goldmining business we established within Dallhold. It became one of the world's top 10 goldmining groups, and within that organisation the greatest achievement was the building of the Super Pit in Kalgoorlie. As well as saving the town, it revolutionised the industry by using open cut techniques that were previously thought to be impossible. We applied lateral thinking to that challenge and showed the world what could be done. I am also very proud of how we developed the Chile Telephone Company and the benefits it brought to that nation.

Much of the excitement I enjoyed in business came through being a pioneer and what that achieved. For example, the Swan Brewery deal led to me building the first aluminium can plant in

Western Australia. Back then WA was said to stand for 'Wait Awhile', but I set out to change that. For years and years the brewery had been importing cans, but when I took over I asked the logical question, 'Why do we have to do that? Why can't we build our own aluminium can plant?' I went out and found some people who could build a can plant and commissioned them for the job. It saved Swan a lot of money.

The Lanesborough Hotel development in London was another great achievement, and the vision of the Chifley Square development in the heart of Sydney was special. Yet while it can be said that we built landmarks, buildings don't really matter to me — someone can always build a bigger and better building.

The question often asked is where Bond Corporation and Dallhold were destined to end up if the collapse had not occurred, and I say without any hesitation that Bond Corporation was on a course to be the largest company in Australia. It had the capability to grow to such an immense size that we would have had worldwide influence over a number of important business sectors.

We were working on a 50-year strategic plan for both Bond Corporation and Dallhold. I had a worldwide brewing company within Bond Corporation, and we would also have spun off an oil company because we recognised that one of the big exports that could come from Australia was energy. And then we had a media company that would have held all our media assets, a company that would have seen exceptional growth in the years ahead. Our plan was to have Bond Corporation become a holding company, holding all these pieces. At the same time Dallhold was heading towards even greater things. We had taken the mining business out of Australia and onto the world market by listing it on the New York Stock Exchange, a move that was opening up opportunities in the international capital market, and one that would have benefited both Bond Corporation and Dallhold.

In reality this is a hypothetical scenario that does not matter.

What matters is that today Alan Bond is a happy man with new values in life, values that have come from experiences that few people can imagine. And today, when I look back on every amazing aspect of my life, I know that my greatest pride rests with my family, what they have achieved and how they have stuck by me. They are my greatest achievement, my pride and joy.

INDEX

A
Abeles, *Sir* Peter, 94–95
Aboriginal inmates, 259, 295, 299
academia, 140
accounting and auditing, 168–170, 219, 237–239, 263, 287
A.C. Goode, 169
Adams, John, 36–37
Adelaide Steamship Company, 37, 232, 235, 246
Admiral's Cup, 72–73
Advance (yacht), 110
Aga Khan, 150, 310
AGL (Australian Gas Light), 88, 92
airplanes, 149–151
Airship Industries (UK), 177–180
Aitken, *Sir* Max, 65–66, 310
Allied Lyons, 219, 225, 246
aluminium can plant (WA), 316
America (yacht), 308
American Eagle (yacht), 72
American Express, 234
Americans *see also* United States

American society, 111–112
   attitudes to Australia, 122–123
   attitudes to business, 139
   unpopularity, 132
America's Cup challenge
   1974, 48–53, 57, 68, 76–79, 96
   1977, 78–81
   1980, 81–84
   1983, 15, 86, 104–126, 130–131, 283, 315
   1987, 126–129
   Hall of Fame, 311–312
   Jubilee Regatta in Cowes, 308–311
   winged keel, 106, 110, 113, 121, 123
   Yanchep Sun City, 69, 71–75
AMP Insurance Company, 28, 245
Anderson, Campbell, 88–89, 91
Andreotti, Giulio, 190
Anglo American Group, 34–35
Anheuser-Busch, 163, 165, 166
Antwerp (Belgium), 35

INDEX

ANZ Bank, 37, 191–192
AOL Time Warner, 245
Apollo (yacht), 49, 64–66, 68–72
Apollo II (yacht), 72
Argus, Don, 169–170
Argyle Diamond Mine, 35
Arnott's Biscuits, 11
Arthur Andersen & Co, 239, 263
Ash Wednesday bushfires (Vic), 186–187
Asia, 138–139
Aspinall, David, 174, 197, 218
Aspreys (London), 207
asset stripping *see* Bell Resources asset stripping
auditing *see* accounting and auditing
Australia (yacht), 80–84
Australia II (yacht), 107–123, 125, 143, 308–311
Australia IV (yacht), 128
Australian Broadcasting Tribunal, 174
Australian Consolidated Press (ACP), 136
Australian Jaycees delegate, 33–34
Australian legal system, 212
Australian Maritime Museum, 142
Australian Occidental, 133
Australian of the Year (1978), 284
Australian Rules Football, 101–102
Austria, 123
AWA, 173

B

B-Sky-B satellite channel, 171–172, 227
Babson College (US), 132
Bach Choir (London), 185
Bailey's Beach Club (New York), 112
Ballas, Jacob, 37
Bank of New South Wales, 60
Bank of Nova Scotia, 267
banks and financial institutions
   America's Cup challenge, 131
   Asian banks, 42
   Australian banking system, 97–98, 248
   Bell Resources, 232–233
   Chile Telephone Company, 198
   Lonrho report, 220
   Minsec, 59–60
   private banker *see* Bollag, Jurg
   Queensland Nickel, 200–213
Barrow Island oil fields, 133
Basin Oil, 89, 93–94
Bass, Perry, 87, 88, 133
BCI *see* Bond Corporation International
Beaman, Dianne, 157
Beashel, Colin, 111, 122
Beaverbrook Newspapers, 67
Beckwith, Peter
   Bond Brewing, 163–165
   Bond Corporation, 98, 216–218
   Bond University, 136
   death, 286
   Kwinana petrochemical plant, 254–255
   La Promenade, 261–264, 273
   NCSC, 224
   Price Waterhouse, 239
   Rothwells, 231, 247–255
   Santos oil and gas project, 93
Bedouins, 41

Bell Group *see also* Bell Resources
  asset stripping
  BCI subsidiary companies in, 176
  originally Bell Brothers, 26
Bell Resources asset stripping
  Holmes à Court, 26, 220–227,
    231–233, 286
  Bond Corporation restructuring,
    166
  Bond Corporation purchases
    shareholdings, 220–223
  WA government purchases
    shareholding, 221–228
  NCSC investigation, 221–228,
    231, 247
  Sulan Inquiry, 221, 227–231,
    243, 261
  Bond Brewing assets purchased,
    229–232, 245–246
  bondholders in Bell Group, 234
  Bond Brewing assets revalued,
    234–237
  receiver appointed to Bond
    Brewing by NAB, 237–239
  legal action, 261, 270–272,
    286–291, 308
  plea bargain, 286–291
  Polish brewery, 302–303
bendy mast, 82–84, 105
Bertrand, John, 75, 82, 84,
  105–109, 115–120, 122, 312
Beverly Hills Estate (Perth), 25
BHP, 90, 91, 165, 191, 227, 303
Bic and Biro ballpoint pens, 77
Bicentennial celebrations, 143
Bich, *Baron* Marcel, 76–77, 158,
  161

B.I.G. *see* Bond International Gold
Birchmore, Alan, 255
birth, AB's (22 April 1938), 4
Bjelke-Petersen, *Sir* Joh, 136–137,
  142, 173–174
Black Swan (launch), 114, 118–119,
  121
Bliss, Diana, 153–157, 233,
  276–277, 293–294, 298, 305,
  308–312
Boeing 727, 150–151
Bogard, Gary, 72
Bollag, Jurg
  Dallhold, 185, 200, 204–205
  Dow Chemical Bank
    (Switzerland), 200
  federal government, 213
  his company, 204, 212
  HK& SBC first charge, 207–213
  Metallgesellschaft (Germany),
    204–205
  Portrait of Captain Cook (Webber),
    185
  private banker, 199–200,
    206–207
  Queensland Nickel debt, 200,
    203–213
  Standard Chartered Bank (UK),
    204
  Susanne, 206
Bond Brewing, 160–163, 229–232,
  234–237, 245–246, 248
Bond Building (Perth), 183
Bond Centre (Hong Kong), 173
Bond Corporation
  accounts, 237–238 *see also*
    accounting and auditing

INDEX

America's Cup challenge *see*
  America's Cup challenge
Australian state, 228
Bell Resources asset stripping *see*
  Bell Resources
Bond Corporation Development
  Program, 134
Dallhold, 97–98, 216, 244,
  262–267, 316–317
employees, 241
floats, 90–91, 216
gloom, 144, 165, 190–191, 198,
  200
Kwinana petrochemical plant,
  220, 231, 253–256
La Promenade (Manet) *see La
  Promenade*
liquidators, 185, 237, 247,
  281–282
Lonrho, 219–221, 232–234, 246
Polish brewery, 303
Queensland Nickel *see*
  Queensland Nickel
reasons for collapse, 219–221,
  227–231, 236–237, 243–245,
  268, 272, 284, 292
receivers, 237–241
Robe River iron ore mine *see*
  Robe River
Rothwells *see* Rothwells
Runme Shaw, 37
Santos oil and gas project *see*
  Santos
Scheme of Arrangement, 247
Stock Exchange, 215, 224–225,
  228
subsidiary companies, 176

Swan Brewery purchase *see* Swan
  Brewery
Taylors Lakes development,
  57–58
West Australian Land Holdings,
  37, 42
Bond Corporation International
  Chile Telephone Company, 198,
    216
  holdings, 227
  Hong Kong TVB, 38–39,
    172–173, 216, 227
  Rome property development,
    173, 188–191, 216
  sale to Taiwanese group, 191
  tax-effective domiciles, 176–177
Bond Corporation University Act 1986
  (Qld), 137
Bond, Craig (AB's son), 32, 52–53,
  147–148, 157, 163–165, 237
Bond, Eileen (née Hughes, AB's
  wife)
  meets and marries AB, 13–14,
    22–23
  raises family, 30, 32, 43, 53, 307
  response to AB's sentence, 258,
    277
  role in AB's business, 25, 52, 54,
    122, 147, 186–188, 199, 237
  divorces AB, 153–155, 157
Bond, Frank (AB's father), 2–4,
  6–10, 21
Bond, Geraldine (AB's sister), 4–7,
  10, 22
Bond International Gold, 100, 193,
  209, 213, 216
Bond, Gemma, 53, 157

INDEX

Bond, Jody (AB's daughter), 43, 53–54, 111, 147, 157, 307
Bond, John (AB's son), 22, 30, 52–53, 139, 147, 157
Bond, Kathleen (née Smith, AB's mother)
    accounting and business skills, 5, 13, 21
    investments, 10, 28
    meets and marries Frank Bond, 3–4, 8–9
    religious beliefs, 6, 12–13
    views on education, 11, 134
Bond Media, 169, 175–176, 227, 239
Bond Motor Corporation, 227
Bond Petroleum, 132–133, 254
Bond, Susanne (AB's daughter), 43, 53–54, 146–147, 151, 157, 206, 306–307
Bond University, 134–142, 173, 315
Bond University, The Beginning, 1985–1991 (Orr), 142
Bonython, John, 89, 93, 94
Boos, Bill de, 60
Borghese family (Rome), 189
Bosch, Henry 'Big Ears', 223–227
Bourke, Marcus and Adrian, 25
boxing kangaroo flag, 108, 121, 125
BP oil refinery (Fremantle), 24
branding, 16, 164–165
brick business, 33
Brisbane freeway, 137
British Associated Foods, 145
British Satellite Broadcasting, 171–172, 227
Brunei, Sultan of, 213

bureaucrats, 47
Burke, Brian, 226, 247, 249, 250, 256
Burleight Forest plantation (Qld), 136
Burmah Oil, 87–91, 95
Burnside QC, Julian, 272, 275
Burswood Casino (Perth), 253

C

CAGA, 56
Callinan QC, Ian, 285–286, 288–291
Cambria (yacht), 310
Cambridge University, 135
Canadian Imperial Bank of Commerce, 72, 92
Cardington (Beds, UK), 178
Carlton and United Brewery, 102
Carlton Football Club, 102
cars (AB's liking for), 30–31
cash flow *see also* debt to equity ratios
    benefits, 234
    credit squeeze, 55, 58, 88
    creditors payments, 26
    ensuring, 20, 158–160, 196, 202, 221, 232, 255
    fluctuations, 91, 170, 265
    management fees, 62
    transactions between companies, 229
Casley, Leonard George, 28–29
Castlemaine–Tooheys, 136, 159–163, 173
Casuarina Prison (WA), 141, 276, 290–302

Catholic Church, 12–13, 187–191, 249, 252
Challenge 12 (yacht), 107, 110, 111, 118
Channel Nine National Network, 167, 175–176, 227
Channel Nine TV (Qld), 159, 167, 173
Channel Nine TV (WA), 167, 170–171
Chapter 11 (US legislation), 165–166, 239–241
charitable donations, 186–187
Chemical All-State Bank (US), 264–267
Chifley Square development (Sydney), 228, 316
Chile, 151, 176, 191–199, 292 *see also* Pinochet, *General* Augusto
Chile Telephone Company, 45–46, 173, 194, 208, 216, 242–243, 316
Chilean Ambassador (Canberra), 199
China, 37, 172, 227
'Chinese mogul' *see* Shaw, *Tan Sri Dr* Runme
Chisholm, Sam, 171
Christian Democrats (Italy), 190
Churchill, Winston, 44
Citibank, 56–57
Claremont Yacht Club (Fremantle), 21
Cleveland-Cliffs (company), 62
coalmining, 1–3, 19
Coco's restaurant (South Perth), 148
coeliac disease, 306

Coles, 181
Collins, Joan, 150
Commonwealth Director of Public Prosecutions, 290–291, 304
Compañía de Teléfonos de Chile *see* Chile Telephone Company
Connell, Laurie, 248–258, 260, 286
Conner, Dennis, 83, 107, 114–120, 128–129, 312
Connery, Sean, 125
consultancies, 313
consumers, 92–93, 167
convertible bonds, 223
Cook, Captain James, 142–144
Cook Islands, 176
Coppin, Brian, 90, 174, 247, 250–252, 256
corporate world, 134
corporations law (takeover provisions), 158–159, 223, 224
Cottesloe Surf Club (Perth), 52
Cotton, George, 21
Courageous (yacht), 76, 81
Court, Sir Charles, 49, 55
Cowes (UK), 67, 68, 72, 308–311
credit squeeze, 55, 58, 88
Crusade (yacht), 65–66
Cudmore, Harold, 118
Cuneo, John, 75
currency transactions, 218–219
Cutty Sark Trust (London), 144
Cwmtillery (South Wales), 1–3, 19

D

Daily Express (London), 67
Daily News (Perth), 227

INDEX

Dallhold
  America's Cup challenge, 109
  Bollag, 185, 200, 204–205
  Bond Corporation, 97–98, 216, 244, 262–267, 316–317
  Dow Chemical Bank (Switzerland), 200
  El Indio mine (Chile), 191–199, 209
  employees, 241
  gloom, 144, 190–191
  goldmining holdings, 214, 315–317
  Irises (Van Gogh), 183–185, 237, 302
  La Promenade (Manet) *see La Promenade*
  liquidators, 185, 237, 247, 281–282
  Price Waterhouse, 239
  Queensland Nickel *see* Queensland Nickel
  Super Pit Kalgoorlie, 99–100, 204, 316
  Windsor Resources, 98
dancing lessons, AB's, 13–14
David, John, 310
Davies, Wynn, 211
De Beers, 35
de Boos, Bill, 60
de Savary, Peter, 108, 110
Deakan, Cam, 35–36
debt to equity ratios, 55, 162, 166, 177, 184, 193, 200–201, 203, 206–213, 231, 313 *see also* cash flow
Dempster, Dallas, 253–255

depositors in Rothwells, 249, 251, 257
depression, 288–289
diamond business, 35
Diamond, Neil, 152
Dickinson, John, 249
divorce, 153
Dow Chemical Bank (Switzerland), 200
Dow Chemicals (US), 254
Dowding, Premier, 226
'Down Under' (song), 118
Drexel Burnham Lambert (US), 162
drug surveillance, 177–180
drugs in prison, 260, 295, 301
Drumbeat (yacht), 238–239
Dunraven, Lord, 68
Durak Mines, 34–35

E
Edmonds, Bill, 28
education, AB's, 5, 10, 11, 18
Edwards, *Dr* John, 157
Edwards, Kevin, 249, 250, 253
EIE Corporation (Japan), 139
El Indio mine (Chile), 191–199, 209
electoral influence, 135, 221, 227
11 September 2001, 132
Elizabeth II, Queen, 182, 185
Elliott, John, 102
employees *see* workers
employment creation, 92, 133, 134, 141, 191
Endeavour project, 142–145, 315
England, Richard (liquidator of Bond Corporation), 185, 281–282

325

INDEX

'Entrepreneur of the Year' (1985), 132

F
failure, 79, 95–97, 245
farming, 28–30, 32, 36, 48, 54–55
Fastnet Race (Admiral's Cup), 73
federal government
    Bollag, 213
    El Indio mine (Chile), 192
    foreign investment guidelines, 55
    investigators, 287, 290–292, 304
    private education, 140
    Queensland Nickel, 202
    Sulan Inquiry, 221, 227–231, 243, 261
Fewster, Damien 'Knuckle', 111, 122, 157, 307
Fewster, Jody *see* Bond
Film and Television Institute (Fremantle), 10
Financial Times (newspaper), 172
financing projects, 19, 26–28, 43, 56–59, 92, 159, 179, 183, 192, 196–197, 208–210, 243, 313 *see also* floats
Fischer, Syd, 72, 110
Fitzhardinge, John, 78
floats *see also* financing projects
    Bond Brewing, 163, 166
    Bond Corporation, 90–91, 216
    Bond International Gold, 100, 193
    Bond Media, 169
    Rothwells, 250–251
    West Australian Land Holdings, 42
Fluor Daniel, 191–194

Forbes, Dave, 65
Forbes, Malcolm and *Forbes* magazine, 152
Foss, Peter, 141
Fosters beer, 159–161, 166
XXXX beer (Qld), 136, 159–162
Fraser, Andrew, 273–274, 275, 289
Freedom (yacht), 83–84
Freeman, Cathy, 86
Freemasons' Lodge (Fremantle), 11
Fremantle Boys' High, 10
Fremantle City Council, 14
Fremantle Harbour Trust, 14, 23
Fremantle shopping centre project, 27, 45
Fremantle Technical School, 11
Fremantle (WA), 9, 127–129
French Impressionists, 182–183, 302

G
gambling, 248
Garnett, Bob and Joan, 283
gas prices, 92–93
Geraldton railway station (WA), 23–24
Germany, 33, 73, 204
Gibney's Dry Cleaners (Fremantle), 15–17
Gillan, Neil, 189
Ginkgo (yacht), 72
Gold Coast (Qld), 135
Gold Mines of Kalgoorlie, 98
'golden handcuffs' (contract), 217–218
Gooseberry Hill (Perth), 25
government contracts, 23–25

INDEX

Grace Brothers, 181, 263
greenmail, 232
Gretel II (yacht), 69, 80
Griggs, *Dr* Ted, 64

H
Halvorsen, Trygve, 65
Hammer, *Dr* Armand, 146
Hancock, Lang, 60–61, 99, 201
harbour walls, 50
Hardy, Jim, 69, 74–76, 80, 82, 84, 107–109, 114, 116–117, 121, 122, 312
Harriet Oilfield, 133, 254
Harrington, Melissa H., 123
Harvard University, 134–135
Hawke, Bob, 130–131
Healy, Max, 260
Heath, Edward, 65
Heileman Brewing Company (US), 162–166, 177, 216, 229, 240
Hello (magazine), 157
Hennessy cognac, 310–311
herpes, 259–260
High Court (Canberra), 304
Hill, Danny, 101
Hill, Geoff, 245–246
Himalaya (ship), 9
Hinze, Russ, 137
HM Bark *Endeavour* Foundation *see* *Endeavour* project
Holmes à Court, Robert, 26, 220–227, 231–233, 286
Hong Kong and Shanghai Banking Corporation, 191–194, 198, 206–213, 220, 240–243, 249, 312

Hong Kong as AB's base, 216
Hong Kong TVB, 38–39, 172–173, 216, 227
horse racing, 102, 248
hostile takeovers, 219–221
Hudson, Hugh, 92–93
Hughes, Bill 'Doozer', 14, 19, 23, 27, 102
Hughes, *Father* Don, 14, 157, 188
Hughes, Eileen *see* Bond
Hughes, John, 30
Hughes, Maureen, 13, 32
human rights atrocities, 194–195
Hutt River Province (WA), 28–29
Hyundai motor vehicles, 227

I
IAC (Industrial Acceptance Corporation), 28, 56–58
immunity offers, 270–271, 287–288
Indonesia, 201–202
insolvency and Chapter 11, 165–166, 239–241
insurance premiums, 90
interest rates, 96, 175, 190–191, 231, 234, 245
International Energy Bank (London), 92
International Forum (US), 132, 177
International Yacht Racing Union (IYRU), 114
investigators, 287, 290–292, 304
Iran, 39–42
Iraq, 86
Irises (Van Gogh), 183–185, 237, 302
Ishizaki, *Dr* Bungo, 139

INDEX

J

J. Paul Getty Museum (US), 184–185
J. R. Cluff and Son (WA), 133
Jackson, Bruce, 90, 91
Jackson, *Dr* John, 94, 132, 218
jam jar business, 6, 45
Jamison, Jim, 60
Japan, 139, 184
Jaycees World Congress, 34
Jessica (yacht), 150
Jewish business mentality, 17
John Paul II, Pope, 188
Jones, Warren, 39–41, 80, 109, 113, 114, 121, 122, 171, 309, 311
Journeyman's Ticket, 18
Junior Chamber of Commerce (Fremantle), 33
jury trials, 275–276, 286–287

K

Kalamunda (Perth), 25
Kalgoorlie (WA), 10, 98–100, 204, 316
Karnet Prison (WA), 276–284, 286, 290–291, 301, 304–305
Kennedy, *Justice* Antoinette, 272–273, 276, 285
kidney infection, 273
Koch, Bill, 310
Kookaburra (yacht), 128
Krantz, Harold, 17
Kuala Lumpur Kepong Amalgamated Group, 35–36
Kwinana petrochemical plant (WA), 220, 231, 253–256

L

L. J. Hooker's, 20–21, 25
La Croix Mineral Water (US), 163
La Promenade (Manet), 261–270, 272–276, 285–290
Lanesborough Hotel development (London), 216, 316
lateric nickel ore, 46, 201, 206
Law Faculty, Bond University, 141
Leederville Tech School (Fremantle), 11, 18
legal actions against AB
  AB's memory loss, 211, 259, 268–269, 273–274, 312
  arrest for trespassing, 20
  Bell Resources asset stripping *see* Bell Resources
  La Promenade charge, 261, 264, 267–270, 272–276
  prison sentences, 155–156, 187, 199 *see also* Casuarina Prison; Karnet Prison; Yatala Prison
  Rothwells success fee, 251–252, 256–258
  television licence revoked, 174
legal actions by AB's companies
  in Appellate Court, 260
  in arbitration court, 93
  Australian judicial system, 247
  Bond Brewing, 237–239
  Chemical All-State Bank, 264–265, 274–275
  Citibank, 57
  high-risk medical inmate, 279
  Hong Kong and Shanghai Banking Corporation, 212

La Promenade trial and appeal,
    268–269, 285–286
legal advice, 228, 230, 238, 282,
    287–288
Macquarie Bank, 266
over Bjelke-Petersen writ,
    173–174
against publican leaseholders,
    161–162
Robe River Limited, 62
Leighton Beach Surf Club
    (Fremantle), 11, 14
Leonard, *Prince* (Hutt River
    Province), 28–29
Leone, Armand, 146
Lesmurdie (Perth), 25, 28
Lessheim, Kurt, 15–17, 28, 33, 77,
    161
Lexcen, Ben
    1977, 1980 America's Cup,
        79–84
    1983 America's Cup, 105–107,
        109, 111, 113–115, 120–122
    Apollo, 64–66, 68–69
    Apollo II, 72
    Southern Cross, 76
    Susanne, 307
Liberty (yacht), 114–120
Lightning (yacht), 73
limestone quarry, 45, 50
Lindsay, Mike, 29, 40–41, 54–55, 156
Lipton, *Sir* Thomas, 68, 312
liquidators, 185, 237, 247, 281–282
live sheep exports, 39–42
Living Next Door to Alan (CD), 311
local government, 47–48
London blitz, 4–5

Longley, John 'Chink', 108, 122,
    143–144
Lonrho, 219–221, 232–234, 246
Louis Vuitton Cup, 110, 111, 122,
    308, 311
Lucas, Bill, 63
Lucas, Peter, 218, 247, 267

M

McAllister, Scotty, 111
McAlpine, *Lord* Alistair, 36
McCusker *QC*, Malcolm, 252, 256
McKechnie, John, 257–258, 261,
    271–272
Macquarie Bank, 265–267
Mallesons, 210
Marconi, 245
Margaret, *Princess*, 185–186
Maritime Museum (Fremantle), 309
markets (the market), 42, 44, 97,
    160–162
marriages, AB's, 22, 156–157
Maxim's (Paris), 151, 186
media
    AB's relationship, 257–258, 274,
        278, 305, 313
    America's Cup, 78–79, 113–114
    Bell Resources, 224–225, 272
    Bond Corporation, 241–243
    Bond University, 140
    electoral influence, 227
    La Promenade, 269, 285
    publican leaseholders, 162
    Robe River iron ore mine, 60
    Santos oil and gas project, 91
    Taylors Lakes development, 57
    Ted Turner, 81

Mediterranean Restaurant (Perth), 148–149
Melbourne shopping centres, 42
Melville (Perth), 10, 22, 28, 32
memory loss, 211, 259, 268–269, 273–274, 312
Men at Work (band), 118
Merszei, Zoltan, 254
Metallgesellschaft (Germany), 204–205
Michael, *Prince*, of Monaco, 150, 152
Mid-East Minerals, 200–213
Midland Brick, 27, 33
Miller and Whitworth (company), 64
Miller, Bob *see* Lexcen, Ben
Millers brewery (US), 162, 164–165, 166
Mineral Securities (Minsec), 58–60
Minister for Energy (WA), 223
Minister for Mines (WA), 256
Minister of Communications and Finance (Chile), 196
Ministry of Defence (UK), 178–180
Mitchell, Peter
    Bell Resources, 225, 230, 270–271, 302–303
    Bond Brewing, 163
    Bond Corporation, 98, 217–218
    Bond Media, 169–170
    Chile Telephone Company, 197
    Kwinana petrochemical plant, 254–255
    La Promenade, 261, 273, 285, 288
    Rothwells, 247

monopolies (value of), 16
morphine dependence, 306–307
Mosbacher, Emil 'Bus', 72
Mukinbudin railway station (WA), 24
Munk, Roger, 180
Murdoch, Rupert, 94–95, 122, 132, 171–172
Museum of Contemporary Art (Sydney), 156

N

NASDAQ (US), 242
National Australia Bank, 41–42, 165, 169–170, 237–239, 247, 250–251, 253
National Companies and Securities Commission (NCSC), 221–228, 231, 247
National Nine Network, 167, 175–176, 227
National Portrait Gallery (Canberra), 185
Netherlands, 107, 176
Nevill, *Lady* Angela, 182–185
Nevill, *Lord* Rupert, 182
New Caledonia, 201–202
New, Rick, 27, 33
New York Stock Exchange, 100, 193, 317
New York Yacht Club, 68, 71, 74, 75, 81
    America's Cup challenge (1983), 104, 110, 112–114, 117, 122–124, 127
Newport to Bermuda yacht race, 68–71, 73

Nichol, Peter, 64
Northern Mining, 35
Norwegian joint venture, 39
Nu-Signs, 19–21, 23–26

O
Oates, Tony
  Bell Resources, 230, 233–234, 270–271, 302–303
  Bond Brewing, 163, 238
  Bond Corporation, 98, 217–218
  Kwinana petrochemical plant, 254–255
  La Promenade, 261, 265, 273, 275, 285, 288
  Price Waterhouse, 239
  Rothwells, 247, 249, 250
Oblate Order of the Roman Catholic Church, 12–13, 188–190
Occidental Australia, 146
offers of immunity, 270–271, 287–288
offshore funds, 199, 228, 237 *see also* taxation
offshore oil and gas exploration, 132–133
Ogilvy, Angus, 187
open-heart surgery, AB's, 259
Order of Australia, 283–284
Orr, Brian, 136–137, 142
O'Sullivan, *Father*, 12
Oxford University, 135

P
Packer, Kerry, 136, 167–171, 175–176
Packer, *Sir* Frank, 68, 69, 77, 312

painting business, 14, 17–18
paintings, AB's collection, 182–185
  see also Irises; *La Promenade*
paintings by AB, 12, 15, 22, 141, 182, 301–302
Panamuna (yacht), 63–64
Parker, David, 223, 226, 249–251, 253–256
Parmelia Hotel (Perth), 36–37, 153
Parnell, Fred (Parnell Signs), 11, 14–15, 17–18
Parry, Kevin, 128–129
passport, AB's, 213
payola in Chile, 197–198
personal wealth *see also* shareholders
  at 28 years old, 43
  America's Cup challenge, 80, 127
  Bell moneys, 199, 228, 237
  cache of paintings claim, 272
  Endeavour project, 144
  family companies, 57
  Hong Kong and Shanghai Banking Corporation, 209
  La Promenade sale price, 267
  Nu-Signs capital, 19
  Swan Brewery purchase, 158–159
Perth City Council, 47–48
Perth home (Watkins Road), 58, 146–147
Petrochemical Industries, 253–254
petrochemical plant project *see* Kwinana
philanthropy, 186–187
Phillips Brothers, 62
Pilbara exploration leases, 34–35, 60

INDEX

pine forest plantations, 136
Pinochet, *General* Augusto, 191, 194–199
Pittsburgh Brewing Company (US), 162
planes, 149–151
plea bargain, 286–292
Poland, 303
political donations, 250
political parties in Chile, 197
political prisoners, 292
politicians, 135, 146
politics (electoral influence), 135, 221, 227
Pontypool (Wales), 2
Portrait of Captain Cook (Webber), 185
Powers Brewery, 160–162
Pratt, Dick, 107, 118, 250
Price Waterhouse, 239
Prince of Wales Trust (UK), 187
prison officers, 278, 301
prison phone calls, 294–295
prison sentences *see* legal actions against AB
Prisons Department (WA), 281
privatisations in Chile, 195–196
public interest, 273
Public Works Department (WA), 25
publican leaseholders, 161–162
Purves, Willie, 193–194, 208–210

Q

Quartermaine, Murray, 156, 167
Queensland government, 202
Queensland land deals, 42
Queensland Nickel, 46, 173, 200–213, 220, 312
Dallhold, 206–213
lateric nickel ore, 46, 201, 206
pollution from lateric nickel, 202
Queenslanders (attachment to XXXX), 160–162

R

Rabbit Warren prospect (WA), 101
Race of Discovery (Bermuda to Bayonne), 71
racehorses, 102, 248
radio stations, 227
Ragamuffin (yacht), 72
railways, 23–24, 50–51
Rainier, *Prince*, of Monaco, 150, 152
Reagan, *President* Ronald, 124, 131–132, 177
receivers, 237–241
Red Hill (WA), 33
Reed, Noel, 265, 275
Reef Oil, 89, 93–94
religion, 6, 12–13
Republic National Bank of Dallas, 92
Reserve Bank, 55
restructuring, 217
rezoning, 48–52
Rhodes, Cecil, 99
Richmond Football Club, 102–103
Robe River Iron Ore Associates, 61
Robe River iron ore mine, 45, 58–62, 99, 201
Robe River Limited, 61–62
Roberts, Ed, 234
Robins, Noel, 80–81
Rowe-ham, David Sir, 132

Roma restaurant (Fremantle), 31
Romagna, Vic, 69
Roman Catholic Church, 12–13, 187–191, 249, 252
Rome, Lord Mayor of the City, 189–190, 251
Rome property development, 173, 188–191, 216
Rose, Andy, 75
Rosehill Estate (Guildford), 32
Rothwells
  Bell Group, 220–221, 226–227, 231, 247–258
  Bond Brewing deposits, 248
  Connell, 248–258, 260, 286
  Coppin, 247, 250–252, 256
  Dempster, 255
  depositors, 249, 251, 257
  float, 250–251
  Kwinana petrochemical plant, 220, 231, 253–256
  McKechnie, 257–258, 261, 271–272
  shareholders, 250–251
  success fee for Bond Corporation, 251–252, 256–258
  WA government, 220–221, 226–227, 231, 247–258
Rowland, Tiny, 220–221, 232–234, 246
Roxborough, Kerry, 249
Royal Air Force (RAF), 3–4
Royal Perth Yacht Club
  America's Cup, 72, 123, 126–129
  Panamuna (yacht), 63–64
rugby league, 11, 102
Ryan, Susan, 140

S
St Joe Gold Corporation, 98
St Malo (France), 72–73
St Patrick's Catholic Church (Fremantle), 12, 22, 146, 157, 182
sand dunes, 50
Sandberg, *Sir* Michael, 209, 213
Santos Limited (Regulation of Shareholdings) Act (SA), 93, 95
Santos oil and gas project, 45, 72, 87–95, 158–159
satellite communications, 46, 150, 171–172, 194
Saudi Arabian market, 167
Schnackenberg, Tom, 109, 111, 122
Schools' Fund of the Catholic Church, 249
Schooner XXXX (yacht), 150
seawalls, 50
self-belief, 78–79
September 11 2001, 132
Shah of Iran, 39, 41
Shanghai, 38
share trading, 218–219, 242, 257, 278, 298
shareholders
  AB, 244, 247, 261, 315
  Bell Resources asset stripping, 228–229, 232, 235–236, 244, 246
  Bond Corporation, 177, 198, 216, 241, 244, 245, 285, 314
  Chapter 11 (US legislation), 240
  Hong Kong and Shanghai Banking Corporation, 220–221
  La Promenade contract, 263–264

large public corporations, 314
Lonrho, 233
Rothwells, 250–251
Santos Limited (Regulation of Shareholdings) Act (SA), 93, 95
Stoll Moss Theatres (London), 222–223
taking out dividends, 43
Shaw, *Sir* Run Run, 37–39
Shaw, *Tan Sri Dr* Runme, 37–39, 42, 59
sheep transporters (ships), 39–42
Shell Exploration, 94
signwriting apprenticeship, 11, 14–15, 17–18
Simmer, Grant, 111, 122
Singapore, 37–39, 41
Singleton, John, 145
Skase, Christopher, 222–223, 284
Skipper Mayday (hire business), 39–40
Sky Channel, 171–172
Smith, Kathleen *see* Bond
Sopwith, *Sir* Thomas, 68
Sotheby's (New York), 183–185
South Africa, 7–8, 34
South Australian government
  extradite AB, 297–298
  gas prices, 92–94
  interview AB in prison, 281–282, 297
  oil reserves, 87–88
  Santos oil and gas project, 45, 72, 87–95, 158–159
  Sulan Inquiry into Bond Corporation, 221, 227–231, 243, 261

South Fremantle Football Club, 102
Southcorp, 225
Southern Cross (yachts), 75–76, 149–150, 152, 189
Spalvins, John, 232, 235, 245–246
Spanish telephone company, 198
sport and Australia, 85–86
Standard Chartered Bank (UK), 100, 204–205, 207
Stanford University, 134, 140
Stannard, Bruce, 142–145, 315
State Government Insurance Commission (WA), 221, 223, 249, 252–253
State Superannuation Board (WA), 253
Stephens, Olin, 114
Stock Exchange (Perth), 37
stock market collapse (1987), 96, 183, 193–194, 209, 210, 215, 219, 247
Stoll Moss Theatres (London), 222–223
strip searching, 293–294
student unions, 140
success and failure, 79, 95–97, 245
Suharto family, 201
suicides in prison, 300–301
Sulan Inquiry into Bond Corporation, 221, 227–231, 243, 261
Sulan *QC*, John, 229
Summers, Jack, 64
Sunday Express (London), 67
Sunflowers (Van Gogh), 183
Super Pit Kalgoorlie, 99–100, 204, 316

INDEX

Swan Brewery, 102, 158–159, 166, 167, 180, 238, 316
Sydney to Hobart yacht race, 65–66, 73, 238–239
Sylvester's Dry Cleaners (Subiaco), 10, 16

T
T. M. Bourke (company), 25
Taiwan, 39
Takahashi, Harunori, 139
tapped phone lines (Chile), 197
taxation, 176–177, 203, 205, 212, 218, 262, 263 see also offshore funds
Taylor, Elizabeth, 152
Taylors Lakes development (Melbourne), 56–58
television channels see Channel Nine
Terrey Hills (Sydney), 74
Thatcher, Margaret, 178–179
Thorpe, Ian, 86
Time magazine, 15, 125
Tokyu Corporation (Japan), 50–52, 55, 96
Tom the Cheap (grocer), 27–28
Tooheys, 161–162
Townsville (Qld), 201–203
trade unions, 140, 194, 250
Treharne, Hugh, 108, 111, 120, 122
Tremain, David, 88, 89
Trouble, Bruno, 311
Turnbull, Malcolm, 169–170, 175
Turner, Ted, 72, 73, 80–81, 312
Tyler, Tracy, 154–155, 239

U
United States *see also* Americans
Chapter 11 (US legislation), 165–166, 239–241
government contract for airships, 177–180
State Department, 131–132
Upp Hall (Herts, UK), 157, 237
Uren, Tom, 55

V
Valentijn, Johan, 80
Valiant (yacht), 69
Van Gogh, Vincent, 183–184 *see also Irises*
Varanus Island (WA), 132–133
violence in prison, 295–296, 299
Vuitton, Louis, 110, 111, 122, 308, 311

W
WA Inc. *see* Western Australian government
Walton's retail business, 180–181
Ward, Steve, 105, 107, 143–144
Wardle, *Sir* Thomas, 27–28
Wardley Australia, 249–251, 312
water catchment area (Perth), 42
Waterside Workers' Federation (Fremantle), 19–20, 25
Watson-Munro, Tim, 268
Wendt, Jana, 174
West Australian Land Holdings, 37, 42
West Australian (newspaper), 227, 243

335

Western Australian government
  Bell Resources shareholding, 221–228
  Bond Corporation, 226–227, 292
  Kwinana petrochemical plant, 220, 231, 253–256
  Perth water catchment area, 42
  rail systems, 51
  Rothwells bailout, 220–221, 226–227, 231, 247–258
  WA Inc., 226
  Yanchep Sun City, 49, 52, 55
Western Mining, 90, 91, 191–192
Western Underwriters (Perth), 90
Westinghouse (US), 179
Weston, Garfield 'Garry', 145
Westonia farming land (WA), 28–30, 36
White House (US), 124, 132, 177
Whiteman Brickworks (Guildford), 32–33
Whitlam Turnbull, 231, 235
Wilson, Kevin 'Bloody', 311
Windsor Resources, 98
women, 72–73, 148–149
Woodside, 95
Woolworths, 181
Wooroloo Prison (WA), 258–260, 276
workers
  apprentices team, 11–12
  Chinese labourers, 41
  coalminers, 1–3, 19
  contractors, 28
  in dry cleaning plant, 16
  Endeavour project, 144
  farmers, 30
  financing Chilean, 194
  Indian crew, 40
  Iranian dockworkers, 41
  Kalgoorlie, 99
  maintenance, 25
  Nu-Signs, 20, 21
  Queensland Nickel, 200–206
World Trade Center, 132
World War II, 4
Wormbete (Winchelsea), 54
Wrightson's Dance Studios (Fremantle), 13–14

X

XXXX beer (Qld), 136, 159–162

Y

Yanchep Sun City (WA), 48–52, 55, 71–75, 78, 96, 134
Yatala Prison (SA), 297–298
Yellow Rose of Texas (gold nugget), 100–101
Yonge, James, 207, 210–211, 221, 249, 250, 312
Young, Peter, 30

www.ingramcontent.com/pod-product-compliance
Lightning Source LLC
Chambersburg PA
CBHW022027290426
44109CB00014B/782